The Tales Of The Genii Or The Delightful Lessons Of Horam, The Son Of Asmar, Volume 1...

James Ridley

Nabu Public Domain Reprints:

You are holding a reproduction of an original work published before 1923 that is in the public domain in the United States of America, and possibly other countries. You may freely copy and distribute this work as no entity (individual or corporate) has a copyright on the body of the work. This book may contain prior copyright references, and library stamps (as most of these works were scanned from library copies). These have been scanned and retained as part of the historical artifact.

This book may have occasional imperfections such as missing or blurred pages, poor pictures, errant marks, etc. that were either part of the original artifact, or were introduced by the scanning process. We believe this work is culturally important, and despite the imperfections, have elected to bring it back into print as part of our continuing commitment to the preservation of printed works worldwide. We appreciate your understanding of the imperfections in the preservation process, and hope you enjoy this valuable book.

Vide Volume I. Page 237.
The Lion after dispersing the robbers & destroying the ruffian, fawning at the feet of Urad the fair wanderer.

TALES OF THE GENII.

THE
TALES OF THE GENII;

OR, THE

DELIGHTFUL LESSONS

OF

HORAM, THE SON OF ASMAR.

Faithfully Tranflated From

THE PERSIAN MANUSCRIPT;

And compared with the French and Spanifh Editions, publifhed at Paris and Madrid.

By SIR CHARLES MORELL,

Formerly Ambaffador from the Britifh Settlements in India to the
GREAT MOGUL.

Cooke's Edition.

EMBELLISHED WITH

SUPERB ENGRAVINGS.

VOL. I.

London:

Printed for C. COOKE, No. 17, Paternofter-Row.
And fold by all the Bookfellers in
Great Britain.

AVA 1870

TO

HIS ROYAL HIGHNESS

GEORGE PRINCE OF WALES.

May it please your Royal Highness,

AS this work is designed to promote the cause of morality, I have presumed to lay it at the feet of your Royal Highness; whose early entrance into the paths of virtue, under the conduct of an illustrious and Royal Mother, and the direction and auspices of the best of Fathers and of Kings, has encouraged me to hope, that these Tales will hereafter meet with your Royal Highness's approbation.

I am,

Your Royal Highness's

Most devoted

And obedient servant,

The EDITOR.

THE EDITOR
TO
THE READER.

Kind Reader,

THOUGH Sir Charles Morell has been long since dead, yet it is not in the least wonderful that this work has been kept from the public eye, as his papers were left to relations, who neither knew nor enquired into the value of his works. Nor had they now seen the light, unless they had been put into my hands, with many other papers and parchments, to settle some differences which have arisen in the family.

Having full liberty to use his literary works as I pleased, I have made it my business to become master of them by degrees; and I should have published his account of India long ago, had I not found that work already done to my hands, though not in so masterly a manner, yet sufficient to prevent the sale of any second work. But although this was a very curious performance, and I was vexed that pecuniary prudence should oblige me to withhold it for some time longer from the public, as his elegant drawings alone, relative to the subject he wrote upon, would cost 500l. to engrave;

yet

yet I hope to make it up to the world, by offering them a book, which, if it is less useful to commerce, yet it may be of far more entertainment and instruction to all degrees of men; and this is a translation, in his own hand-writing, of the works, (or, as they are called in the title-page, the Delightful Lessons) of Horam the son of Asmar. Delightful, indeed! whether we consider the matter, the subject, the manner, or the moral of the work.

These lessons are divided into tales; wherefore, in compliment to the taste of the age, I have called them, 'The Tales of the Genii;' and at several times I have inserted some small detached parts of them in the public papers, to try what success they were likely to challenge from the world; which was so just and so great, that I have now been at the expence of printing the whole together, and of employing several very able artists to enrich it with copper-plates.

And now, reader, I hope that these Tales will be as successful in Europe as my friend, Sir Charles Morell, testifies they have been in India; that they will be the means of delighting and instructing the noble youth of both sexes; and that they will give that satisfaction to the learned, which every good work of genius, art, and morality, doth always excite.

THE LIFE OF
HORAM THE SON OF ASMAR.

WRITTEN BY

SIR CHARLES MORELL.

DURING my long and painful residence in many different parts of Asia, both in the Mogul's dominions, and in those of the Ottoman Empire, it was my fortune, several times, to meet with a small Persian work, intitled, 'The Delightful Lessons of Horam the son of Asmar,' a book of great note both at Ispahan and Constantinople, and frequently read by the religious teachers of Mahomet to their disciples, to excite them to works of morality and religion.

I confess, being chiefly conversant in trade, I had very little appetite to read the religious doctrines of Pagans; and it was not till I had met with the work in almost every part of Asia, that I was tempted to examine a book recommended on the score of their religion. But a few hours reading in it made me repent my former want of curiosity; as the descriptions were lively, the tales interesting and delightful, and the morals aptly and beautifully couched under the most entertaining images of a romantic imagination.

Having got this treasure in my possession, it was my next study to translate it into my native language, intending it, when completed, as a present to my wife and family in England. But business calling me to Fort St. George, I unfortunately left part of the manuscript behind me at Bombay. I was sensibly affected at this loss, and the more so, as I found it impossible, through the multiplicity of my affairs, to replace my translation: so I gave over all thoughts of my intended present, and contented myself with frequently reading the enchanting original.

But

But if my voyage to Fort St. George deprived my family of the translation, it doubly repaid my loss, by the addition of a very valuable friend, with whom I got acquainted at Fort St. George. This was no other than the great Horam, the author of the book in question, who then resided in the Blacks Town, and was esteemed as a saint by all denominations, both Pagans and Mohammedans, and who was very intimate with the English belonging to the fort.

As I was extremely desirous of his acquaintance, and very assiduous in pleasing him, he soon distinguished me from the rest of my countrymen; and he would often, in our walks through the gardens, at the back of the fort, entertain me with his elegant and instructive conversation. At these times I did not fail, at proper intervals, to lament his disbelief of our Holy Christian Faith. To this, for some time, he made no answer; but whenever it was mentioned, he seemed more thoughtful and reserved. But I considered the subject of too much consequence to be laid aside, merely on a point of punctilio, and therefore seldom omitted to bring it up in all our private conversations; till at length, one day, after I had been for some time expatiating on the blessings of Christianity, he stopped short, and falling prostrate on the sandy walk; in a solemn and audible voice, he pronounced as follows in the Persian language---

' O Alla! thou most powerful and merciful Being; who, although thou spannest the heavens with thy hands, dost nevertheless endue the pismire and the bee with wisdom and knowledge; vouchsafe also to enlighten the understanding of the reptile that adores thee; and if it be thy will, who canst cause the light to arise out of darkness, that these men should teach that with their lips for truth, which they will not acknowledge by their lives, have mercy both on me and them: on me, who cannot be convicted by precept without example; and on them, who mock and deny thee, under the semblance of faith and obedience! Are not the Christian vices, O Alla, more hateful in thy sight, than Pagan blindness? and the eyes of those who boast superior sight, more dim than the eyes of him who gropeth in darkness

and

and error? Are these men, who are sharp and greedy in worldly gain, lavish and profuse in heavenly riches? And would they, who covet the dust of India, offer us an eternal exchange for our mouldering possessions? Surely the purest and wisest religion cannot be revealed to the most unthankful and ignorant of mankind. The pearl would not be cast to the swine, and the children of Alla be deprived of their inheritance. But the worm must not fly, the ignorant judge, nor dust presume!'

After saying this, which, I confess, affected me strongly, he continued some time in awful silence, prostrate on the ground; and at length arose, with tears in his eyes, saying, ' Be the will of Alla the law of his creature!'---It was some minutes before I could muster up words and resolution to answer Horam, so much was I awed by his just, though severe imprecations; but observing him still continue his meditations, I ventured to begin.

'My friend,' said I, ' God is just, and man is sinful. The Christian religion is professed by millions, and all are not like the merchants of India. If these prefer wealth to religion, there are many who have suffered for the cause of Christ; who have preferred an ignominious death in his faith, to all the glories of infidelity. I, indeed, am not like one of these; but I trust, O Horam, that my faith, though weak, is not dead; and that my obedience, though imperfect, will yet be accepted, through his merits whom I serve.'

' If all Christians were like my friend,' said Horam, ' Horam would embrace the faith of Christ; but what are those who mingle with infidels, whose days are the days of riot, and whose nights are the nights of intemperance and wantonness? who teach truth, and practice deceit? who, calling themselves Christians, do deeds unworthy of Pagans?' ' These,' said I, ' my friend, are most of them unhappy men of strong passions, and small instruction, who were sent here as forlorn hopes; but even of these many have turned out sober and religious, and have spent the latter part of their lives in piety and devotion.'

' What!'

'What!' interrupted Horam, 'they have served their lusts first, and their God last! Alla, whom I worship, likes not such votaries; he requires the earliest offerings of a pious heart, and prayers and thanksgivings that rise to Heaven ere the dews of the night disappear. The man who serves the all-glorious Alla, must prostrate himself ere the watchful sun accuse him of sloth by his reviving presence, and continue his adorations when the lamp of day is no longer seen. He must enter into the society of the faithful, while manhood delays to seal him for his own; and persevere in his march, as the Rajaputas of the east.'

'O, Horam,' answered I, were the God whom we worship, to be worshipped in perfectness, the whole length of our lives would not suffice to lie prostrate before him. But our merciful Father expects not more from us than we are able to pay him. True it is, that we ought to begin early, and late take rest, and daily and hourly offer up our praises and petitions to the throne of his grace. But better is a late repentance than none; and the eleventh hour of the day for work, than perpetual idleness unto the end of our time: and this is not obtained to us, but through the mercies of our Lord and Saviour; not the prophet only, as Mahomet represents him, but the King, the Priest and the Saviour of mankind.'

'What Saviour is this,' said Horam, 'of whom you speak so often, and in such raptures? Can one then save another from the wrath of God, when you yourself acknowledge the best of men to be his unprofitable servants?'

'As a man only,' answered I, 'he cannot, but as God and man he was able; and did offer a full atonement, not only for my sins, but your's also.'

'It is certain,' said Horam, 'that all flesh is weak and corrupted; and, as the creatures of God, we cannot suppose that he, who is all goodness and perfection, should make us unable to perform what natural sense informs us is our duty both to Alla and his creatures: that some supernatural power was necessary to relieve us, I grant; but I see not why we should go so high as to suppose that power must be divine.'

'If

'If the offence,' answered I, 'was against God, God could only remit the punishment, and no creature of God could possibly pay him more service than was due from an entire dependant on his Maker. Therefore, neither angel, nor saint, nor prophet could redeem; for all they could do, was but the discharge of their own moral debts, and cannot be called a work of mediation for another, with regard to a prophet or any private man. Give him the utmost power and favour with God; suppose him to be born perfect, to pay an unsinning obedience, yet he still has paid but the service of one man, and therefore can satisfy but for one: and with regard to angel, genius, or superior being, though superior to man, he is but a servant of God, and a debtor to his Creator, to whom he must for ever owe all possible service and obedience. Considering an atonement in this light, O Horam, you see no possible Saviour but one equal to God; and to suppose that there be many gods, is to derogate from his honour, and to deny his government and power. Therefore, we Christians are taught, that the Son came from the Father, the Messias, whom David wished to see, and called him Lord; of whom all the prophets in the books of the prophesies of the Israelites did prophesy, took upon him our flesh, that he might be enabled to suffer for the infirmities of mankind. And truly, I think, O Horam, that this stupendous instance of mercy cannot be looked upon as absurd or unreasonable, though it be the most supreme declaration of God's mercy and forgiveness. For when God condemns, who can ransom but God himself? or to whom, think you, the glory of man's redemption could be, with any propriety, attributed, but to the Lord of all mercies?'

'Mr. Morell,' said Horam, 'there is reason and truth in the words of my friend; but I am persuaded few of the Christians I have seen think so seriously of these things as you do: profession without practice, and faith (I think you call it so) without a true belief, contents your brethren. If your religion is true, how wicked are the greatest part of the Europeans! I compare them only to silly women, who

who strive to shut out the glories of the meridian sun, that they may poke over the dull light of an offensive lamp.'

My friend and I had many such conversations, but this in particular I took down as soon as I left him; because, I confess, I was very much shocked at his judicious remarks; and, I am sure, if they make as much impression on others as they did on me, they will not be unserviceable to the world, should ever these sheets see the public light. And now I am in the vein of writing, and recollecting these passages between Horam and myself, which gave me great pleasure, I cannot omit mentioning one particular, which passed between us previous to his relation of his own adventures to me.

We were disputing, as usual, on religion, and Horam was remarkably strenuous in contending for his Prophet Mahomet, when I said to him, ' Tell me, then, O Horam, since you are so bigotted to the Mohammedan religion, what invitations have you to propose, should I be willing to enter into your faith?'

' O my friend,' answered Horam, shaking his head, ' I too well understand the meaning of your deceitful request! Yes,' continued he, ' I know the professors of my religion are apt to propose a multitude of wives, and the pleasures of women, to those who will embrace our faith; but these, O Morell, I dare not promise, for I am scandalized at the Mohammedans, when I reflect, that worldly pleasures are all that we promise to those who will take the name of Mahomet for their prophet; but surely the young only can propose such pleasures, and the young can only be captivated by them. Worldly joys are mean incitements to the love of Alla, and impure embraces but little sign of purest faith. Had I an inestimable gem, should I honour it by placing it in the mire! or would any one believe that I had treasured it up amidst the filth of the earth!'

The more I conversed with Horam, the more reason had I to admire both his natural and acquired talents: he was a bigot to no religion, and had as few prepossessions as ever I met with in man. By his discourse,

discourse, I found he had travelled into many parts of the world; and, by his sensible reflections, perceived that he had made a noble use of his studies and travels. This made me very desirous of hearing an account of his life; which, after some length of acquaintance, he indulged me in.

'I came,' said he, 'from the confines of the Caspian Sea; and the mother which bore me was the widow of Adenam Asmar, the Iman of Ferabad: she lived on the contribution of my father's friends, who was adored, when living, for his piety and devotion; and those who supported her, spared no pains or cost in my education, that I might tread in the steps of Adenam my father. At twelve years of age, my friends sent me in the caravans to Mousul, to study under Acham, the most learned of the teachers of the law of Mahomet. With this sage I continued for nine years, and officiated for him in the mosques of Mousul; till Alhoun, the bashaw of Diarbec, taking occasion to quarrel with our cadie, marched towards Mousul, and utterly destroyed the place, carrying away with him four hundred of the inhabitants, whom he sold for slaves. Among this number was Horam, the friend of thy bosom; who, though an Iman, was nevertheless sent to Aleppo by the avaricious bashaw, and sold to an English merchant. With this person, whose name was Wimbleton, I lived for several years; but having a ready memory, I applied myself to learn the English language, and served him in the quality of an interpreter. My master finding me more faithful and useful, soon employed me to traffic for him in the inland countries, and I travelled with the caravans into most parts of Amasia, Turcomania, Armenia, Curdistan, and Persia; and, executing my commissions to the satisfaction of my master, he gave me my liberty, upon condition that I would, during his life, serve him in the capacity of steward. I accepted, with thanks, his bounteous offer, and Alla made the time of my servitude as the shadow before the sun.

Within two years my master died, and commanded me on his death-bed to make up his effects, and send or carry them to England to his brother, who, he
said,

said, but little deserved them, (but the grave should not be entered by those who were at enmity) allowing me a quarter part for my subsistence: "For freedom," said he, "without property, is but an obligation to change, perhaps a good master for a worse." I was greatly affected at the death of my master, and resolved to undertake the journey to England in person, reserving only one-tenth of my master's fortune, which was sufficient to satisfy the desires of one whose hope was not fixed on the pleasures of life.

'Having collected my master's effects, I passed through the Mediterranean to Leghorn, and from thence to Paris, and so by Calais to London. In the countries which I passed, I saw, with surprize, the magnificence of the Popish religion; where, however, ceremony seems to possess the seat of moral duties, and superstition is clothed in the vestments of faith. I was surprized to find such absurdities in Europe, where I was warned by my master to expect the most rational customs, and the purest light of virtue and religion. But the female glance will not always bear to be exposed, and the veils of the east would well become the faces of the European ladies. I often perceived a customary monotony in the prayers of Christian priests, and the fervour of devotion was buried in the unmeaning gestures of its votaries. In the east we fall low before Alla, we are earnest in our petitions; but in Europe, Christians seem as unconcerned in their temple as in their houses of refreshment, and often as loquacious and familiar. But this I have observed more frequently in England, than in any other part of the world. Indeed, the English behaved as though they were wiser than the God they pretend to worship; they attend him with great indifference; and, if the face is an index of the mind, a by-stander may perceive, that when they meet together to worship their Deity, they think of every thing but religion. Perhaps a variety of attitudes is, among Christians, a mark of the highest adoration; if so, the English are the most meritorious devotees I ever beheld. Some are sitting, some are standing, some are lolling, some are yawning, some are even sleeping, and all these varieties are to be met with in the same part of their worship; so that a stranger would imagine, that there was a great diversity of opinion among Christians, even in the same church, which was the most decent and becoming posture for a sinner to use before a God of purity; for so I think the Christians call their Deity. But I will not trouble you with my observations, which are chiefly religious, as my first studies in life naturally led me to observe the different modes of religion among mankind.

' I waited upon the brother of my deceased master with a faithful account of his effects, and informed him how generous my master had been to me, in allotting me one quarter of his effects. Mr. Edward Wimbleton changed colour at my relation; the death of his brother did not seem to effect him so much, as my declaration, that my master had been so beneficent to me. I was grieved to observe this behaviour in a Christian; and to find that a man, in the most enlightened kingdom of the earth, should think so avariciously of riches, and shew so little respect to his benefactor and brother. But I hastened to relieve his disquietude, as it is my maxim to make every one as happy as I can, leaving justice and judgment to the eternal Alla.'

"Though my master has been thus indulgent, Sir," said I, "yet I did not think it decent in me to reward myself so amply as his partial fondness might fancy I deserved; and therefore I have only taken one tenth part, and the rest I am ready to deliver up to you."

' Mr. Edward Wimbleton was pleased at my answer. "Modesty and decency," said he, "are the most useful attendants on those who were born to serve; and I commend your fidelity to my brother, in not presuming to take that, which sickness only, and an impaired judgment, might influence him to lavish and squander away. He always was too generous, he hurt his fortune here in England formerly by the same vice, and much good counsel have I given him ere now on that topic, when he wanted to persuade

suade me to lend him money, to make up his broken affairs; but I rather advised him to seek his fortune out of the kingdom; and if I had supplied him here, he never had gone to Aleppo, or been the man he was when he died." He then commended my fidelity to my master, and commanded me to wait upon him the next morning. This I did, and took with me the will of the deceased, wherein my legacy was specified; and I found it not useless to me.

' Mr. Edward Wimbleton, when he saw me in the morning, abused me much; calling me many names, which were a reflection on my country, and my religion. These I submitted to patiently, considering how often the Christians are abused and stigmatized by the followers of Mahomet. But his threats were succeeded by more alarming severities; for opening his counting-house door, he beckoned to some ruffians, who called themselves officers of justice, and commanded them to seize me, and carry me to prison, as a debtor to him. I insisted that I owed no man any thing. To this my master's brother answered, that I had cajoled him with a false story of my honesty and moderation, and under pretence of not taking a quarter of his brother's fortune which was left me, I had taken a tenth part, when in reality none was left me.

' To this I answered, that I could produce my master's will, which was properly attested; and that I had a friend in London, a gentleman who had been long resident in Aleppo, who had cautioned me to be watchful of his dealings; that if the officers had the power of the law, they might use it; but if not, my friend would inform against Mr. Wimbleton, if he did not meet me on the Exchange by two o'clock.

' At this instant we heard a violent knocking at the door; at which Mr. Wimbleton turned pale; and the officers, if such they were, looked aghast. I took advantage of their consternation, and hurried out of the counting-house to the street-door, and saw my dear friend with several gentlemen behind him.

"Sir," said I, "you are come in time to save me from the designs of several ill-looking men. Mr. Wimbleton charges me with imposition; but I have in my pocket the will of my master."

"Where is Mr. Wimbleton?" said my friend; "is there no servant in the house?" And he knocked again.

"This, Sir,"? said I, "is the counting-house," (pointing to the door;) "I left him in it with several men, whom he called officers of justice." My friend then rapped at the door of the counting-house, and was told from within, that Mr. Wimbleton saw no company, nor did any business that day. "Well," answered my friend, "I am not much concerned about that, as I have rescued a poor stranger from destruction."

' We quitted the house of my master's brother, and my friend carried me to the 'Change, and declared to every one the usage I had met with, and the right I had to insist on a quarter of my master's effects. But how was I surprised to find, that my behaviour, so far from being applauded, was laughed at by every one! "It is a pity he should have any," said one, "since he knows no better how to make use of it."--- "'I should suspect," said another, "that he really had no right to any; for what man upon earth, who might have had a quarter, would be satisfied with a tenth?" ' In short, every one asked to see the will, which being read, cleared all doubt and dispute.

' But now a different clamour arose, and my friend, and all that were present, advised me to prosecute Mr. Wimbleton for my whole legacy.

"Gentlemen," said I, "I never wished for more than I have; every man ought to set bounds to his desires; mine are, I bless Heaven, amply indulged: to have more than enough is needless, is burdensome; too much rain does not nourish, but causes the fruits of the earth to rot and decay. There is a wind which filleth the sails of the mill, and there is a wind which destroyeth by over-much power. "The man," said they all, "is beside himself; he has
fooled

fooled away his wealth, he knows not the value of riches."

" Beside," continued I, " gentlemen, I cannot accept of such obligations as are unreasonable: the bounty of my master bore no proportion to my merit; though his munificence was great, yet it should not destroy the humility of my own thoughts; but, exclusive of all these considerations, I have already given up the remainder to my master's brother; I have resigned all pretensions to that which I never thought I merited or deserved."

" That, indeed," said they, " is bad; but did you sign any such release? did you say it before witnesses? has Mr. Wimbleton any proof to bring against you? If it was only between yourselves, the law will take no notice of his evidence, and you may proceed safely against him."

" Mr. Wimbleton's proofs," said I, " are of little consequence to me, I bear within myself a witness and record of all my actions; one who will not acquit me, though the judgment of princes should pronounce me guiltless."

" This poor man," said they, " has a comical way of talking and thinking, but I believe we may venture to pronounce, that he will never rise in the world." ' After this most of them left me: and one of the few that staid, said---

" Stranger, I admire your notions, your contentment, and your modesty: but give me leave to say, you are neglecting the public welfare, while you endeavour to provide only for your own private advantage. To bring an infamous man to justice is a debt you owe to the public, and what you recover from him, you may reasonably lay out in some public service. This is the great law of society; and to do good to multitudes, is far more preferable than the private satisfaction of eating or drinking to ourselves alone."

" Sir," answered I, " your notions also are right; but in the present case what opportunity have I of bringing an offender to justice, unless I demand from him what I have already freely delivered up to him?

The

The public surely cannot require the sacrifice of my conscience, nor can public justice be exalted through private vices."

"Sir," said he, "I shall say no more than this; the law has befriended you in your present case. Mr. Wimbleton is in your power, and you are to blame if you let him escape: nay, let me tell you, the world has reason to expect this from you; and he who hides an offender from justice, is little better than the knave who commits the offence."

'At this they all left me, and a new set of gazers succeeded, whom I avoided as soon as possible, by leaving the place; and having returned to my lodgings, I began to reflect on the scene that was passed.

"The refinements of Europe," said I, "are too subtle for the grofs understanding of an Asiatic; and I was mistaken when I thought that virtue had the same outlines in every community.

'Traffic is the prophet of the Europeans, and weatlh is their Alla. I will, however, remain among them till I have learned their sciences, whose roots first grew in Asia, but whose fruit is with these sons of care."

'With this resolution, I applied myself to the cultivation of those sciences which are so justly admired in the East. I studied the power of figures, and found my mind enlightened by the application of a few magical Arabic characters; with nine figures I was taught to measure the great parent of day, and to calculate the distance of the stars of heaven; to foretel the baneful eclipses of the sun and moon, and to prophesy unto kingdoms and nations the loss of the light of heaven: by these talismans of science could I measure the inaccessible heights of the mountains, and the wide surface of the deep, and threaten the earth with the portentous appearance of terrifying comets. Think not, therefore, O Morell, that I spared either trouble or time to arrive at the depths of mathematical knowledge. I adored that bright constellation of the North, the heaven-taught Newton, with whom I often held such converse, as the inhabitants of the East are said to hold with the

Genii

Genii of mankind. I saw him bring down the moon from the realms of night, to influence and actuate the tides of the sea, and heard him read in his books the laws of the tumultuous ocean; he marked the courses of the stars with his wand, and reduced excentric orbs to the obedience of his system. He caught the swift-flying light, and divided it's rays; he marshalled the emanations of the sun under their different-coloured banners, and gave symmetry and order to the glare of the day; he explained the dark eternal laws of Nature, and seemed acquainted with the dictates of Heaven.

' Such a master over-paid all the toils I had taken in my voyage to England; and what I could not find in the public resorts of the merchants, I discovered in the closets of the learned.

' It was matter of great surprize and joy to an ignorant and bigotted Asiatic, to be thus let loose from his narrow prejudices, into an immeasurable system of planets and worlds; to look with contempt at the Caspian Sea, delineated on the artificial globe, which was once like a boundless prospect before my eyes, and discover, with a motion of my finger, all the kingdoms of the earth exposed to my view. But then, when the wide extent of sea and land had filled my mind, to look on all as a small attendant planet on the sun, and on the sun itself as but one among a thousand stars, of equal, if not superior magnitude; my whole soul was lost in the long, long extended idea; and I seemed but as an invisible atom amidst ten thousand worlds! Nor did my researches end here: I attended my friend to Cambridge, and examined with him the systems of the natural philosophers. I was pleased to see facts preferred to hypotheses, and Nature dictating her own laws. I traced with admiration the principles of mechanism, and saw the regular scale of multiplied power by which Archimedes would have moved the earth. The secrets, too, of chemistry, were laid open before me; inert matter was engaged in warlike commotion, and fire was brought down from heaven to entertain me. But it was not amusement without instruction, nor

the

the cause of admiration unfruitful in knowledge; I had the reasonings of the philosophers on these subjects, and considered their conclusions; and I often smiled to see opposite opinions arising from, and supported by, the same experiments. This taught me at once the beauty of nature, and the folly of man. I found ignorance growing on knowledge, and that the mazes of learning were leading me to their original entrance.

'I arrived at the same place of uncertainty from whence I set out; with this difference, I was assured of human ignorance, while others were preparing to be deceived by a shew of learning. I left this seat of knowledge, pursuing their circle of studies; concluding, from what I had seen, that science is no farther useful, than as it conduces to the improvement of life; and that to know, and not to practice, is like him who is busy in the seed-time, and idle in harvest.

'Having joined a knowledge of physic and history to the sciences I was before master of, I began to pant after my native land, where there was a wide field open to display my knowledge. But war, which is the bane of science, prevented my journey to Aleppo. The regions of Asia being barred from any approach in the Mediterranean, were yet open in the East-Indies: a fleet being destined for those parts, I entered as a passenger in one of the company's ships, and arrived, after a tedious passage, in the bay of Bengal.

'In the progress of my voyage my intellectual knowledge was confirmed, and I was pleased to add experience to science. The wonders of the deep are not less magnificent than the rude and enchanting scenery of the majestic mountains; and waves are hurled on waves by contending storms, till mimic Alps appear equal in horror to the true; but he who is certain that his life is never a moment in his own power, will be as calm in the tempest as when he runs before the breeze. It is of little consequence, whether the worm or the loud thunder destroys us; whether the earth open and swallow up a nation, or

whether

whether that people go down to their graves the single victims of death.

'I resided some time in Bengal before I could find any opportunity of proceeding to the Mogul's court, where I had resolved to seek for preferment. The monarchs of the East are fond of the European sciences! they in some measure tolerate the religion of the Jesuits, that they may be benefited by the ingenious labours of that insinuating society; but they are no friends to the Christian faith, and the missionary who was to depend on his religion only, would soon fall a sacrifice to either the Mahommedan doctors, or the Indian bramins. But at present religion is the pretended motive of the Jesuits travels into India, though perhaps they are as little zealous to propagate the true doctrines of Christianity as those they serve are to believe them. They are good mathematicians, but bad saints, unless where they expect some temporal advantage from the propagation of their faith.

'Nothing, therefore, but their useful knowledge, could prevail upon the Eastern monarchs to caress a society whom all Asia despises. The machinations of these fathers, though carried on by art, are yet betrayed by the proud spirit of those who conduct them, and their fate is determined whenever the Asiatics shall have learned their sciences. These reflections induced me to study the European arts, and I made no doubt but that my presence would be acceptable at the court of the great Mogul. My surmises were not unjust. I made myself known to the nabobs and vizirs of the court, and being provided with an entire set of the best mathematical instruments, and a portable apparatus in philosophy, I was heard with pleasure, and attended to with admiration; my fame soon reached the Mogul's ears, and that mighty monarch ordered the wonderful philosopher of the East into his presence.

'My knowledge and experiments raised the suspicion of the Mogul, and he fancied that I was a Jesuit disguised. Ten learned Mohammedan doctors were ordered to examine me. I went through my ablutions

tions and purifications, and the hidden ceremonies of the religion of our prophet. I explained to them my birth and manner of life, and told them under whose instructions I had imbibed the precepts of the faithful. I painted to them the days of my slavery, and my education in Britain, the land of science. I declared to them finally my desire of implanting in Asia the seeds of that learning which I had gathered in Europe, and besought their assistance to cultivate and ripen the great design.

' My brethren were amazed at my discourse, and rejoiced at my success; they hastened to discover my intentions to the Mogul, and to assure him of my uprightness and truth. That powerful Monarch was enraptured at my design, and immediately ordered me a building in his palace. He daily sent for me to exhibit the amazing effects of my art, and employed me in mathematical and astronomical labours.

' Being returned to my own religion, I begged leave again to officiate as an iman of our law. I preached to the people at my leisure, and read in the book of our prophet before them. Alla prospered my labours, and my fame extended over Asia. Respect and honour were on my right-hand, and my left was as the handmaid of science. Aurengzebe, the great conqueror of the earth, was my friend, and he placed the Sultan Ofmir, his son, under my tuition. Ofmir was but five years old when the Mogul entrusted him to me.

" Let virtue be the basis of knowledge, and let knowledge be as a slave before her." ' Such were the words of Aurengzebe: I heard, and fell prostrate; and applied myself to the instruction of my infant charge.

' And now it was, O Morell, that I conceived the purpose of disguising the true doctrine of morality under the delightful allegories of romantic enchantment. Mine eye had seen the great varieties of nature, and the powers of my fancy could recal and realize the images. I was pleased with mine own inventions, and hoped to find that virtue would steal

into

into the breast, amidst the flowers of language and description.

'My lessons, though designed only for the young prince, were read and admired by the whole court. Osmir alone was displeased at them; his mind was not disposed to attention: he cursed the hours of his confinement; he read without benefit; he admired vice in all it's deformity, and despised the lessons of virtue and goodness.

'In the mean time, Asia received with pleasure the Lessons of Horam the son of Asmar; but yet what was Asia, or the whole world, while one unconquerable mind was left, for whom alone they were first intended! But although various countries were my admirers, the maxims of Horam had no effect on the lives of those who commended my writings.

'Osmir grew up under my care, and I had the mortification to be called the preceptor of the most abandoned of mankind. In a few years he became a monster, and a man. It was then Horam was destined to feel the weight of his malice. Aurengzebe perceived the haughtiness and the vicious principles of his son, and made no doubt but that he would soon aspire to his throne. This made the prudent monarch resolve to take all power from him. Osmir was confined by the order of the Mogul, and but a few chosen attendants suffered to see him.

'This malicious prince, finding himself curbed by the authority of his father, and supposing me to be the cause of his confinement, accused me to his attendants of advising him to seize on the throne of India. The pretended confession was carried to the Mogul, and ignominious chains thrown over me. The sultans and the nabobs were all pleased at my fate. I wondered not at the fickleness of the courtiers, but was astonished at the malice of Osmir.

'In a few days I was drawn out of a dungeon, whither I had been ordered, and brought before Aurengzebe. That monarch had assumed the imperial frown, but I saw the beams of mercy in his eye. He ordered my chains to be taken off, and commanded the slaves and courtiers to withdraw. When we were alone, I prostrated myself before him, and remained on the earth.

"Rise, O Horam," said Aurengzebe; "rise, thou faithful servant; I do not believe the accusation against thee. Declare thine own innocence, and I shall be persuaded of the truth."

"Rather," said I, "O master of the world, let Horam thy slave perish, than that the truth of Osmir thy son be questioned. Yes, I do confess, I have often counselled the prince to aspire to the virtues of truth, wisdom, justice, and moderation, the great ornaments of thy throne; and I think my life should pay the forfeit of my presumption. Ill-fated Horam," continued I, bursting into tears, for my heart was overcharged, "how are thy endeavours frustrated, and how is the fruit of thy labour blasted!"

"Blasted, indeed, thou good old man!" said Aurengzebe; "for I must either accuse my first-born of the utmost meanness, or my faithful slave of rebellion. There is one way left to me. Depart from the court, Horam; thou shalt have yearly a thousand sequins of gold. But on thy faith declare to me, that thou wilt never leave my empire: I cannot myself employ thee; and yet, O Horam, I cannot lose thee."

' I fell again prostrate at the feet of Aurengzebe; I thanked the merciful prince for his continued goodness, and I prayed aloud to the great Alla to change the heart of the ill-fated Osmir.

' Aurengzebe gave me a ring from his finger, and bid me depart silently in the night to the utmost confines of his empire.

' I obeyed with cheerfulness; and, by the assistance of a nabob, who was my friend, and whom Aurengzebe had ordered to take care of me, I travelled to the mouth of the Ganges, and from thence, by sea, to this settlement of your countrymen; where I have bought up every copy of my unavailing instructions that I could meet with, and have committed them to the flames, to be devoured by the god of Pagans!'

THE

THE TALES OF THE GENII.

VOLUME THE FIRST.

PATNA and Coulor, the children of Giualar, the Iman of Terki, were the pride of their parents, and the wonder of the inhabitants of Mazanderan. Their aged father took them daily into a grove of oranges and citrons, which furrounded a fountain in his garden, and feating them under the fhadow of thofe fragrant trees, befide the pure bafon, after he had firft dipped them in it's waters, to wafh away the bad impreffions of the world, he thus began his inftructive leffon :---

'Hearken, ye tender branches, to your parent
' ftock ; bend to the leffons of inftruction, and imbibe
' the maxims of age and experience ! As the pifmire
' creeps not to its labour till led by its elders ; as the
' young eagle foars not to the fun, but under the
' fhadow of its mother's wing; fo neither doth the
' child of mortality fpring forth to action, unlefs the
' parent hand point out its deftined labour.

' But no labour fhall the hand of Giualar appoint
' unto Patna and Coulor, except the worfhip of Alla
' the firft of beings, and of Mahomet the great pro-
' phet of the faithful.

' Bafe are the defires of the flefh, and mean the
' purfuits of the fons of the earth ! they ftretch out
' their finews like the patient mule, they perfevere
' in their chace after trifles, as the camel in the defart.
' As the leopard fprings on his prey, fo doth man
' rejoice over his riches, and bafk in the fun of floth-
' fulnefs like the lion's cub.

'On the stream of life float the bodies of the careless and intemperate, as the carcases of the dead on
the waves of the Tigris.

'The vultures of the sky destroy the carcase, and
man is devoured by the sins of his flesh.

'Retire from men, my children, like the pelican
in the wilderness, and fly with the wild ass's colt
into the deserts of peace.'

As Giualar uttered these words, he perceived an unusual fragrance issue from a large citron tree, which was planted opposite the tender parent and his attentive children, which in a moment dropping its leaves, the trunk swelled into human proportion, and discovered to their view a bright female form.

'Giualar,' said the Genius, 'I approve your care,
and am pleased to see your little progeny thus instructed from the mouth of their parent. A father
is blessed in the wisdom of his children, and the
tongue of a fool shall pierce the heart of his mother.
But why is Giualar so careful to prevent his offspring from entering into life? Alla has made
them the children of the world, and their labour is a
debt which they must not refuse their fellow-citizens. To drive them into the desart would be indeed to make them the companions of savages and
brutes, but the wise purposes of Alla must not be
prevented. No man is master of himself, but the
public is lord over him; and to endeavour to defeat the purposes of Heaven is madness and folly.
Rightly does Giualar caution his children to avoid
the follies and vices of life, but they must be subject
to temptations ere their worth be approved. Suffer
me, therefore, good Iman, to carry your children
where they shall hear the lessons of humanity from
the lips of our immortal race, and where they shall
learn from the failings or virtues of others, to guide
their steps aright through the vallies of life.'

Giualar was transported at the offer of the Genius, and falling down before her, was about to offer her

his

his prayers and praises; but she raising him up---' O
' Iman,' said she, ' pay thy vows to Alla alone, and
' not to the beings which, however thy superiors, are
' yet the work of his hands. The moon is now be-
' tween us and the eye of day; ere it surround the
' inhabitants of earth, Patna and Coulor shall return
' unto their parents; rejoice at the favour shewn unto
' thy race, and rest in peace till a new moon bring
' them back into thy arms.' So saying, she embraced
the young Patna and Coulor, and leaping into the
fountain, disappeared with her charge.

In a few moments the children of Giualar found
themselves on a wide extended plain, which was terminated at one end by a noble palace. Moang, the
Genius who led them, bid them observe that building.
' It is there,' said the kind female, ' that Patna and
' Coulor must learn to know good from evil, light from
' darkness. But one thing observe, my children, that
' silence be upon your lips; hear, see, and learn, but
' offer not to mingle speech with the Genii of man-
' kind.'

As soon as they arrived at the palace, Moange led
her little charge into a spacious saloon, where, on
twenty-eight thrones of gold, sat the good race of
Genii; and beneath, on carpets covering the whole
saloon, were numberless of the lower class of Genii,
each with two or more of the faithful under their
charge, who were permitted to hear the instructive
lessons of that useful race. Iracagem, whose throne and
canopy was more exalted than the rest, first began.

' O race of immortals,' said the silver-bearded sage,
' to whose care and protection the offspring of clay
' are committed, say what hath been the success of your
' labours; what vices have you punished; what vir-
' tues rewarded; what false lights have you extin-
' guished? Helpless race of mortals; but for our pro-
' tection, how vain would be your toils, how endless
' your researches!---Say virtuous companion,' said he
to the Genius that was seated nearest him, ' let us
' hear

'hear what have been the effects of thy tutelary 'care?'

At these words the Genius arose from his throne, and standing before it with a decent awe, thus began his pleasing adventure---

'At your command, O sage Iracagem, my voice
'shall not remain in silence: small as my abilities are
'in the preservation of the human race, yet have I
'endeavoured to act according to the precepts of our
'master Mahomet; and the success that has attended
'my labours, may be in some measure known from
'the History of the Merchant Abudah.'

TALE I.

The History of the Merchant Abudah; or, the Talisman of Oromanes.

IN the centre of the quay of Bagdat, where the wealth of the whole earth is poured forth for the benefit of the faithful, lived the fortunate Abudah, possessed of the merchandize and riches of many various nations, caressed by the mighty, and blessed by the indigent; daily providing for thousands by his munificence, and winning daily the hearts of thousands by his charity and generosity. But however magnificently or royally the days of Abudah might be spent, his nights were the nights of disturbance and affliction. His wife, who was fairer than the greatest beauties of Circassia, and his children, who were lovelier than the offspring of the Fairies, and his riches, which were greater than the desires of man could consume, were unavailing to drive from his imagination the terrors of the night. For no sooner was the merchant retired within the walls of his chamber, than a little box, which no art might remove from it's place, advanced without help into the centre of the chamber, and opening, discovered to his sight the form of a diminutive old hag, who, with crutches, hopped forward to Abudah, and every night addressed him in the following terms---' O Abudah, to whom Mahomet hath
'given

' given such a profusion of blessings, why delayest thou
' to search out the talisman of Oromanes? the which,
' whoever possesseth, shall know neither uneasiness
' nor discontent; neither may he be assaulted by the
' tricks of fortune, or the power of man. Till you
' are possessed of that valuable treasure, O Abudah,
' my presence shall nightly remind you of your idle-
' ness, and my chest remain for ever in the cham-
' bers of your repose.

Having thus said, the hag retired into her box, shaking her crutches, and with an hideous yell closed herself in, and left the unfortunate merchant on a bed of doubt and anxiety for the rest of the night.

This unwelcome visitant still repeating her threats, rendered the life of Abudah most miserable and fatiguing: neither durst he tell his grievance, lest the strangeness of the adventure should rather move the laughter than the compassion of his friends. At length, however, wearied out with the strange and importunate demands of this nightly hag, he ventured to open his mind; and in the midst of his friends, asked publicly, as he was feasting in his saloon, who could give any account of the talisman of Oromanes, or the place where it was preserved. To this question his friends could return him no satisfactory answer: they had all indeed heard of it's virtues, but despaired of finding it. So that Abudah was forced to return again to the upbraiding of his nocturnal hag, and knew not what course to steer in the pursuit of the appointed treasure.

The next day he caused it to be cried publicly in the streets of Bagdat, that Abudah the merchant would give much riches to the man who could inform him where the talisman of Oromanes was lodged. This declaration was made for many days successively, but no one appeared to satisfy the enquiries of the impatient Abudah.

After many days, a poor traveller, who had been spoiled of his goods by the Arabians, passing through Bagdat,

Bagdat, heard the publication, and immediately offered to go to Abudah, and make known the place where the talisman of Oromanes was preserved. The friends of the wealthy merchant joyfully carried the poor travaller to the palace of Abudah, and with great tumult introduced him to the merchant, who was sitting on a low sopha, and seemed entirely indifferent to the music which played before him, the desert of elegancies which were prepared for his food, and the caresses of his wife and children, who endeavoured by their tenderness and affection to divert the gloom that overshadowed him.

' Abudah,' cried his friends, (lifting up their voices together.) ' behold the discoverer of the talisman of
' Oromanes.'

At their voices the afflicted merchant looked up, like one awakened from a dream.

' This,' said his friends, presenting the poor traveller to him, ' this is the man who will engage to point
' out to you the talisman of Oromanes.

The traveller was now about to begin his relation, when Abudah, having eyed him round, commanded the apartment to be cleared, that no one but himself might enjoy the discovery. His family and friends obediently departed; and the traveller, being left alone with the merchant, thus began his tale.

' Your fortune and attendance, O wealthy citizen
' of Bagdat, allow of your search after the talisman of
' Oromanes; but to the poor and needy, to the out-
' casts of fortune, no such happiness is permitted: they
' may indeed wander, and examine, but the talisman
' is for ever shut up from their search; for infinite are
' the expences which attend the discovery, and the
' large rewards which must be given to them who
' help the inquirer forward in his adventure after the
' sacred talisman. Myself, O merchant, have slaved
' through life to obtain a sufficiency for that great end
' and purpose; but since the prophet has repeatedly
' blasted

' blasted my designs, and reduced me to my original
' state of want, I must endeavour to wean my af-
' fections, and rest contented, though unblest.

' But, my friend,' said Abudah, ' you neglect to in-
' form me where I may find or purchase this heavenly
' talisman.

' It is lodged,' replyed the poor traveller, ' in the
' valley of Bocchim; princes are it's guardians, and it
' is treasured up amidst all the riches of the earth:
' you cannot obtain admittance there, without you go
' loaded with every variety that is costly and expen-
' sive; which you must present to the Genii, who keep
' a watch over this earthly paradise of riches; and if
' your present be not sufficiently costly, your labour
' is lost.'

' I have,' cried Abudah, (rejoiced to hear the talisman might be obtained by riches) ' nine thousand
' acres of pasturage around the rivers of Bagdat; I
' have twelve thousand estates of fruits, and oils, and
' corn; I have twenty-two mines of the finest dia-
' monds, and six hundred vessels which fish for and
' produce the most costly pearl; I have, moreover,
' eight hundred warehouses, and four hundred store-
' rooms, filled with the most precious bales of silks and
' brocades; besides these, the fortunes of nine vizirs
' mortgaged for an hundred years, and all the beauti-
' full slaves of Circassia are at my dipoſal.'

' O happy, happy Abudah!' interrupted the poor
traveller; ' thine then, and only thine, is it to pur-
' chase a passage into the valley of Bocchim.'

' If so,' continued Abudah, overjoyed at the traveller's exclamation, ' direct me instantly to the en-
' trance of the valley.'

' Alas, Sir,' answered the traveller, ' it is in the de-
' sarts of Arabia, many days journey from hence,
' besides your presents are not ready, nor your guard,
' lest the Arabs spoil you of your riches, and prevent
' your application at the entrance of the valley of Boc-
' chim: but if you will permit your servant to direct

you

'you in the choice of the presents, some of which will take much time in preparing, by the next spring you may set forward, and speedily find an issue to your journey.'

Abudah acquiesced in the arguments of the traveller; and having given orders that he should use as he pleased his immense riches, he gave himself entirely up to the meditation of the intended journey. The poor traveller, having sufficient powers, disposed of the riches of Abudah to purchase the necessary presents, and hired nine thousand archers to accompany the wealthy caravan of the merchant into the desarts. The appointed time being arrived, and every thing prepared, Abudah took a tender leave of his wife and family, and began his journey with the poor traveller to the valley of Bocchim.

The Merchant Abudah's Adventure in the Valley of Bocchim.

ON the ninth day of the third month, ere the sun was rising on the mosques of Bagdat, was the sumptuous caravan drawn up in long order through the streets of that city, which Abudah beheld from his windows. Five hundred archers, mounted on the fleetest coursers, led the van; behind whom were twelve thousand oxen, thirty thousand sheep, and two hundred of the finest horses of Arabia. Next to these came six hundred armed with pole-axes and scymitars, with silken banners, displaying the blessings of pasturage, and the utility and conveniency of cattle for the service of man.

After these were driven two hundred camels, laden with all manner of dried and preserved fruits; a thousand more with all sorts of grain; a thousand with the richest wines; and five hundred with the most pure oil; five hundred more with spices and perfumes; and behind these a thousand armed husbandmen, singing the blessings of the earth, burning in censers the most costly perfumes, and bearing flaxen and silken

banners,

banners, representing the seasons and annual labours of husbandry.

These were of the first day's procession; the second began with five hundred miners armed with sledges and hammers, whom a large car followed, drawn by twenty strong oxen, having within it all the implements of iron; and above, in the upper part, an hero, who commanded the armed men in the whole cavalcade. Then came five hundred artificers, and after them a car drawn by twenty mules with the implements of lead, and a curious artizan on the top of the car, singing the uses of metals. Behind these came five hundred more artificers, with their different tools, and a car drawn by twenty horses with cast figures, statues, and implements of brass, and a cunning artificer on the top of the car. After these followed a thousand artificers in silver, and a sumptuous car of solid silver drawn by twelve unicorns, and laden with plate and silver coin; also an hundred camels behind, laden also with silver; and on the car sat the steward of Abudah.

At a small distance from these came forward a thousand armed cap-a-pee, after the manner of Saracens; and behind these followed, on sumptuous mules, five hundred of the principle foreign merchants, richly habited, with the emblems of commerce curiously wrought in their garments, who were followed by an enormous car drawn by four elephants, laden with golden emblems and devices, with great quantity of that precious metal; the car also was of beaten gold. And into this, taking leave of Abudah, ascended the poor traveller, arrayed in purple and gold, and pointed with a golden rod toward the valley of Bocchim: and these compleated the second days procession.

On the third day issued forth from the gates of Bagdat, the final procession of the caravan of the merchant Abudah: a thousand archers began the ceremony, preceded by a martial band of music, and bearing among their ranks fifty silken streamers interwoven

with

with gold, and having the emblems of Abudah's family wrought in their centres. Next to these came fifty carriages laden with the richest silks and brocades, and two hundred surrounded the carriages arrayed in the different habits of two hundred nations; after whom came fifty negroes on dromedaries, bearing about their necks strings of the most costly pearl. After these a thousand armed soldiers, after the European manner, who at a small distance were followed by an hundred mutes, behind whom came in two hundred palanquins as many beautiful slaves from Circassia, each guarded by four eunuchs, and clad in the richest robes.

The next in procession was the merchant Abudah, drawn in a chariot of pearl of the most curious workmanship, by ten milk-white steeds, whose trappings were of gold. As to the garments of the merchant, nothing could be conceived more magnificent; but the splendor of the jewels that were interwoven with the clothing, exceeded the most lavish description: on each side the chariot a hundred musicians attended, and fifty slaves burning the choicest perfumes; various splendid banners waved around him, and two hundred friends behind of the highest rank in the city of Bagdat, attended the illustrious and wealthy Abudah; after whom a thousand archers, and numberless camels laden with all manner of provisions, water, and wine, brought up the rear of this magnificent cavalcade.

On the thirteenth day they halted in a plain, bounded on it's sides with lofty mountains, and at the farther end with a deep forest of cedars and palms. Here the poor traveller descending with Abudah, walked forward toward the forest before them.

The traveller led Abudah into the forest through thickets almost impervious, save the blind path which guided them forward. In this manner they passed till the evening, when the traveller, entering a cave, disappeared from the wondering Abudah. The merchant essayed to follow him, but looking into the cave, he found it had no bottom, therefore he was obliged to desist.

The

The sun was now sinking from the mountains, and the glowing skies seemed to tip the woods with their reddening light. Abudah being fatigued, first sought out a tree, and climbed into it, resolved there to wait the dawn of the morning. But the severe fatigues had so much exhausted him, that although he had resolved to watch till the morning, yet sleep soon overpowered him, and made him forget either the wonders or the dangers that surrounded him.

Abudah, in the morning, when he awaked, was surprised at an unusual glitter about him; and looking more stedfast, he found the tree wherein he sat to be of pure gold, and the leaves of silver, with fruit like rubies hanging in clusters on the branches. Looking around, he also beheld the face of the country as though it had been changed; for on every side appeared the most glorious palaces that eye could conceive, glittering with silver, gold, and precious stones; so that the whole appeared more like an heavenly than an earthly situation.

Descending full of wonder from the tree, he found the ground he trod on to be gold dust, and the stones pearls: these were covered with flowers which seemed formed of vegetable crystal, emeralds, and amethysts. Trees and shrubs of silver and gold met his eye, growing almost visibly about him. At the farthest end of the prospect he beheld a vast and expanded dome, which seemed to cover a whole plain, and rose to the clouds. The dome shone so brightly by the reflection of the costly materials of which it was composed, that he could hardly look toward it. However, as it seemed most to take his attention, he advanced up to the dome.

The dome, which was of entire gold, stood upon three hundred pillars of precious stone; one emerald formed the shaft of one pillar, one diamond the capital, and one ruby the pedestal; the intermediate spaces between the pillars were of crystal, one piece between each pillar; so that the inside of the dome was visible

from

from all parts. The architrave was of solid pearl, inlaid with curious emblems, composed of festoons of amethysts, topazes, carbuncles, rubies, emeralds, sapphires, and the most sparkling diamonds.

Abudah, though the richest of mankind, was struck with astonishment at the profusion of riches and beauty which he beheld; and entering at one of the four portals, (for the dome had four, one to each quarter of the heavens) he beheld an ancient form, seated on a throne, which looked too bright to distinguish what glorious materials it was made of. A great number of crowned heads attended him; and these were supported by inferior beings, all clad in the most superb vestments. All around the dome were placed, with great beauty and symmetry, numberless heaps of wealth and riches; and the very pavement on which he trod was covered over with tapestry carpet, representing the riches of the earth, all in their natural colours.

Abudah, as abashed at this amazing magnificence, and beholding such personages within the dome, was retiring, when one of the chief of the attendants, who stood nearest the throne, advancing, beckoned Abudah forward. The merchant obeyed with trembling, and, as he came forward, bowed himself to the ground; which the royal personage perceiving, who sat on the throne, spake thus to him---

' Fear not, Abudah, thou hast ever been a favourite
' of the genius of riches. I am thy friend; and this
' journey which thou hast undertaken in honour of
' me, in hope here to find the talisman of the great
' Oromanes, should not go unrewarded.---And first,
' lead Abudah,' said he to the genius who had presented the merchant, ' through all my stores, and let
' him view the riches of the earth: a sight that so
' many thousands long ardently to enjoy.'

The inferior genius obeyed; and taking Abudah by the hand, he led him toward a royal palace,, facing the eastern side of the dome. Here, as Abudah entered

tered the palace, the walls of which were of the pureſt ſilver, with windows of cryſtal, he beheld incredible heaps of that precious metal, all ſeemingly compoſed like branches of trees.

'What thou feeſt here,' ſaid the genius, 'is tri-
'fling; for theſe heaps, which ſeem to lie on the
'ſurface of the ground, really are of the ſame depth
'with the centre of the earth: ſo that of this metal
'alone, there is laid up more in value than all the
'viſible riches of the world.'

The genius next carried Abudah to a ſecond palace, built of pure gold, having windows like the firſt. Here, alſo, Abudah beheld the like profuſion of gold; which, like the ſilver, continued down to the centre. Next he was ſhewn, in an huge building of adamant, a ciſtern filled with the fragments of all manner of precious ſtones and diamonds.

'Theſe, alſo,' ſaid the Genius, 'are not terminated but by the centre of the earth. Now,' continued he, 'as you obſerved in the two firſt palaces, the ſilver and gold are the little branches which drop from the trees of this vegetable valley of riches; as all things on earth are ſubject to decreaſe, which are here carefully collected, (for the rich are not exempt from toil) and placed in theſe repoſitories, the bottoms of which, at the centre of the earth, are grated, and let out ſparingly theſe ſmaller fragments: ſo likewiſe of the jewels, which fall like fruit from the trees, and break into little pieces; theſe are all thrown together to ſerve the earth, but none above ſuch a ſize are admitted, nor indeed could they paſs through the grating below. Thus theſe metals and jewels mixing with the earth, and being diffuſed in its bowels, are at length ſtopped by the rocks and ſtones, and ſo form mines in different parts of the world, each requiring the induſtry and labour of man, that they may be brought the more ſparingly into the world.'

Abudah, having viewed theſe things, returned; and being preſented to the Genius of Riches,—

'Now,' said the Genius, bring forth the iron chest, wherein it is said the talisman of Oromanes is lodged.' At the command of the Genius, ten of an inferior order brought in an huge chest with fifty locks upon it; the chest itself was of iron, and bound round with the strongest bands, which were harder than adamant. 'There,' said the Genius to Abudah, 'there is thy reward: return to Bagdat, and live in peace all the days of thy life.'

'Must I then,' replied Abudah, 'O beneficent Genius, carry with me the chest also? or is it permitted that I take from thence the talisman of Oromanes?'

'Wouldst thou then,' replied the Genius, 'take it from its place of security? Whilst thou dost possess the chest, the talisman is thine own, and the force of man cannot bereave thee of it? Why, then, should curiosity prevail over security? It is written in the chronicles of time, that he who possesseth the talisman of Oromanes shall be happy: seek not, therefore, to disentangle the talisman from it's present state of security, till it fail thee of its promised efficacy. Take, however, these fifty keys; but beware lest thy curiosity alone tempt thee, for what mortal can say if its refulgence be not too much for man to behold!'

Having thus said, the Genius commanded Abudah to lie down on the chest, and immediately his eyes closed, and not till the morning after did he awake, and find himself in a tent, on the plain where he had left his immense caravan; but now he found but forty camels and forty servants to attend him.

Abudah enquired of his servants, what became of the riches and attendants that had travelled from Bagdat with him to that plain; but they could give no answer. They said, indeed, that they had heard of such a caravan, and that they had for some time missed their master from Bagdat; and that although they went over-night to their rest in his house at Bagdat, they found themselves with the tents and forty camels,

laden

laden with provision, on that plain in the morning; and that coming into his tent, they saw him sleeping on an iron chest, and had removed him to the sopha. 'And is the chest here?' cried Abudah. 'Here is, Sir,' replied the slave that spoke, 'an iron chest of prodigious size, and secured with many locks.'

Abudah immediately arose; and though he could not unravel the mysteries of his journey, yet seeing the chest, and finding the keys which the Genius had given him, he was contented, and ordered them to strike their tents, and begin their march for the city of Bagdat. The chest was by long poles made fast to four camels, which were placed in the centre of the caravan.

The mind of Abudah, though in possession of the chest, was yet not without it's apprehensions that the wild Arabs might come down upon his little party, and bereave him of his treasure. The first day the caravan reached a pool of water, and on it's banks the careful Abudah ordered his retinue to pitch their tents, and unload the camels from their burdens; and at the same time placed four of his slaves as centinels, toward the four different quarters of his encampment; and ordered the chest, for the greater security, to be buried in the sand under his tent, while he endeavoured to compose himself for slumber. Nor were his fears unreasonable, for at the hour of midnight a small party of Arabs stole down toward them, in order to encamp there for the benefit of the water.

Abudah had notice from his slave, who looked toward the west, of their approach, and was likewise informed that their number was small; but such was his anxiety and irresolution, and fear of losing his treasure or his life, that he dared not order them to be attacked, or prepare for flight. During this ineffectual altercation and struggle of Abudah with his fears, one of the slaves, more daring than the rest, finding his master fearful, encouraged his comrades, and

marshalling

marshalling them in order, led them toward the robbers.

The Arabs, who were not more than twenty in number, at sight of a force so much superior, turned their backs, and left Abudah's slave in quiet possession of their tents. But now the slave seeing the Arabs flying from before him, and observing the fear of his master, and the great concern that he had for the iron chest, addressed himself to the rest of the slaves, and declaring what immense treasures there might lie hid in that chest, seeing their master had left Bagdat to search for it, and had secured it with so many locks, persuaded them to rob Abudah, and depart with the riches to some other country, where they might enjoy the fruits of their rapine. This being easily agreed to, they all in a body advanced to the tent of Abudah, who came out to meet and thank them for their gallant behaviour.

The bold slave thus made answer to his master's thanks---

' The danger, O Abudah, of defending thy riches, contained in the iron chest with many locks, fell all upon thy slaves; while thou, who wert to enjoy the comfort of those riches, didst lie trembling in thy tent: wherefore, we, who have borne the burden, mean also to share the profits with thee; but that thou mayest see that we are just, one equal share shall be thy portion, and the rest belong to those who have preserved to thee even the share that will be appointed thee.' These words being ended, without any regard to either the threatenings or prayers of Abudah, they dug up the chest; and having cleared away the sand, demanded of him the keys of the fifty locks.

Abudah, finding them inexorable, besought them that they would at least give him a day to consider of their proposal. 'What,' replied the bold slave, ' a day? Why, merchant, long ere that will a thousand Arabs be upon us, invited by those that are fled; and we shall suffer death, and you and all entirely lose

the

the valuable possessions which are doubtless contained in that strong chest of iron.' It was in vain that, in return, the merchant assured them, that there was nothing therein but a poor talisman, whose virtues they could not know; and promised them all liberty and riches if they arrived safe in Bagdat with the chest. They had gone too far to trust his promises; and the slave who was their ring-leader, ordering all to retire, left Abudah for half an hour to think of their proposal.

Abudah, as soon as they had left him, threw himself upon the chest, as one who was grasping all that was dear to him, and with a loud sigh began to lament his fate; when, as before, a sleep overtaking him, he sunk motionless on his treasure. At midnight he awaked, and turning his eyes around, perceived he was in the apartments of his seraglio at Bagdat, and that his wife was sleeping near him on the sopha. The recollection of his happy escape immediately got possession of his mind; and he doubted not but he should find his chest as he had done before. Wherefore, before he saluted, or indeed thought of his wife, taking one of the sweet-scented lamps, that always were burning in the centre of his apartment, he perceived the chest in the very corner where, before, the box which had caused him so much uneasiness, used to remain fixed.

Abudah now feeling for, and taking out the fifty keys, thought himself the happiest of mankind. The danger which he conceived the talisman might be in, from lying in a chest so conspicuous, and which he had already experienced, determined him, at all hazards, to unlock with his fifty keys the iron chest, and take the talisman out, and always wear it concealed about him. With this view he began to try the first key, which, to his amazement, would fit neither of the fifty locks. At this he began to suspect that either the Genius of Riches had mistaken, which he could hardly suppose, or that some evil Genius had changed them in his bosom. 'However,' said he to himself, 'perhaps as one key will open none, one also may open all:' so taking one by one, he tried them all, but neither of the fifty keys would open a single lock.

Abudah, at this discovery, flung himself on the sopha, and began to lament his miserable fate. But he soon resolved to try the keys a second time: 'for,' said he, 'some key I have possibly missed, and such a treasure cannot be expected without much labour and pains.' At this he rose up, and was going toward the chest; when, starting at a noise in the centre of the room, he beheld the little box, which had been the first cause of all his grief; and was saluted by the old hag, who hobbled out from her confinement, and began to terrify the afflicted merchant in the following terms.---

'O, senseless Abudah! to hope that the talisman of Oromanes might be bought with riches. Thou hast indeed a chest, but thou has neither a means, nor canst thou force open this chest to search for thy treasure: what then art thou the better for thy possession, or happier for thy chest of iron? It will, indeed, convey thee where thou desirest, and thou mayest rest upon it; but waking, thou feelest the tortures of anxiety, and feelest them the sharper, because thou fearest to lose what thou canst not enjoy: go, then, and search till thou findest the keys of the fifty locks; but be not so senseless as to suppose, that the Genius would have parted with the treasure, could he have made any use of it. In a far different country must thou hope to find those keys which will unlock that chest; a joyous country, where serenity ever dwells, and pleasure reigns eternal.

'A short respite will I give thee; but ere this moon be passed, let me find you active, or I shall invent double horrors to surround you.' Having thus said, the box closed, and in an instant Abudah beheld it mounted on the chest, which he vainly hoped would have drove such a troublesome guest from his house.

And

COOKE'S EDITION OF
THE TALES OF THE GENII.

The Jinn appearing to Abudah when in search of the talisman.

And now Selima, his wife, awaking, beheld with surprize her husband Abudah drowned in tears by her side. She instantly pressed him in her arms, and, in transports, enquired by what happy fate he was returned.

'Why, know ye not,' replied Abudah, 'that the third morning, as I mounted the car, which the traveller had prepared for me, and was arrayed in my best vestments of gold and diamonds, having a procession the length of two days before me, and such a numerous retinue of all the nobles of Bagdat, and having archers innumerable attending my splendid caravan, which was moving toward the valley.——'

'O my dear Abudah,' said Selima, interrupting him, 'with what madness hath that wicked enchanter possessed you? What car? what vestments? what procession doth my lord talk of? There came, indeed, (brought by those who called themselves your friends) a poor wretch here, who has embezzled the greater part of your riches, and who often talked in private with you; and this continued for some months, during which time you never attended to the speech of your friends, but seemed wrapped up in that specious villain, who at last took you to the room fronting the gateway of the city, and there for two days you continued looking out, and seemed to be in raptures, talking of more riches than the world contains; and the third day, though he still continued by you, you persisted he was gone. Yet he went forth, and you followed him; and getting into a little vehicle, he placed himself behind you, and your family have from that day lamented your absence.'

At this recital Abudah turned his face on the sopha, and spake no more for several hours. At last, rising from the sopha, 'Fool, indeed, that I was!' said he, to trust the account of a miserable impostor, or believe that the talisman of Oromanes might be purchased with riches!'

'O, rather,'

' O, rather,' replied Selima, ' may my lord find peace in this city, and comfort from his family who adore him.'

' It was there,' answered the merchant, ' that I once hoped to find it; but satiety, which I will not suffer to breed disgust, forces me at least to be indifferent to the pleasures which surround me. No, Selima, I have a nocturnal monitor, who will not permit me to rest till I have made myself master of the talisman of the perfect Oromanes. It is some knowledge to perceive our errors; and, at least, I am nearer the possession of the talisman, as my last journey, though it has not given me the talisman itself, has yet furnished me with the means of obtaining it.'

Having thus spoke, he seemed for a time easy and resigned, and endeavoured by love and tenderness to sooth the affliction of the weeping Selima. The moon passed in all those endearments which holy love inspires, when the persecuted merchant was again awakened by his midnight hag, and commanded to pursue his journey after the talisman of Oromanes.

Abudah was about to reply, when on a sudden he heard the most ravishing music, and immediately subtile and precious perfumes filled the chamber, and a small cloud gathering from the roof descended, and expanding, produced to his view a most exquisite beauty, habited like the eternal Houri's, bedecked with chaplets of delicate, ever-living flowers, holding in one hand a crystal cup, and with the other pressing out the sparkling juice from a swelling cluster of delicious grapes.

' Here, faithful Abudah,' began the lovely form, ' receive from these humble hands the cup which will inspire you with the knowledge of the talisman of Oromanes; quaff off this delicious draught, and reclining yourself on the iron chest, that faithful treasure will, at a wish, convey you to those happy realms, where, without a guard, the keys of all thy pleasures are preserved.'

At

At these words, with grace ineffable, she advanced to the transported merchant; who, with thrilling joy, received from her ivory hands the rich, sparkling draught, and sucked it in with mad delight. The Houri immediately disappeared, and Abudah falling senseless on the chest, resigned himself to sleep, and to a second adventure.

The second Adventure of the Merchant Abudah, in the Groves of Shadaski.

ABUDAH awaking at the chearful sound of innumerable birds who sat around him, and strove for mastery in their sweet notes, found himself lying in a lovely pavilion strewed with fresh lilies and roses, and filled with the most ravishing perfumes: the downy sopha on which he reclined was of the finest silk, wrought with curious devices, and executed with such life and spirit, that flowers seemed in the mimic work to spring forth from under him. The rising sun, which appeared over the blue distant hills, and warmed the awaking day; the choristers of the groves, whose melody was softened by the gentle motion of the air; the unspeakable elegance of the pavilion, which seemed formed by the powers of harmony; and the delicious fragments of the air; transported the merchant with the most pleasing sensations: he could not for some time believe his existence, but supposed that he was still under the influences of the delightful vision which had the night before taken possession of him. He turned his eyes on all sides to meet with new delights; which, though sumptuous and costly, owed more lustre to their delicacy and disposition, than to the expensive materials out of which they were formed.

But if such were the ravishing delights within, Abudah thought them much realized, when he was convinced he was awake; and by stepping forward out of the pavilion, he beheld every enchanting object that art and nature could unite. The pavilion itself stood upon a rising mount, in the midst of a most beautiful green, and was partly shaded by some upright palms; and a scattered grove of oranges and citrons, which on all sides, by beautiful brakes, gave a view of the neighbouring paradise. The centre of the pavilion opened to the lawn, which was beset with elegant tufts of the most delightful verdure.

Blushing and transparent fruits peeped from between the foliage, and every coloured, every scented flower, in agreeable variety, intermingled with the grass, and presented to Abudah's eyes the garden-work of luxuriant nature. Here roses, with woodbines entwined, appeared in beauteous contention: here luscious grapes adorned the barren branches of the stately elm; while beneath strayed the rich flocks, or birds of various feather; some in numbers upon the ground, and some paired in trees, which added a new variety to the scene. At the bottom of the lawn ran a clear and transparent stream, which gently washed the margin of the green, and seemed to feed it as it passed. On the other side a grove of myrtles, intermixed with roses and flowering shrubs, led into shady mazes; in the midst of which appeared the glittering tops of other elegant pavilions, some of which stood just on the brink of the river, others had wide avenues leading through the groves, and others were almost hidden from the sight by the intervening woods.

Abudah directing his steps towards the stream, found there an elegant barge, manned by ten beautiful youths, whose garments were of azure, trimmed with gold. They beckoned the happy merchant, and received him with the utmost affability into their bark; then all at once plying their refulgent oars, they made the chrystal flood sparkle with their ready strokes. The boat rode lightly on the buxom stream, and as it passed through the meanders of the current, every moment presented a new and striking prospect of beauties to the delighted Abudah. Hanging rocks of
different

different hues; woods of spices, and perfumes breathing sweetness over the cool stream; fruits reflected in double lustre in the clear waves; shrubs dropping their roses on them as they passed; flocks and herds standing gazing at their own images in the deep; others drinking of the transparent waters; and some, more satisfied, frisking on the lawns, or chasing each other in sport among the trees.

At length the stream growing wider, opened into a spacious lake, which was half surrounded with a rising hill, on which might be seen intermixed with groves, various gay pavilions, palaces, theatres, rotundos, obelisks, temples, pillars, towers, and other curious marks of elegance and luxury; various pleasure-boats were sailing on the surface of the lake, some with gawdy banners fanning the winds, others with pleasing structure for shade and entertainment; in one boat gay music; in another banquets; in a third deserts of the finest fruits, viands, cooling liquors; and gay company in all, who looked more blooming than the sons of the Genii, or the daughters of the Fairies. At the extremities of the swelling hill, ran glittering cascades; and o'er the pendant rocks, dropped down the most luxuriant vines, whose modest leaves attempted in vain to hide their luscious and transparent fruit from the curious eye of the observer. At the extremity of the lake, which, by its pure waters, exposed the yellow golden sand on which it wantoned, two streams ran toward the right and left of the hill, and lost themselves amidst the grove, pasturage, lawns, hillocks, and romantic scenes of the adjacent country; where lofty gilded spires, swelling domes, and other curious labours, were partly concealed, and partly discovered by the blue expanse of sky, which at last seemed blended with the country, and terminated the prospect of the groves of Shadaski.

The beautiful watermen, who in alternate song kept time with their oars, were now almost at the farther side of the lake, and in the centre of the shore

where

where Abudah had beheld the mixed groves, temples, and pavilions. A little creek, shaded with myrtles and cedars, was the place where Abudah was destined to land. Here, as he approached, ten beauteous fair ones, dressed like the Genii of the woods, stood ready to receive him, which they did with the most amiable and pleasing address.

The boat having landed the merchant, shot again swiftly over the lake, and mixed with the gay pageants on the water, while the fair strangers invited Abudah toward the palaces which were scattered on the hill.

Having passed through several fragrant avenues of trees, laden either with shade, fruit, or flower, they brought him toward an elegant building, whose front faced the lake from whence they came; here, amidst parterres and beds of flowers, a broad plat led them to the entrance of the palace, where all the lavish ornaments of art and sculpture were displayed in the most refined symmetry; light polished shafts, airy devices, highly finished entablatures, and other fanciful decorations, formed the building, which was more calculated to give the ideas of pleasure than magnificence, and had more ease than labour conspicuous.

Toward this mansion the ten beauties led the way, and introduced Abudah into a grand hall adorned with lively groups of delicate statues, in all attitudes and actions: some representing the lovely wood nymphs; some the naked beauties of the flood; others pursuing lovers; others the coyly willing virgins, who seemed, even in the ivory in which they were carved, to shew a soft reluctance.

Between the statues were pictures of every joy the heart conceives; the luscious banquet; the wild effects of the enlivening grape; the various pleasures of the different seasons; the country and the court; the amorous swains; the gentle fair; the mixed dance; the various seraglio; the gay-decked sultana, and the joys of sweet retirement with the favourite nymph.

These

These all were so lively in their different colours and complexions, that they seemed to the eyes of Abudah as moving pictures.

Next the ten beauties led the merchant into an inner apartment, adorned with the softest sophas, whose walls were one entire mirror, which reflected the ten beauties to the amorous Abudah ten thousand ways; while smiles and soft languishing looks darting from on all sides at once upon him, ravished his senses beyond the power of description. From this apartment a door opened into a spacious rotundo, lighted from the top by the sun, and the sides supported by emblematic pillars. In the middle of this rotundo Abudah beheld a bath, and round it were eleven doors, which led to as many sophas. Into one of these the ten beauties led the merchant, and prepared him for the bath; and in the others, the ten put off their own superfluous garments; after which they brought the ravished merchant, and plunged him in the bath, which was prepared of warm and sweet-scented waters.

The nature of Abudah could scarce resist the languishing powers of this place, and he sunk into the arms of his fair attendants, who now led him onward to the other side of the rotundo into a wardrobe furnished with the most airy and fanciful dresses; here every one chose as they liked. Abudah was presented by the ten beauties with a pink suit, embroidered with myrtle twigs of silver, and flowers of pearl; but first they sprinkled him with sweet-smelling essences, and with a fragrant wash renewed his complexion, and gave to him a second youth.

They next arrayed themselves in costly robes of divers colours, and like Abudah, added by that fragrant wash a new bloom to their elegant complexions. From the wardrobe a door opened to a spacious saloon: here Abudah was invited to a sopha, and immediately each fair beauty was laden with dishes; every luxury, every rarity was there. Abudah and his fair company began the banquet, while Genii invisible administered to them rich sparkling wines, high sauces, congealed liquors; fruits of every kind, the nectarine, the Persian apple, the lordly pine, the luscious grape, the cooling pomegranate, the juicy pear, were heaped before them, till Nature was not only satisfied, but tired with profusion. Then followed the full and racy wines, forbidden indeed by Mahomet, but not forbidden in the groves of Shadaski; the sweet-meats and preserves, and beside these, every luxury which could stimulate and rouze the jaded appetite.

During this repast, the beautiful companions of Abudah began to challenge each other with lively songs and mirthful jokes; while the rapturous merchant, with sparkling eyes, the quick effects of wine and song, beheld each with equal flame, and knew not, in such exquisite variety, where to fix his choice. The banquet bringing on satiety, after washing they arose, and this lovely train led Abudah (the evening drawing on) into the gardens of the palace.

After walking by several cooling fountains and sweet-smelling groves, they came to a magnificent terrass, crouded with gay youths and beauties, in the most fantastical masquerades. All nations might be seen upon this variegated terrass, and the beauties of every clime; all conversation was here indulged, though the pleasures of life was the universal topic. Cooling liquors, fruits, cakes, creams, and wines, were spread on the flowery banks on each side the terrass, and in arbours of oranges and myrtles, or sweet jasmines, where any company, as they pleased, retired; behind the trees and shrubs were placed large bands of music, sometimes inspiring, and sometimes melting the hearts of their auditors.

The sun was setting, just as Abudah had gained the centre of this extensive terrass (for his companions had left him to join what company he pleased). Here he perceived on a large green planted round with lofty palms, under which grew every kind of shrub, a most

extensive

extenfive building, of an oblong form, and fupported by feven hundred magnificent pillars, where the crowd from the terrafs were retiring. Abudah entered with the reft, and advanced into the room, which was lighted up with numberlefs luftres, and furnifhed all round with filken canopies, each having under it fophas of the richeft velvet. Here the gay affembly, as foon as the mufic from the gallery ftruck up, began the dance, nor could the pleafed merchant refrain from the enlivening motion. Thus paffed the fleeting hours, till exercife renewed their appetites for the banquet.

On a fudden, while each fair-one, and her enamoured partner, were refting on the fophas, which furrounded the room, a noble banquet was fpread, to which Abudah was about to rife, when his partner pulling him by his garment, bid him wait till the queen of pleafures honoured that bright affembly with her prefence. Ere long the fofteft mufic began to found, an hundred choirifters in mafquerade habits entered the affembly, finging the pleafures of women, company and wine. Thefe were followed by forty young maidens, fcattering rofes and violets around; after which came forward, under a canopy fupported by twelve beautiful boys, the queen of pleafures; at her approach the company arofe, and with the utmoft adoration proftrated themfelves before her.

When the queen was feated on a throne at the upper end of the room, and the banquet was about to begin, fhe ordered her maidens to find out the ftranger who came yefterday to vifit her dominions. Immediately Abudah was brought before her, who proftrating himfelf at her feet, fhe, with a fmile, gave him her hand, and commanded him to rife.

'O, happy Abudah,' faid the queen of pleafures, whom the fates ordained to bring into thefe delightful regions the cheft of the valley of Bocchim! The fuperior Genii envying the happinefs which we unreftrained Genii enjoyed, contrived to divide the keys and the cheft, which, as tradition declares, contains the talisman of Oromanes; and you, O Abudah, are the man who art destined to unite them. Worthy, Abudah, for such services, of the love of thy slaves. Come then, thou prince of my affections, and share with me the pleasures of these happy groves.'

She then commanded the company to pay Abudah the honours they used to pay her; and, with a pressing tenderness, obliged him to share with her the throne of pleasure. Abudah now conceived himself the happiest of mankind; the alluring charms of the queen of pleasures, whose beauties were almost too exquisite to behold, caused his veins to boil in mad delight; but when, with all the fondness of a doating mistress, she seized him by the hand, and with eyes, brim full of love, she seemed to gaze with transports upon him, his passion knew no bounds, he commanded the entertainment to cease, and with tumultuous haste, led the yielding queen to the remotest canopy. And now the company retiring, each under their canopies, the room was all hushed and silence. Thus passed away the night in the groves of Shadaski: the morning brought reflection and satiety; and Abudah, with some impatience, besought the queen of pleasures to surrender him the keys of the iron chest.

'My ever-loved Abudah,' replied the queen, 'behold the chest in the centre of my temple, and here are the keys for my adventurous hero; go, happy Abudah, and purchase a perpetuity in these never-fading arms, by the possession of the talisman of the pleasure-giving Oromanes.'

Abudah, having received the keys, jumped forward from the pavillion to the middle of the temple; and, like a man just entering on a new pursuit, with great impatience began to open the fifty locks. The locks, being only touched by the keys, flew from their staples, and the merchant, in a few minutes, had conquered forty-nine of the obstacles of his happiness: as he was opening the last—'O queen,' said he, 'come forward,

TALES OF THE GENII.

*Abudah's disappointment in the
Temple of the Queen of Pleasure.*
Vol. I. p. 98.

Painted by T. Kirk.   Printed for C. Cooke, Paternoster Row, March 28, 1796.   Engraved by C. Warren.

ward, and fee me finish this desirable adventure!" The last lock tumbled off just as the queen arrived at the chest, and Abudah besought her to share with him the pleasures of exploring the treasures of the chest. But no sooner did the merchant stoop to open the lid of the iron chest, than a sudden darkness ensued, and in a moment the loud thunder cracked around him, and streams of crooked lightnings, with horrid blaze, encircled the astonished Abudah.

The shrieks and cries of the once-gay set, who were indulging under the canopies, next struck his ears; some, already blasted by the lightning, withered away others, the ruins of the temple falling in huge fragments, half buried in the earth; the rest in madness running to and fro in despair, tore each other to pieces. The red angry lightning still continuing, Abudah, in the utmost anguish, looked toward the queen; when, O fearful sight! he saw her soft form parching and contracting by the flames, and her whole body diminishing, till by degrees, instead of eyes brimful of love, he beheld the little old hag, with fury flashing from her looks.

'Wretch, as well as fool,' said she, with a voice that pierced his inmost sense, 'how darest thou to presume to seek the talisman of Oromanes amidst the vanities and intemperance of this filthy grove! But I leave you to enjoy the situation you are so fond of, be this dungeon of lust your prison, here wander, and contemplate the pleasures you have chosen.'

Thus saying, she struck Abudah with her crutch, and vanished from his sight; the touch of her noxious crutch filled him with aching pains, and the dead bodies and the groans of those dying around him, inspired the wretched merchant with the utmost horror and despair. He wandered for a long time in what he now believed an endless cavern, without light; and to add to his wretchedness, every step he took, he trod on some venomous creature. The serpents hissed at him as he passed, the toads spit malignant fire, and the asps

twining

twining round his legs, spewed their venom on him, and marked Abudah with a thousand blotches. Thus continued he wandering to and fro, with great caution, about the dismal cavern, not more tormented with the groans of others, than his own dismal and heart-aching thoughts, which made him weep and tremble every step he took. After many weary searches for an end, or place to escape, he felt somewhat larger than common seize him by the leg, upon which the poor wretch supposed he was in the gripe of an enormous serpent, and began shrieking with fear and terror, when a voice, like that of despair, spoke as follows—

' What wretch art thou, who yet remainest alive, in this cavern of desolation and death?'

Abudah, though still in terror, was yet somewhat comforted, to find some companion in his miseries, and thus answered him—

' I am, indeed, a wretch misled in my searches after the talisman of Oromanes!'

' What,' answered the voice, ' wast thou fool enough to suppose, that vicious pleasure was the road to that noble jewel? It were then,' continued the voice, ' an easy purchase; but rough is the path, and high the mount, on which that treasure is preserved.'

' Alas!' answered Abudah, ' it matters not to me, where or how this talisman is disposed, who am thus for ever inclosed in these walls of wretchedness.'

' We may rise, but cannot sink lower,' answered the voice, ' when we are at the bottom, and perhaps the most barren ground will yield the richest mine; be thou but resolved to tread the crooked and laborious path, and I will instruct thee, for within these caverns begins the winding ascent.'

' O friend, or Genii, or whatsoever else thou art,' returned the merchant, ' place me but in the track, and no dangers shall deter me: for what has he to fear, who is beyond hope?'

' Take,

'Take, then,' answered the voice, 'thy way as the cavern descends, and fear not to stoop in order to rise, for in the lowest part of this cavern is situated the opening you must ascend.'

As the voice ended, Abudah found his feet at liberty, and began to feel out for the cavern's descent. The lower he went, the more filth and stench he found; to which, submitting with patience, he, by a long passage, sometimes crawling under rugged arches, sometimes wading in mud and dirt, and in total darkness, attained the end of the cavern, where he stumbled on some narrow steps, but could see no light, and was nearly suffocated with the noisome vapours. The winding ascent was so intricate, and clogged with dirt and rubbish, that the merchant worked like a mole in the dark; but by his industry, he gained ground considerably: yet what mostly tormented him, was, that as often as he endeavoured to mount, the steps would slip from under him, and he would come tumbling down with a weight of dirt upon him, and then had all his work to do over again. Nothing but his intolerable situation and lost condition could have supported the merchant in this odious undertaking; but meanness and wretchedness know no evils greater than themselves.

After various labours Abudah arrived at a little kind of resting-place, from whence the steps began to enlarge, and by degrees he perceived from above a glimmering light; to which ascending, the nearer he drew to it, the plainer he could hear a confused sound of voices ecchoing from the top, which increased as he rose, till he could plainly distinguish it must proceed from some great concourse of people without. When he had reached the uppermost step, over which an hole opened sufficient for a man to crawl through, the clamours without were so terrifying, that he feared to proceed: at last, considering that death must be the consequence of remaining in the cavern, he boldly ventured forth.

The Merchant Abudah's Third Adventure, in the Kingdom of Tafgi.

NO sooner did the merchant Abudah appear through the opening of the cavern, than ten thousand voices cried out all at once—'Long live our sultan, whom the mountains of Tafgi have brought forth!' And Abudah looking around, saw an infinite concourse of people round the mountain, and beyond them a most plentiful country, with cities and towns scattered among the vallies which opened to his view.

A number of eunuchs and vizirs stepped forward to disengage Abudah from the mouth of the cavern, who was so spent with his infirmities, sores, and fatigue, that he was obliged to be supported. Immediately a princely robe was thrown over him, and a costly turban put upon his head; the concourse still crying out, with extacy and rapture—'Long live our sultan, whom the mountains of Tafgi have brought forth!'

Silence being commanded, the grand vizir, with a long train, came toward Abudah; and, with all the people, prostrating himself before the merchant, thus addressed himself to Abudah—

'Behold, O thou, before whose presence even the sun is darkness! behold, O wonder of mankind, most sacred progeny of Tafgi! thou miracle of beauty! thou mirror of perfection! thou most glorious sultan of earthly princes! thou diamond of nature! thou guardian of the world! behold thy prostrate slaves; whose wish is only to lay down as thy foot-stools, and to be trodden under thy feet as the dust of the plain! Thine, O sultan, is all earthly happiness! thine, every perfection of body and mind! thine, all power from the mountains of thy parent Tafgi, to the parching desarts of Shezrallah, which forbid the approach of the stranger to the kingdoms of our invincible sultan. Rule, therefore, thy slaves, according unto thy pleasure, and know but one will in the plains and cities, which by thy permission and bounty thy slaves inhabit.'

As the grand vizir, still prostrate with the people, uttered these words, they all with one voice repeated—'O sultan, whom the mountains of Tafgi have brought forth, rule thy slaves according to thy pleasure!'

Abudah, filled with conceit, and bloated with pride, had almost forgot his pains and infirmities in this flattering applause; he set his foot on the neck of the vizir with the utmost haughtiness, and commanded him to conduct him to the seraglios of his ancestors. A number of slaves and eunuchs brought a magnificent throne of ivory, with a canopy of golden embroidery thrown over it, into which Abudah ascended, and was borne on the shoulders of the grandees and vizirs of his new acquired kingdom. The retinue winding round the hill, brought Abudah in sight of an extensive encampment, which, after the eastern manner, was of different colours; one division yellow, one blue, another white, some red, some green, and all adorned with silver or gold. In the centre of this splendid armament stood the royal tent, which shone with the lustre of the gold and lively blue velvet, of which it was composed, and looked rather like a palace than a tent.

Here Abudah was seated on his throne, and the nobles having done obeisance, Abudah commanded all but the grand vizir to depart. The rest being gone, the grand vizir again prostrating himself before Abudah, cried out, 'May my lord, the sultan of Tafgi, ever rule over Harran his slave.'

'Harran,' answered Abudah, 'arise and declare to me the cause of this encampment, and why the armies of Tafgi are thus scattered on the plains.'

'Our renowned Sultan Rammasin,' replied the vizir Harran, 'made it his custom to take the field in summer, to terrify his foes; but in the midst of this campaign, it pleased the powers, who preside over the mountains of Tafgi, to call him from us, and bless us with the presence of my lord, before whom I stand.

For

For since the time that the descendants of Mahomet involved our kingdom in perpetual bloodshed, we have been warned by the oracles of Tasgi to expect a king from the womb of the mountain, that no division of families, or contention among brethren, might disturb the peace of these happy kingdoms.'

' And who,' said Abudah, ' are the neighbours of my kingdom beyond these mountains?'

' They are,' replied the vizir, ' O Sultan, an harmless inoffensive race, which was the cause that the Sultan Rammasin would not make war upon them, although their territories extend to the sea-coast, and would be a noble addition to the kingdom of the Sultan of Tasgi.

' Rammasin, then,' answered Abudah, ' wanted a nobleness of soul, to sit down contented with less than he might have enjoyed: but Abudah, your present sultan, will give their lands to the slaves of Tasgi, and extend his dominions even over the waves and the tempest.'

' My royal master will thereby,' answered the vizir, ' gain the hearts of his soldiers, who have long pined in the inglorious lethargies of peace.'

' Go, bid the trumpets sound then,' said Abudah, ' and let it be proclaimed in the camp, that your Sultan Abudah will revenge the injuries which the inhabitants of Tasgi have received from their perfidious neighbours. Go, Harran, and denounce war against the——'

' Shakarahs,' said Harran, bowing, ' who have insulted the mountains of Tasgi.'

Abudah was going on, but his pains and weakness obliged him to order them to prepare an inner tent for his reception.

While the eunuchs and slaves were attending their new sultan, his vizir Harran caused the royal mandate to be proclaimed within the encampment, and commanded the leaders of the army to be assembled together to deliver to them the orders of the sultan Abudah.

The

The whole kingdom of Tafgi, was rejoiced at the news of their sultan's expedition against the helpless and innocent Shakarahs; so little do subjects weigh the merits of war! and the old and decrepid parents stirred up their children to engage in a service, where cruelty and destruction were honoured with the titles of virtue and the love of their country. Ere the sun began to smile upon the harvests of the Shakarahs, the tents of Abudah were moving to destroy them; the loud cymbals were clanging in the air, and the brazen trumpets, with their shrill notes of liveliness, seemed to inspire the armies of Tafgi with a thirst of glory, and not of blood. The order and discipline of the troops, the regularity of their march, and the sprightliness of their looks, utterly disguised the rapacious purposes of the royal plunderer; who, though but just master of one kingdom, was so eager to get possession of a second, that he destroyed many of his men in forcing a march over the mountains which nature had placed as the boundaries of their nation.

The Shakarahs having notice of their motions, sent an embassy to meet the Sultan of Tafgi, beseeching to know the cause of his coming; making the humblest professions of peace; and offering, if any thing had offended him, to make the fullest satisfaction they were capable of; and imploring him, that he would not make war upon a nation who were ever the friends of the Tafgites, and to whom that kingdom had never declared any hostile intention.

To these humble remonstrances Abudah replied, that he was not to be taught and directed by such base slaves as the Shakarahs; and that whatever intention he might have had originally in entering their kingdom, he now declared he came to punish the insolence of that people, who dared send such dictating embassies to the Sultan of Tafgi. He then commanded the ambassadors to be driven from the encampment, and ordered his army to begin their hostilities on the presumptuous Shakarahs.

The

The leaders of the armies of Tafgi being ignorant and imperious, every kind of tyranny and cruelty was practifed, till the wretched Shakarahs being made prifoners, and their wives and families ravifhed or murdered, the Sultan Abudah returned to the kingdom of Tafgi, with the fpoils of the conquered country, amidft the acclamations of the army and it's leaders; who were fo lavifh of their praifes and adulations, that Abudah efteemed himfelf at leaft equal to the prophet of Mecca.

After Abudah arrived at the metropolis of Tafgi, his vizirs came to enquire of him, where he would beftow the miferable Shakarahs, moft of whom they had led home in chains. Abudah was for fome time doubtful of their fate, and was at laft going to order a general execution, when he recollected the iron cheft which was buried in the mountains of Tafgi.

'Let the Shakarahs,' faid the Sultan Abudah, 'be condemned to work in the mountains of Tafgi, till they find an iron cheft with fifty locks.'

At thefe words the grand vizir Harran bowed before the fultan, and faid—'Will my lord dare to fend the Shakarahs into the womb of Tafgi, which his own fubjects are forbidden to approach!'

'Take the rebel Harran,' faid Abudah, in indignation, 'and let his head be fevered from his body, and his tongue let the dogs devour.'

The other vizirs gladly faw this execution performed on Harran, and returned to the fultan, and faid—'Far be it that a monarch of the eaft fhould be governed by his flaves. Be the will of the Sultan Abudah for ever obeyed, as it is in the deftruction of the traitor Harran, as it is in the labours of the Shakarahs in the mountains of Tafgi.'

Abudah hourly fent his vizirs to infpect the miners in the mountains, who returned with accounts of the death of thoufands, over whom the mountain crumbled, and fmothered them in it's caverns.

The Tafgites, jealous of their mountain, which they fuppofed was fomewhat divine, began to murmur at the impiety of their fultan; which, when Abudah knew, he commanded the leaders of his army to chaftife them, and to put every tenth man throughout his kingdom to the fword. At length the fainting Shakarah's dug out the cheft of iron, and brought it to Abudah, who commanded every engine or force to be applied to it to break it open, but in vain; the cheft refifted all their endeavours, and would not yield to the utmoft force the art of man could bring againft it.

Abudah then publifhed a reward to any that fhould make the keys to fit the locks. This feveral undertook, and fucceded, but as foon as one lock was opened, it fhut while the artificer was employed about the fecond. Abudah, puffed up with pride, was enraged at this difappointment, and commanded fifty men to take the fifty keys, and all attempt it at once; which they did, and were all immediately ftruck dead; he then commanded a fecond fifty, but none but his army were near him, for the reft were fled from the tyrant's prefence. Abudah now ordered fifty foldiers to approach; when the leaders of the army, moved by his cruelties, and feeing he was about to facrifice his army as well as his fubjects, uniting together, came toward him in a body; which Abudah perceiving, and expecting no mercy, leaped on the cheft, and trufted himfelt to it's flying power. Immediately the cheft moved aloft in the air, and Abudah being ftupified and giddy, fell into a deep fleep, and was wafted far from the army and kingdom of Tafgi.

The Merchant Abudah's Fourth Adventure, among the Sages of Nema.

ABudah found himfelf on the iron cheft beneath a rock which hung over him, and was covered with a pleafant fhade of palms; at a little diftance a gentle rill ran bubbling over the ftones, and took it's courfe along a narrow valley, which on each side was bounded by rocks and verdant hills. Here, as he eyed the rural scene, and reflected on his escape from Tasgi, he observed a venerable sage gently moving forward along the valley, and, to appearance, directing his steps toward the rock under which he was sitting. Abudah's conscience was so alarmed at the sight of an human form, which during his tyrannical reign he had so often defaced, that he strove to hide himself even from the approach of a weak old man; but the sage still advancing with ease and composure, Abudah, after some hesitation, suffered him to join him.

The sage, with great obsequiousness, bowed before Abudah, (who had still the royal turban upon his head, and the ensigns of the regal power about his shoulders) and said—' O prince, who deignest to visit these retreats of learning and philosophy; whether thou art he whose knowledge was universal, the glory of the east, the sagest of sages, the indefatigable Solomon; or whether thou art here arrived from any neighbouring realm in quest of science, and art willing to honour our school with thy august presence; permit one of the lowest of the sons of knowledge to conduct you to the temple and seat of learning, which the great Solomon here founded in the desart, for the investigation of truth and the discoveries of nature. This vale, which is our only retreat from the sultry sun, or the wide-extended desart, winds round to the entrance of our seminary, where every science is taught, and all the fountains of knowledge are displayed.'

As he spake these words, the sage led the way; and Abudah somewhat recovered from his hurry and confusion, said within himself—' O prophet, how blindly have I wandered! yet here surely, among these springs of knowledge and learning, is the talisman of Oromanes to be discovered!'

Abudah arriving with the sages at the end of the valley, beheld the mansions of philosophy. A grand portico first presented itself to his view, gilt after the
model

model of the Grecian architecture; to this, with the sage, he ascended by a grand flight of steps, and entering the doors of the inner portico, found himself in a spacious hall. 'Here,' said the sage, 'must even kings remain, till the director of this seat of learning is acquainted with the arrival of a stranger, and his motives for seeking entrance into the sacred college of science.'

'Give, then, this message,' answered Abudah, 'to your director: that the Sultan of Tasgi,' (for Abudah's penitence had not entirely humbled his pride) 'studious of knowledge, seeks, in his philosophic seat, to find the talisman of the perfect Oromanes.' The sage, after having made obeisance to the supposed sultan, went in quest of the director, and left Abudah in the hall, where were many other candidates for admission into the college of philosophy, and each had his particular sage or introducer.

Abudah's instructor shortly returned. 'Our director,' said he, 'rejoices to find so great a monarch studious of truth, and bids me declare (as is customary) that the talisman of Oromanes is the ultimate end of all our researches, and therefore invites the Sultan of Tasgi to seek it, in whatever science he thinks most likely to contain it. But,' added the sage, 'happily for the Sultan of Tasgi, he has met with Abraharad, who can unfold to him the secrets of nature, and teach him in what recesses the talisman of Oromanes is inclosed.'

'And are you then,' answered Abudah, 'the renowned Abraharad, whom my subjects of Tasgi have often described to me as the man who knew the properties of all herbs and roots, and the minerals of all the earth?'

'These, O prince,' replied Abraharad, 'are the plainest precepts of nature; but I will unfold to thee such of her secrets, as none, since the magnificent Solomon, have been allowed to view: for what was Oromanes, the founder of this talisman, but the magician

gician of fire, the great alchymift of the firft and moſt powerful element! However, I will not wafte your time in words, when I can work wonders to convince you.—Defcend then, O prince, with me, into the area of this inner building, in which every fcience has it's feparate offices and aparments, and I will bring you to the knowledge of the inmoft fecrets of nature and art.'

Abudah, rejoicing in his new acquaintance, followed Abraharad into an extenfive court, furrounded by porticos, in each of which he beheld feveral fages teaching their refpective difciples.

Abraharad led Abudah to the portico of his own fcience, where many were bufied in the various branches of his art. 'Even in this veftibule,' faid Abraharad, ' could I furprize the Sultan of Tafgi; but I lead him at once to the myfteries of fcience.' So faying, he opened a door that led to an inner apartment; and Abudah entering, the alchymift clofed the door of his laboratory. While Abudah's attention was diverted by the variety of inftruments and apparatuffes which he beheld in this mimic fhop of nature, the alchymift began to order his materials, and fet them in furnaces; compounding falts, and earths, and fpirits, and varying his experiments according as he faw occafion.

'Patience and perfeverance, O Sultan,' faid Abraharad, 'are the tools of an alchymift, without thefe he could not work, as hidden caufes fo often vary and perplex his operations. The fecret which I am now preparing, is what gave the great Demogorgon power to diffolve all nature: but as it is a tedious procefs, and the furnace as yet gives but the third degree of fire, I will fhew you what great effects lie hidden in the meaneft caufes, that you may conquer the prejudices which cuftom may have rooted in your mind againft any particular modifications of matter; for the whole earth that you view, is one confufion of materials, out of which, by feparation, conjunction, affimilation,

unity,

unity, or disjunction, may every appearance of nature, and many which she had never discovered, be formed. You see the seed drawing to itself atoms, capable of forming wood, and various fruits: from this seemingly tasteless earth arises first the harsh, and then the sour; and, lastly, the luscious grape, concocted, meliorated, and perfected, in these different stages, by the subtile alchymy of the sun. You see in others, the bitter, the salt, the tart, and the sweet, all drawn from the same earthly bed or well: so likewise, O Sultan, is the generation of all things; the semen is a kind of standard which marshals each under it's particular banner. Now as these are all, by affections and sympathies of size or quality, naturally led by these causes to conjunction and unity, so also have they all aversions, that is to say, particles discordant which are capable of separating them, whereby their cohesion, unity, and substance, is destroyed, and they themselves are rendered discontinuous and resolvable into their first principles or rude atoms: thus, what we call corruption, is really no more than a new modification of matter, which, according as it is agreeable to our senses and perceptions, we call by names, conveying agreeable or disagreeable ideas; thus the ferment of the grape, we call a making, or creation of wine; and the ferment of vegetables, which resolve themselves to a kind of muck or manure, we call putrefaction, though they are begun by one and the same process in nature; so again, the change of an egg into one living animal or bird, we call breeding; but the change of another, by staleness, into a thousand maggots, we call corruption. But yet, whatever may be our notions and ideas, they are never lost or destroyed materially, though they are formally; all returns to the common bed of nature, and there lies dormant, till called forth by sufficient causes into different forms.

 Hence it is, O sultan, that the alchymist, taking this universal bed as the ground-work of his science, and acting, as nature does, by the force of the nobler

and

and more vivifying elements, teaches mankind the powers of separation and composition; and hence he is able to proceed or move backward in his work, and can either stop, reduce, or drive forward, the matter which he guides. Thus, O Sultan, you perceive those two bottles of transparent liquors; you see, by mixing them, they instantly change and become red: so the small plant which you set in water, though fed by that element only, produces green leaves. Now these waters may again be rendered transparent by other mixtures, may be disunited, and reduced to their former state; or by other additions, you see, I render them blue, or black, or green, or yellow; yet all these beautiful colours and phenomena are caused by a few common and natural causes.'

Abraharad then ordered the laboratory to be darkened, and immediately the sultan beheld, among vivid flashes, this writing in fire upon the walls—' The Sultan of Tasgi will be satisfied.' At this sight Abudah was transported; whereupon Abraharad said—' O sultan, let not appearances either slacken, or too rashly inspire your researches: this luminous appearance is natural, drawn from the most refuse of materials, and may serve to convince you, that wonders lie hidden in the most disagreeable formations of matter. But I see the colours arising in the furnace, all that is bright to the eye! What flashes of red, blue, green, yellow, purple, white, arise from my work! brighter, O sultan, than the rubies or the emeralds of thine empire!'

Abudah looked at the furnace, and saw the most glorious colours arising from the crucibles of Abraharad.

'These,' continued the sage, ' are signs that my universal menstruum is near perfection; and now all nature will be open before me.'

' What,' answered Abudah, ' is the mixture you are making in the furnace an universal dissolvent?'

' Yes,' said Abraharad, ' it is.'

' Then,'

'Then,' replied the merchant Abudah, 'the talisman of Oromanes' will soon be my own.'

'It may possibly,' resumed the sage, 'require some time to seek out where it is deposited.'

'That,' said Abudah, 'I know; for it is inclosed in the iron chest which you saw me sitting upon under the rock, which has hitherto resisted every application of force or art.'

'Hast thou then, O royal sultan,' cried Abraharad, 'the chest of adamant with fifty locks, said to contain that precious jewel, that philosophic talisman, which can give life, immortality, riches, honour, and happiness, to the possessor? But see, my work is finished; the bluish vapour rises, and my menstruum, the key of nature, is compleated. Let us then hasten with it to this chest, and release the treasures of my royal sultan.'

'Rather,' replied Abudah, 'will I go and bring it here, which, by it's virtues I am able to perform, and Abraharad shall exercise his authority over this stubborn matter, and reduce it to its former atoms.' Abudah then leaving the sage, returned to his chest, and seating himself thereon, was, at a wish, conveyed with his treasure into the laboratory.

The sage Abraharad having viewed the chest with rapture, took out his crucible, full of the universal menstruum.

'Alas,' said Abudah, 'O sage, be not deceived. Can that which dissolves every thing be confined by a crucible?'

The sage grew pale at the merchant's reproof; and, with the utmost vexation, threw his menstruum on the ground, where the harmless liquor continued, without altering itself, or the earth that supported it.

'Alas,' said Abudah, 'where now is alchymy!'

'I have a cold fusion,' answered Abraharad, 'though an hot one is denied me; for I will send the lightning, which melts the sword, and leaves the

scabbard

scabbard unhurt, through that stubborn piece of mechanism.'

A new apparatus being now fixed, the sparks and flashes began to issue through the sides of the adamant; and Abraharad exulting, and impatient to hasten the effect of his mimic lightning, stepped nearer to the chest, when the flash altering it's course, drove violently through the temples of the sage Abraharad, and reduced him to ashes. At this dreadful catastrope, Abudah, whose hopes were raised to the highest pitch, ran out of the laboratory with frantic wildness, and filled the area with his groans and complaints. Here, as he wandered about, tormented by passion and disappointment, a sage, with a steady and composed mien, advanced from one of the porticos toward him, and, with great seeming unconcern, said—
' O wretch, why will you neglect the possession of the talisman of Oromanes, which it is in your power to enjoy!'

' Canst thou assure me of that?' answered Abudah, in transports.

' I can assure you,' replied the sage, ' that you are, at present, incapable of making use of it.'

' And therefore, it is, I suppose,' said Abudah, ' that I am thus for ever deceived, when I think it within my grasp.'

' It is even so,' answered the sage. ' Then teach me, O friendly sage,' continued the merchant, ' how I may come to the true enjoyment of this valuable treasure.'

' Must not happiness,' said the sage, ' be seated in the mind?'

' It must, it must,' replied Abudah, ' and I have neglected my mind, to search for it among bodily enjoyments. O what a new scene have you, O greatest of sages, opened to my view! But proceed, O heavenly instructor, and perfect the cure you have begun.'
' Cool

'Cool and moderate your grief this night,' answered the sage Gherar, 'and to-morrow, if I find you dispassionate, I will unmask your mind, which at present is beset by worldly objects.' Thus saying, the sage Gherar introduced Abudah among his scholars, and provided him apartments in his portico.

Early the next morning the sage Gherar attended Abudah, and led him forth towards the valley that fronted the building dedicated to science and instruction.

'How delightful,' said Gherar, 'are the sweet dews that are again rising at the call of the morning sun! The groves seem, like man, refreshed by the silence of the night; the grass is capable, by this relief from nature, to stand against the fiery beams of the noon.'

'It is, indeed,' answered Abudah, 'a glorious morning, and looks more like a new creation, than a scene which has already lasted such numberless ages. O how happily might man spend his days in such sweet retirements! no cares to molest him; no storms to beat upon him; no human desolations to suffer from!'

'Such,' answered Gherar, 'are the dreams of folly, and the conceits of infirmity; conscious of your weakness, I led you to this scene, in order to convince you, how incapable you are of happiness: if the brightness of the sun, and the vapours of the morning, can so affect you with pleasure, the want of them will be painful unto you. In these gratifications the soul is totally passive, and must be fed by the senses: thus she is taught to rejoice at the wanton touches of a finger; at the tickling of a luxurious palate; at the odours of a fading flower; at the sounding undulations of the circumambient air; or at the accidental objects that play upon the eyes of a trifling, circumscribed animal.

'But

'But the purity and immortality of the soul teaches the philosopher to govern the corruptions of the flesh, and not to suffer the body to be the master of the mind; the momentary pleasures or evils of life are alike indifferent to him, who, conscious of his perfections, and compleat in his own virtues and immortality, can smile amidst the horrors of dissolving nature, and preserve a firmness and indifference, when even the whole earth is crumbling to it's original chaos; and if these things affect not his self-fortified breast, how little will he regard the common accidents and vexations of life! If he drops a limb, his immortal part is nevertheless unimpaired; if he suffers hunger, still his mind is fed with never-failing pleasures; if power throw it's arbitrary chains around him, his soul is still free, and can mock the tyrant's rage, and defy his malice. In short, O Abudah, the true philosopher is capable of every pleasure, and released from every ill; the beauty of virtue has eternal charms for his contemplation and possession; the changes of mortality have nothing that can move, transport, or disquiet him; he neither hopes nor fears; he neither admires nor dreads; and always wears within his breast a contentment more invariable, and unshaken, than all the treasures upon earth, because nothing earthly can disquiet him.'

As the sage Gherar spoke these words with an heart-felt pride, Abudah, transported at his doctrines, was about to answer, when a fierce tyger bursting from the thicket, with his eyes flashing dreadful fires, and a mouth begrimed with human gore, sprung violently towards the sage and his pupil. Abudah, who had not so entirely forgotten his worldly wisdom, as to stand perfectly undaunted, leaped into the brook that divided the vale, and swam across, as knowing the tyger would not follow him through the water. Having reached the opposite bank, he looked towards the sage Gherar, whom he saw running with the utmost precipitation before the voracious tyger; but his

flight

flight was vain, the monster overtook him, and leaping upon the sage, tore him limb from limb, while Gherar filled the woods and the vallies with his piteous cries and lamentations. ' Alas!' sighed the merchant Abudah, as he beheld the wretched end of Gherar, ' how vain is it for weakness to boast of strength; or for man, who is infirm, to deny the reality of what he must hourly feel!. to boast of a power over nature, is, I see, the end of philosophy, which should only with wonder contemplate what it cannot scan; much less ought the reptile man to vaunt itself superior to the blessings or scourges of Him who is the ruler of the universe.'

With these reflections Abudah arose, and being fearful to venture on the other side of the brook, he advanced up a lawn, which winding between two mountains, brought the merchant into a spacious plain; where he beheld innumerable flocks feeding upon it's surface, and shepherds and shepherdesses tending their innocent charge. ' Here,' said Abudah to himself, ' here is neither pomp, nor luxury, nor vanity ; here is rural peace, and quietness, and tranquillity, which know no sorrow.'

As thus Abudah mused within himself, he advanced toward the shepherds and their flocks; when one passing near him, immediately ran with the utmost precipitation among the rest, crying aloud— ' Fly, fly, O my wandering and distressed friends, for the tyrant of Tafgi, not content with driving us out from the land of Shakarah, is come down to bereave us also of our flocks and herds.'

Abudah was touched to the soul at this scene of distress and confusion, which his former passions had occasioned, and called to the poor wanderers to stay; but they, fearful, and lamenting, drove their flocks along the plain, and with dread, looked back, expecting to see again the cruel armies of the Tafgites.

One old, venerable, bramin alone, unable through age to follow the Shakarahs, whom he had for many

years

years instructed, sat, with a majestic composure, on a square stone which stood at the entrance of his cell. As Abudah advanced, he rose, and made obeisance, saying, 'Know O sultan, I rise not to the tyrant of Tasgi, but I bow before him whom it has pleased Alla to set over his people. But wherefore shouldest thou seek to do evil, that thou mayest reap good? Are then bad actions capable of salutary ends, and is evil predominant, that purity may triumph? Alas, O sultan! not such are the means of obtaining the talisman of the great and perfect Oromanes: purity and perfection, such as man may attain unto, true virtue and benevolence, and a faithful religion, are the means of possessing that treasure. Hasten therefore, O man, to the tomb of the prophet, and there confess the follies and iniquities of thy researches; and learn from that fountain of purity and truth, the will of him who ordained you to this hitherto ineffectual toil.'

'Good and pious bramin,' replied Abudah, 'much have I abused both the gifts of Providence, and you, and your poor, innocent, and distressed nation; but direct me in my journey to Medina, for I seem hitherto to have trodden on the enchanted ground.'

'The chest of adamant will convey you to Medina,' answered the bramin.

'I left it,' replied Abudah, 'in the mansions of philosophy, which may not be found without crossing the brook, and risking the fury of the tyger.'

'There is,' answered the bramin, 'a path that leads from hence, round the brook, to the back of that mansion, into which a small bridge will carry you over the brook; and may Mahomet prosper your undertaking!'

Abudah then took leave of the sage, assuring him, that the Tasgites knew not of his place of retreat; and that he might rest with the Shakarahs safely there, for no evil was intended them. The bramin blessed Abudah as he parted.

The

The sultan-merchant hastened to the seminaries of learning, where taking possession of the chest, he threw himself on it, in full assurance that he should awake in the temple of Medina. In a short time the merchant Abudah found himself in an awful mosque, reclining on the chest of adamant: on one side stood the box which used to haunt his chamber with the diminutive hag; and on the other a large cistern of water. Presently, with mildness in his aspect, stood the Genius Barhaddan before him. 'At length,' said he, 'Abudah, receive the true keys of the adamantine chest.'

At these words the merchant Abudah approached the Genius; and having prostrated himself before him, received the long-expected keys.

'Begin,' said Barhaddan, 'O Abudah, and search for thy treasure.'

Abudah obeyed; and in a moment the locks of the chest flew open. Abudah with a consciousness and dread, lifted up the lid of the chest, when instantly flew out a thousand feathers, so that they covered the whole pavement of the mosque.

'Now,' continued Barhaddan, 'put in thine hand, and draw forth the contents of the chest.' Abudah obeyed, and first he took up a beautiful, but bleeding hand, with a curious bracelet of diamonds.

'That hand,' said Barhaddan, 'was severed from the body of a fair sultana, by a slave who could not unlock the bracelet. Dost thou think, Abudah, the wearer was the happier for that ornament?'

As Abudah was going to draw again, out stepped a poor wretch, laden with his bags of gold, trembling and looking behind. Next, on a sudden, a gay youth, with a poniard, stabbed the miser to the heart; upon which several women, in loose attire, came and shared with him the spoil, and began dancing and singing. These were followed by a crowd, among whom was a crowned head, who ordered his soldiers to fall on them and destroy them; then came a surior force, and put a bowstring around the neck of him that was crowned, and another stripped the crown from his head. After these came several madmen; some with wings on their shoulders, some with wheels, which they strove always to keep in motion: some looking unto the skies, some drawing circles in the air with straws, some jabbering ridiculous notions, that the same quantity was both more and less than itself.

When these were passed, Barhaddan asked Abudah— 'Dost thou understand these things?'

'I understand by them,' answered the merchant, 'and also by my travels, that neither riches, nor gaiety, nor honour, nor power, nor science, nor learning, nor obscurity, is free from the common accidents of life; and that, therefore, these can never lead us to the perfect talisman of Oromanes.'

'What didst thou understand by the feathers?' said Barhaddan.

'I knew not their meaning,' answered Abudah.

'They,' continued the Genius Barhaddan, 'were the thousand light, airy, inconsistent hopes and wishes, which lie on the top of every man's heart, which have some kind of tendency to the talisman, and so they are the first on the top of the chest.'

'And now, O merchant Abudah!' said Barhaddan, 'art thou convinced that the talisman of Oromanes could not be treasured among such refuse as these? Shut down, therefore the chest, and attend with silence to the scene which will follow.' Abudah obeyed, standing like a mute with his hands before him.

'Now, thou wicked hag,' said Barhaddan, 'thou evil Genius, who lovest to torment and mislead mankind, come forth.' At these words, the little box fell to pieces, and the hag came trembling out on her crutches before Barhaddan.

'I know,' said the pure Genius, 'thy implacable nature, and that thou delightest only in mischief and evil;

evil; but, that you may have some awe for those who regard mankind, stand here, and see me purge the man whom thou hast enslaved with worldly thoughts and desires.'

Barhaddan then commanded Abudah to wash himself in the cistern; which having performed, he ordered him a second time to open the chest of adamant. Abudah obeying, looked in, and saw only a little book; which Barhaddan bid him read, and he read these words aloud—

'Know, O man, that human nature, which is imperfect, cannot attain to perfection; that true happiness, which is the real talisman of Oromanes, being immortal, can be enjoyed by immortals alone. That man, being a creature, is subject to the commands of his Creator; and therefore a knowledge of his will, and a faithful obedience to it, should be the first and last pursuit of mortality, till it please the Eternal Power to remove him from trial to perfection, from earthly misery to the eternal happiness of a glorious paradise.' As he ended these words, Abudah fell prostrate in the mosque, and adored the Eternal Power above, which the Genius seeing, commended him.

Then Barhaddan, turning to the hag—' Go,' said he, ' false and wicked Genius, into that chest, and there, for fifty years, contemplate the happiness you are so anxious to recommend.' The hag trembled and obeyed: the chest closed with violence, the locks fastened themselves on, and the whole was taken up like a whirlwind, and vanished away.

Abudah then looked round to thank the friendly Genius, but he was gone; and what surprised him more, he found himself on his bed at Bagdat, and his wife and family weeping around him. As he moved, Selima in transport ran to him, and asked him, if the life were in him.

' In me!' said Abudah; ' why, woman, I have been travelling these three months: I have seen various countries

tries and kingdoms; I have (but would I had not!) been crowned a sultan!'

'O,' interrupted Selima, 'my lord raves again. Thy children and servants know, O Abudah! that four days thou hast slept upon this sopha, and we feared you were dead.'

'Was what I have seen a dream?' cried the merchant Abudah; then blessed be the prophet, who has added unto me knowledge without guilt. But now, my lovely Selima,' said Abudah, 'I am released from those terrors and uneasinesses, which have made me a burden to thee and myself. Yes, Selima, I have learned to be content, the utmost man must expect on earth; I have learned to be obedient to Alla, to love and cherish my family, and to do good to mankind. At these words he again embraced his wife and children, and the day was spent in decent endearments; nor lived there a happier or more resigned and chearful family in Bagdat, than in the house of the merchant Abudah.

When the Genius Barhaddan had finished his tale, Iratagem arose from his throne, and humbled himself before him; then turning to the august assembly, he thus addressed the pupils of his immortal race—

'Hear, O ye reptiles, whose life is a span, and whose habitation is as the dust in the whirlwind; who look toward the earth, and see not below the sand that covers it; and to the heavens, but the cloud intervened and darkened your search; seek not for durable joys in a world of vicissitude; nor for happiness, which a moment shall alter, as the sea-breeze blots out the writing of a child on the sand. The eye which is mortal cannot see that which is unchangeable, neither can the taste of man be satisfied with variety. Wait then, ye sons of clay, with patience, till ye be translated into the gardens of everliving pleasures, into palaces which moulder not with the storm, into mansions which

time

must for ever admire; and know, that happiness is with Mahomet and Alla; and that the talisman of Oromanes is to obey God, and to love his commandments.'—' Thanks, gentle Barhaddan, continued Iracagem, ' thanks be to thy industry and care: well haſt thou inculcated the leſſons of morality, and the doctrines of truth.—Say then, my nobler brother,' ſaid Iracagem to Mamlouk, ' where has Mamlouk been employed in the ſervice of mankind?'

' To teach the doctrines of truth,' replied Mamlouk, ' has been the endeavour of Mamlouk: how I have ſucceeded, learn from the tale of the Derviſe Alfouran.'

TALE II.

The Derviſe Alfouran.

ALFOURAN, by the ſanctity of his manners, and the abſtemiouſneſs of his diet, had gained the hearts of the whole province of Eyraca; but none was more captivated with the holy derviſe than Sanballad, the ſon of Semi, a merchant in Baſſora, whoſe father intended to bring him up in the mercantile buſineſs, which he himſelf profeſſed. The hermitage of Alfouran was ſituated in a wood, near the ſuburbs of the city. It was formed out of a ſtupendous rock, in the ſide of a mountain, and contained two cells, the outermoſt of which ſerved for the common purpoſes of life, and the innermoſt was ſet apart for the private devotions and religious ceremonies of the ſanctified derviſe.

A ſmall ſpring, which ran trickling down the rock, ſupplied him with the pureſt water, and fell into a baſon, which the induſtrious Alfouran had ſcooped out of the bottom of the rock, from which the water overflowing, deſcended in a gentle rill to the wood, and ran purling among the trees; ſometimes diſcovering itſelf by its glittering ſurface, and ſometimes gliding imperceptibly through the thickeſt buſhes, which grew upon its banks. A little plain opened before the door of the cell, which by the shade of the lofty trees that surrounded it, and the constant attention of the sage to sprinkle its surface, ever preserved a most beautiful verdure. The tall and straight cedars and palms which overshadowed this delightful retreat, at once secured it from the scorching sun, and afforded a most beautiful and majestic appearance, mixed with an awful solemnity, which struck the heart, and demanded the reverence of every beholder.

To this habitation of Alfouran did thousands resort, at the rising of the sun, to hear the instructions of his mouth, and dwell upon the sweet accents of his persuasive tongue: even the labours of the day were forgotten while he charmed their ears; and the poorest subjects of Bassora refused not to follow the sage Alfouran, though the work of their hands was neglected and undone. The pious Sanballad was ever a constant attendant at these captivating lectures, and drank deep of the instructions of the dervise of Bassora. His soul was animated by the example of the self-denying sage: he scorned the mean employments of a dirty world, and sought earnestly to bury himself in the glorious solitude of Alfouran.

One day, after the dervise had been exhorting his hearers to trouble themselves no longer with the concerns of life, nor the transactions of mortality, Sanballad presented himself before him, and having done obeisance to the holy man, he entreated Alfouran to initiate him into the mysteries of his happy life.

Alfouran looked earnestly at the youth; he beheld his complexion, his modest beauties, his eyes streaming with penitential tears, and his heart heaving with the full sighs of sorrow and contrition.

' And canst thou, O young man,' said the dervise ' leave the vanities of this life, to spend in solitude and abstemiousness the sprightly hours of youth?

Canst

Canst thou quit all worldly connections, thy friends, thy relations, thy engagements, thy business, and thy pleasures, and prefer before them the constant company of an aged dervise? If thou art so resolved, let me first have a trial of thy faith and submission. Ascend this craggy rock by the steps which I have hewn in its side, and sit on a stone which is dedicated on its surface to the pure solar fire. There remain while the sun melts thee by day, and the most unwholesome dew falls on thee by night, till three days are accomplished, and I will bring thee of the choicest viands which the rich men of Bassora send daily to tempt my appetite; of which if thou tastest, or to which if thou dost incline thy mind, the curse of the god of fire be upon thee!'

At this command Sanballad arose with joyful looks, and began to ascend the holy mountain. He spent the first day in a solemn silence, not daring even to look up or move from his posture, but kept his eyes fixed on the ground, and in secret implored the strengthening assistance of the founder of his faith.

The second day Alfouran set before him a sumptuous banquet, which his disciples, at his command, had brought from the city: for it was daily the custom of Alfouran to receive such presents at their hands; not, as he said, for his own use, but to fix him stedfastly in his forbearance from those pampering repasts. They stood every day exposed on a table formed out of the living rock in his cell; and at noon the dervise ascended the hill, to burn them at the holy fire, which he kindled from the sun. Sanballad looked not at the tempting viands till Alfouran commanded him, and then persisted religiously in his resolutions; which, when the dervise perceived, he extolled his faith, and exhorted him to continue obedient to the instructions he had received.

The third day the poor youth was nearly exhausted with watching and fatigue: nevertheless, Alfouran endeavoured, by the most artful temptations,

to

to draw him from his purpose, but in vain; the pious Sanballad triumphed over his temptations, and at length fulfilled his commands. But now partly initiated, the dervise, after having fed him, conducted him down from the mountain to the cell beneath; and leaving him for some time to rest and refreshment, he alone ascended with his daily offerings to the altar of fire. In this act of devotion Alfouran continued the remainder of the day; during which time Sanballad heard the most ravishing music, which seemed to descend through the mountain, and filled the cells with its enchanting harmony. And thus was the dervise's time divided: in the morning he preached to the multitude, whilst the careful Sanballad received their offerings, and laid them on the stone table in the cell.

At noon the dervise ascended with the offerings, and the young man was ordered to pursue his private devotions in the innermost cell, and was taught to expect those heavenly sounds, if his prayers were accepted. When the sun left the horizon, Alfouran descended to the place where Sanballad spread some roots on the turf by the spring, and the dervise and the scholar made their single and abstemious meal.

The young dervise was enraptured at the precepts and sanctity of his master; and the inhabitants of Bassora brought daily their riches, and fine vestments and delicacies, that Alfouran might sacrifice those unworthy objects of their affection on the altar of the sun. Nor were the prayers of Sanballad rejected, for he daily obtained a grateful token from the powers he worshipped, and was charmed with the heavenly music which sounded through the rock. In this manner did Alfouran and his pupil dedicate their time to the invincible powers of fire, till the whole city of Bassora was converted to the religion of the dervise; and, neglecting their trade, they all flocked regularly to imbibe the instructions of his lips.

But

But what, even in the midst of his sanctity, preyed upon the heart of Sanballad was, that his master Alfouran did not suffer him to ascend the mountain. When he asked the dervise the reason why he was denied that holy office, Alfouran would answer:—

'Know, O young man, that he only is fit to make such a sacrifice, who, by long and patient abstemiousness, has sanctified his mind, and purged it from the desires of mortality. No, Sanballad, you must serve a longer term of years, and persist in your religion for many suns, ere you be admitted to that, the greatest and noblest work of man: wait, therefore, with submission; and doubt not, but, when thou art accepted, the Deity of Fire will call thee to his service.'

If Sanballad's impetuous desires to serve like Alfouran, in the cell of the worshipper of fire, could drive him, against the inclinations and commands of his parents, to act under the banners of Alfouran, it is not to be wondered, that he was now as eager in desiring to be jointly admitted into all the services of his master.

The bed or resting-place of Sanballad was on the stone table in the outward cell; Alfouran slept on a floor of flints within. It was the hour of midnight, when Sanballad, still revolving his favourite desires in his mind, heard the wind rustle through the grove; the moon played on the surface of the water, in the bason which stood without; when, on a sudden, Sanballad discerned at the door of the cell the figure of a little old man; he immediately endeavoured to cry out to Alfouran, but he found his tongue cleaved to the roof of his mouth. The little figure advanced, and stood before the astonished and motionless Sanballad.

'I am,' said the spectre, 'the good Genius which presides over thy way-ward fate. Alfouran this very night did meditate thy death, and intended to sacrifice thee to his barbarous god. You are, young man, too inquisitive for this mysterious religion, which requires a blind and unsuspicious faith: but, in compassion to thy youth, and being willing to vindicate the truth of thy much-injured prophet, I have taken this opportunity, while he is in his first sleep, to warn thee of thy danger. I must not assist thee farther; for Alfouran possesses the signet of the Genius Nadoc, which he stole from a bramin of the most exalted piety. But if thou art resolute, go fearless into his cell, and boldly thrust thy hand into his bosom, where it ever lies concealed. If thou canst but for a moment snatch it from him, thou art safe; for when it is in thy hand, its virtues will be obedient to you its possessor: be confident, therefore, and forget not, when thou hast it in thy hand, to make a proper use of it.'

' And how it is to be used?' replied the astonished Sanballad.

'Wish,' said the Genius, ' for whatever you desire, and it will not be denied you. But hasten, O young man! for I foresee Alfouran will in a few minutes awake. At this exhortation Sanballad arose from his bed, and entered into the cell of the treacherous Alfouran. He felt gently for his master, who was stretched upon the flints.

Sanballad having found his bosom, boldly put his hand therein, and felt the signet of the Genius Nadoc, which he immediately pulled out, and by the force of his arm awakened the affrighted dervise.

Sanballad seeing Alfouran awake, wished that he had compleated his purpose, that he might have escaped out of the cell while the dervise had slept. No sooner had Sanballad formed his wish, than Alfouran sunk again into a deep sleep; and the young man, perceiving the power which the signet of the Genius Nadoc had given him, blessed Mahomet his prophet, and hastened out of the cell.

On the plain before the door, he met his faithful Genius Mamlouk.

' I see,'

'I see,' said his instructor, thou hast wisely prevailed; and now, O Sanballad, we will together ascend this mountain, and I will convince thee of the folly of thy worship.'

Having thus said, Mamlouk led the way, and having climbed to the altar, on the surface of the mountain, the Genius desired Sanballad to move the altar from its place.

'O Mamlouk,' said Sanballad, 'that is far beyond my strength; for when I sat on this stone, as a probationer before the sun, I assayed with all my strength to move it, and could not.'

'That was,' replied Mamlouk, 'because Alfouran commanded it to continue firm and fixed; but now his power is no more.'

Sanballad then set his shoulder against the stone, and moved it from its place. The stone being removed, discovered a dark winding stair-case cut out of the rock, which descended into the body of the mountain. Mamlouk commanded Sanballad to descend, and fear not: 'For,' said the Genius, 'I will attend you, though invisible, and instruct you in what manner you are to behave, but be resolute in preserving the signet of the Genius Nadoc.'

The Continuation of the Tale of the Dervise Alfouran.

THE astonished son of Sami, emboldened by the presence and speech of the Genius Mamlouk, began to descend into the entrails of the mountain, by circular steps, which wound about a solid pillar of stone.

After he had passed three hundred stairs, he met with a strong wicket, which he commanded to open, and then continued to pursue his way through a dark and close passage, cut out of the living rock. At the end of this passage he found a door of solid iron, which at his command creaked on its hinges, and
opening,

opening, presented to his view a large cavern, illuminated in the centre with an enormous glowing carbuncle. Around this spacious vault hung all the rich and valuable garments which the deceitful Alfouran had begged from the deluded inhabitants of Bassora, as offerings to his god.

'And what,' said Sanballad to his invisible guide, was the design of Alfouran in collecting these riches, since he never makes any use of them?'

'Proceed,' said Mamlouk, and observe.' In one corner of this cavern, Sanballad perceived a chasm in the rock, which he immediately commanded to open, and which let him through its sides into another passage wider than the first, supported by two rows of pillars, and enlightened with a variety of carbuncles.

As soon as Sanballad entered this passage, he heard the sound of many instruments, playing the most plaintive notes; and presently, at the lower end, he saw a number of close-veiled matrons marching with solemn steps along the avenues of the passage.

'May I, O Mamlouk,!' said Sanballad, 'wish that these may receive me as they used to receive Alfouran?'

'Yes,' replied Mamlouk, 'I find thou hast wished it in thine heart, for they already begin to acknowledge thee.'

As Mamlouk said this, the matrons all came round Sanballad, some kissing his hands, some his feet, and others kneeling, and in the highest acts of devotion touching the skirts of his cloathing. Thus surrounded, the fictitious dervise passed to the farther end of the passage, where a spacious portal opened into a gloomy temple, hewn out of a solid rock of adamant: in the centre of this temple was an altar, or hearth, raised from the ground, on which a large fire, fed with oils and aromatic woods, burnt incessantly day and night, and was renewed with all the incense and perfumes

fumes which Alfouran had obtained from the deluded inhabitants of Baſſora.

As ſoon as Sanballad advanced to the fire, the orgies began. The female votaries worked themſelves up into the moſt frantic fits of enthuſiaſtic madneſs, groaning, weeping, laſhing themſelves, falling into trances and fits; till at length, tired and fatigued with their wild religion, they ſunk into ſlumbers round the flame which they had adored.

'Now, Sanballad,' ſaid Mamlouk, 'now muſt thou be reſolute and brave: canſt thou reſiſt temptation?'

'Alas,' replied Sanballad, 'I thought ſo once, but it was a vain opinion, ariſing from the pride of a falſe religion.'

'Your diffidence' anſwered the Genius, 'is prudent, and manifeſts an humble mind; but as temptation may be too ſevere for your new born faith in the prophet, he has permitted me to perſonate Alfouran, and carry you inviſibly through theſe mazes of bewitching error.' Thus ſaying, Mamlouk put on the appearance of Alfouran; and Sanballad having wiſhed himſelf inviſible, ſtood beſide the metamorphoſed Genius.

Mamlouk then waved his hands on high, and clapped them together in the air; at the ſound of his clapping the matrons awoke, and the fictitious Alfouran commanded the cup of love to be produced. Four ancient matrons immediately brought forward a large bowl from the innermoſt parts of the temple, of which the transformed Genius and his females partook. No ſooner were they replete with this liquor, than they began to ſing the moſt prophane ſongs, and by every geſture manifeſted the deſires of their hearts; till at length being worked into a paſſionate madneſs, they threw off their cloathing, and diſcovered, under their formal appearances of ſanctified matrons, the moſt abandoned ſigns of youthful proſtitution.

VOL. I. H The

The Genius having revealed thus much of the mysteries of Alfouran, took Sanballad by the hand, and led him out of that scene of horror to the top of the mountain. As they arose from the cavern, the beams of the sun began to play upon the east, and tinge the dusky clouds with its early light.

'And who,' said Sanballad to his guide, as they arose, 'who are these abominable wretches?'

'They are,' replied Mamlouk, 'weak and deluded women, who have at different times stolen in the dead of night from Bassora, to hear the doctrines of the sanctified Alfouran. But be silent, for I see on the plains before the city of Bassora, the multitudes approaching to hear and adore the hypocritical dervise.'

'And will Alfouran awake and instruct them?' said Sanballad to the Genius.

'No,' answered Mamlouk, 'the prophet will no longer permit his villainies to remain unexposed; but let us hasten to meet the credulous followers of Alfouran.'

Having thus said, Mamlouk descended from the hill, and stood before the cell of the dervise. The crowds gathered around him, for he still personated the form of Alfouran; some blessed him with tears in their eyes, others nearly worshipped the fictitious idol of their affections. In the midst of this ill-placed adoration, Mamlouk lifted up his voice, as though it had been the voice of a whirlwind, and said in the ears of all the inhabitants of Bassora—

'O deluded idolaters, why have ye left the worship of your prophet, to follow the lies and fables of the enchanter Alfouran? As he spoke these words, the Genius shook off the appearance of the dervise, and shone before them in all the native beauty of his heavenly race.

The multitude were astonished at the change, and the Genius proceeded—

'I am

'I am Mamlouk, the guardian Genius of your city, which I have with sorrow of late beheld strangely deviating from the worship of the prophet. The fates decreed that you should be tempted by Alfouran: he came therefore into this grove; and, under the specious mark of sanctity, gained the hearts of your people, insomuch that you neglected the public works of the city, and the social duties which ye owed one to another, and all herded to hear and offer to Alfouran yourselves and your substance. Alfouran was possessed of the signet of the Genius Nadoc, by means of which he has commanded the slaves of that signet to form, in the spacious womb of this mountain, the secret haunts of his wickedness and lust, which I will now disclose unto you.'

Having so spoken, the Genius commanded Sanballad to go into the cell, and awaken Alfouran, which he did, the dervise trembling as he came forth from a consciousness of his guilt. As soon as the multitude beheld Alfouran, they were so infatuated at his presence, that the luminous appearance of the Genius scarce withheld them from worshipping and adoring the dervise; which, when Mamlouk perceived, he said unto them—

'O inhabitants of Bassora, how vain are my labours to bring you to Mahomet! but ere you too foolishly refuse to hear the directions of your prophet, let me expose to your view the entrails of this mountain.'

As he spake these words, the people all looked towards the mountain, which began to crack and open its sides, till by degrees the temple and caverns within were made manifest to the wondering populace. Out of this nest of lust and intemperance came the wild females who had so miserably degraded themselves by their lascivious deeds; but how was the misery of their condition heightened, when they beheld such crowds of their neighbours and kinsmen standing as witnesses of their indecent appearance!

Nor were the men of Baſſora leſs diſguſted, to find among the private hoards of the luſtful derviſe their wives and daughters, who had been thus polluted by his ſecret iniquities. They were now all reſolute in deſtroying the monſter Alfouran from the face of the earth; and ſo incenſed were they againſt him, that they tore the ſaint into ten thouſand reliques; as he was moſt happy who could ſhew the moſt marks of vengeance on the fallacious derviſe.

Mamlouk having ſuffered them to execute their vengeance on the hypocritical Alfouran, exhorted them to follow obediently the law of their prophet, and ever to deſpiſe ſuch teachers as ſhould preach up a myſterious, unintelligible, and hidden religion; or expect that they ſhould blindly give up their ſubſtance and ſocial duties, to follow the direction of a ſanctified and luſtful drone.

As Mamlouk finiſhed his tale, bright flaſhes of light ſtreamed through the lattice-work of the ſaloon; and preſently, with ſmiles of mildneſs on his face, came the illuſtrious prophet Mahomet, and hovered over the auguſt aſſembly.

'Thanks, heavenly Mamlouk,' ſaid the prophet of the faithful, 'thanks do I give thee, in the name of my flock of Baſſora, whom thou haſt reſcued; O may they never again ſtray from the light vouchſafed them; but may reaſon and revelation alike direct them to ſeek the realms of peace, and fly from the deluſions of error and enthuſiaſm—and do ye, favoured flock of Heaven, liſten and imbibe the inſtructions of my ſervants, and obey the voice of their divine morality.'

As he thus ſpake, the royal company all aroſe, and proſtrating themſelves on earth, thus began their hymn of praiſe—

'Glories ſurround the defender of the faithful! Alla, Alla, Alla!

'Praiſe,

'Praise, and honour, and worship, be unto him who giveth sight to the blind, and peace to the sons of care. Alla!

'Be thy reign immortal, prophet of the just! be thy power, as is thy mercy, vicegerent of Alla! Alla, Alla, Alla!

'Happy are thy servants who do the will of their master. Alla!

'Happy are thy servants who hear the voice of their prophet. Alla!

'Happy are they who walk not in error, but are instructed in thy law. Alla, Alla, Alla!'

As the Genii pronounced these words in songs of melody, the prophet arose, and ascended from their sight, while the whole assembly lay entranced with delightful visions. After some time, the company being reinstated, Iracagem thus addressed himself to the Genius Omphram—

'Omphram, let the praises of Mahomet inspire thee in declaring the labours of thy tutelage.'

'Happy shall I esteem myself,' answered Omphram, 'if Iracagem approves of my behaviour in directing the Sultan Hassan Assar.

TALE III.

Hassan Assar; or, the History of the Caliph of Bagdat.

THE royal court of the Caliph Hassan Assar beheld with discontent a long series of gloomy moons. The voice of joy, and the smiles of festivity, were banished the palace, by the severe frowns which sat uninterrupted on the brow of the caliph. The barrenness of his spacious seraglio was the cause of his melancholy; neither the youthful beauties of Circassia, nor the more ripened fruit which his own warmer sun produced, were capable of continuing the race of the Caliphs of Bagdat.

Omphram, the tutelary Genius of his kingdom, saw the perverse will of fate, and could not withstand

stand its decrees; she read in the permanent leaves of that everlasting book, that Hassan Assar would vainly solicit a progeny from Heaven, while he sought after that blessing in the embraces of beauty. Though the day, which as yet had not arisen, was inveloped in the clouds of obscurity, she could still discern the possibility of the continuance of the race of Hassan, but not the particular manner in which it was to come to pass.

As Hassan was administering justice in the divan, the throne whereon he sat was violently shaken with the trembling of the earth, the doors of the divan creaked, the lightening poured down through the windows in sheets of fire, and in the midst of the confusion both of the earth and air, came Omphram riding in the tempest which her power had raised. Hassan bowed at her approach: and, as his heart was unconscious of evil, he regarded not the terrors which surrounded her.

'Hassan,' said the Genius, 'I perceive you are not to be biassed by the outward appearance of things: knowing that only you are accountable for the actions of your subjects, you look with serenity on this confusion of elements, which it was not in your power to prevent. The same trust which enables you to be thankful in the sunshine of affluence, gives you also confidence in the dangerous tempest. Look but as indifferently on all things, and your prayers shall be no longer offered to the unconsenting prophet. He has heard your petition, he believes you are solely desirous of perpetuating his seed, and therefore he commands you to dismiss the beauties of your seraglio, and to give up your whole life and pleasure to the Houri he has provided for your embrace.'

As she finished this declaration, the walls of the palace crumbled into their original clay, the crowds that were gathered in the divan vanished from the sight of the caliph, and he saw no longer the flourish-
ing

ing city of Bagdat, but the wild and fanciful productions of unassisted nature. The lions in the chariot of Omphram roared to the repeated echoes of the forest, and the fairy still observing the courageous Hassan unchanged at his fate, smiled on the caliph, and bid him persevere in his unshaken trust, and no dangers or misfortune should prevent the blessings which the prophet had engaged to shower upon his race.

Although the prospects around him were wild, yet they were beautiful and enchanting. Lofty trees at a distance on one side formed natural temples to the deities of the place; on the other, the adjacent mountains were partly covered with evergreens and flowering shrubs, which grew irregularly, as a covering, above the craggy sides of the rocks, except where a torrent from the summit had worn out a hollow bed for its rapid passage and descent. In the vale beneath, a spacious lake divided the ancient groves from the mountainous side of the prospect; and on the intermediate banks flourished whatever might invite the eye or please the wandering palate; fruits unnumbered of every kind, too heavy for the parent stock whereon they grew; flowers in every varied hue and every varied tint which the sun could form by the many coloured beams of its all-diffusive light.

While Hassan was admiring these luxurious productions of the uncultivated place, he perceived a most beauteous female advancing through the irregular avenues of the spacious grove. 'O, blessed prophet,' cried the enamoured sultan, as soon as he beheld her, what delights hast thou prepared for me, in this vale of plenteousness! surely I am already in thy blissful paradise; and behold the Houri, whom thou hast consigned to my arms, is now approaching to meet my embrace.'

As he said this, he sprang forward to join the blooming fair one, whose delicate limbs stood all confessed

fessed to view, and displayed, in their ineffable symmetry and delicate purity, the utmost harmony of a beauteous creation. She also, as animated by the same inclination and desires, hastened toward the embrace of the all admiring Hassan; but alas! ere the happy couple could meet, the envious earth gave a hideous groan, and the ground parting under their feet, divided them from each other by a dismal chasm.

While the astonished pair stood on different sides of the gulph, viewing the horrid fissure and the dark abyss, wild notes of strange uncouth warlike music were heard from the bottom of the pit; and immediately a flash or vapour of blue flame arose from the cavern, in the midst of which the Caliph discovered an enormous elephant with a turret on his back. When the elephant was level with the surface, the earth closed again: and a black, which sat on the elephant's neck, advanced upon his body to the turret, which he touched with a wand in his hand, and immediately the turret flew into a thousand pieces, and discovered a little hut, out of which came a negro woman, properly accoutred with the implements of war.

The beauteous lady screamed at the sight; and as Hassan was hastening to her assistance, the black who held the wand in his hand, cried out with a voice like thunder,—

'Hassan Assar, forbear! But it matters not, for Omphram has deceived me, and thou art unworthy of the favour of Mahomet: Omphram assured me, that the Caliph of Bagdat was unbiassed by the outward appearance of things; and yet methinks I see you pay a preference to beauty, and neglect to attend on the vigorous Nakin Palata, who is destined for your spouse.'

'What!' cried Hassan in a maze, 'must I leave this perfect original, to take up with that unnatural lump of blackness!' At these words, Nakin Palata, with great wrath, drew forth an arrow from her quiver, and fixing it in her bow, aimed the fatal shaft at the body of the beautiful nymph.

Hassan

Haffan faw the malice, but could not prevent the blow. The arrow pierced through the fnowy heart of the lovely female, and the warm tide of blood and life iffued forth at the unfriendly wound. As the diftreffed caliph drew the arrow forth, and applied his lips to the place, the black jumping from the beaft, ran to him and commanded him to difcontinue his care, or he would for ever lofe the protection of Mahomet.

The caliph looked up in aftonifhment at hearing the command, and was more than ever furprifed to behold the fkin falling from the body of the black, under which he difcovered the features of Omphram his Genius.

'Oh Haffan Affar,' faid Omphram, 'haft thou not yet learnt, that the delights of this world are not to bias your affection and obedience from the will of Heaven. When you prayed to the prophet to continue your race on the throne of you forefathers, did you not promife to give up all other bleffings, if you might poffefs that only defire of your heart?'

'Now, then, what is beauty, when put in competition with her who is to perpetuate the defcendants of the Caliph of Badgat? Waft thou not unhappy, when thou hadft every beauty at command? Didft thou not then defpife fuch faint allurements, and beg from Heaven a more fubftantial bleffing? Behold her, then, who is appointed to blefs thee, and yet thou flieft from her, and art now returning to thofe pleafures which thou haft folemnly renounced; but think not the prophet will fuffer fuch ingratitude! No—enjoy the company of thy beauteous Houri; for no doubt your love is fo exceffive, that you will willingly follow her to the grave.

Having thus faid, fhe ftruck the ground with her wand, and immediately a number of flaves arofe with ftones, and all the materials for building. 'There,' faid the fairy to the workmen, 'inclofe that dying corpfe with a fubftantial monument, and

let

let us see how long this worldly caliph's love will fix him on the body of his mistress. The slaves obeyed, and being Genii of an inferior order, executed their business in less time than a mortal workman could have laid the foundation.

Hassan neither observed their work, nor was solicitous to escape; but still pressing with his lips the fatal wound, suffered himself to be inclosed in those walls of death. Before the roof (which was formed of massive stone) was entirely covered, Omphram called out, and commanded Hassan to withdraw; but the caliph was deaf, and regardless of every thing but the condition of his dear nymph. Wherefore the Genii compleated the work; and Omphram finding him deaf to her commands, left him immured in the mausoleum, with the dead body of the strangely murdered fair-one. Although the workmen of Omphram had totally immured the Caliph Hassan Assar, yet was there left a grate-work of iron in the middle of the tomb by the Genius's command, through which the light might reflect on the deceased body, and give the Caliph a full view of the dead beauties which he had preferred to the will of his prophet.

For several days the love-sick Hassan persisted in his attention to the corpse of his beautiful favourite; but contagious mortality now began to steal away the delicate complexion and graceful hue, which formerly adorned the living Houri's limbs; a noisome stench succeeded, and yellow putrid foulness overspread the whole body; her cheeks sunk, her flesh grew moist with rottenness, and all her frame sent forth the strongest effluvias of corruption and death.

Hassan, whose love and affection was solely supported by lust and passion, having lost the only objects of his desires, began to loath the wretched situation which he had chosen in preference to submission and obedience.

'And is this,' cried the rejected caliph, looking on he corrupted mass, ' is this the natural effect of death
on

on beauty? Is it then only owing to the different modifications of matter, that one mass gives us the highest enjoyment, and another the greatest disgust? Nay, more; are the joys of this world so fleeting and unsubstantial, that the objects of our pleasure to-day, may to-morrow become the objects of our aversion? O prophet! holy prophet!' continued he, 'I now see and acknowledge the justice of thy punishment, I now can discern between the good that thou didst intend me, and the evil which I have chosen.' At these words he sunk on the ground overcome with watching, loathing, hunger, and fatigue. As he lay stretched on the ground, the female negro appeared above at the grate.

'O blind, ill-fated Caliph,' said she, 'how long will it be ere thou seest the follies of thy choice! Wert thou not born to do the will of Heaven; Wert thou not, by thine own desire, consigned over by that will, to fly from the pleasures of life, and give thyself up to the interest of thy race? The prophet doubted the sincerity of thy heart, he therefore placed thee amidst all the natural luxuries which this world affords; luxuries more irresistible than those which art hath made in imitation of them.

'The love which you professed for that noisome body, say, O Caliph, did it arise from virtue or lust? You saw and loved, but you heard not, neither had you knowledge of the perfections or imperfections of her mind. She came only recommended to you, by passion and desire, I came recommended by the will of your prophet; but you foolishly conceived your commands grievous, and your desires natural and reasonable; therefore you were left in possession of your wishes, to convince you that from disobedience and unlawful pleasure, no other fruits can sprout forth but those of corruption and abhorrence. You are sensible this life is short, precarious, and uncertain; it is a life of trial, and not of enjoyment; it is a life in which we must refuse, and not covet the pleasures of

the

the world. Where then is the hardship of obedience, when we are commanded to abstain in order hereafter to possess.

'Think not, O Caliph, I speak this of myself, it is your prophet directs me; he sought me out among many in mine own nation, he snatched me from the arms of one whom I had formerly esteemed for his activity and manly strength.

"Nakin Palata," said a voice unto me, as I was with the utmost pleasure observing the exercises of my lovely youth, "attend to the commands of Heaven, and know thou wert born to fulfil its will." 'At the same time an invisible power plunged me into the earth, and placed me in the hut and turret which you beheld on the back of the elephant.

A black who guided the beast, informed me of the cause of my situation. "You are," said the guide, selected out of thousands for your modesty, your humility and obedience to the Power above, to be mother of a royal race. A great and mighty king shall fill your arms; but then you must never more reflect upon the youth you have left, nor sigh for the enjoyment of your native country. At these words, O Caliph, I sunk with sorrow and disgust; no joys of fortune or riches were in my esteem equivalent to the jetty blackness of my beloved Kafrac.

"What then," said I "must I be condemned for ever to lose the sight of Kafrac, the idol of my soul?"

"No," replied my guide, "you shall see him yet once again, to convince you how blind that choice is, which has only outward comeliness and natural abilities for its object." 'At these words, he took me by the shoulders, and we mounted through the caverns of the earth. The ground opened as we ascended, and presently I was conveyed into the centre of a wood which I remember was near the habitation of my jetty Kafrac.

The

'The black having taken his hand from my shoulder, bid me walk forward to a gloomy part of the wood. I obeyed; but, O caliph, judge the emotions of my soul, when I beheld the traitorous Kafrac locked in the arms of my brother's wife! my blood curdled with horror at the sight, and I stood motionless before the adulterous Kafrac.

'My guardian black perceiving my condition, ran toward me, and again touching my shoulder, the earth opened a second time, and we sunk together on the back of the elephant.' "Well," cried my guide, when he had seated me in the turret, "are you now better disposed to obey the will of the prophet of Mecca?"

"I am," said I, (still terrified with the dreadful vision,) "at the disposal of your prophet, and entirely convinced of my own incapacity to distinguish between real and fictitious goodness." "Then," replied the guide, "you are capable of executing the will of your prophet. Here, take these your national accoutrements," (giving me the bow and arrows) "and when you see the Caliph Haffan Affar pursuing sensual pleasure, and preferring the specious appearance of beauty to the command of Mahomet, direct your shaft at the breast of his mistress, and fear not to destroy her; for she is only beautiful in appearance, but is really no more than an earthly phantom, sent to convince Haffan Affar of the weakness of his heart, and the folly of his sensual lusts." 'Having thus said, we ascended again into the realms of light, and arose just between you and the phantom, which you blindly esteemed beyond the great blessings that are designed for you.'

When Nakin Palata had ended her relation, the caliph prostrated himself on the ground, and thrice adoring Alla and his illustrious prophet, he cried out in the words of Nakin Palata—'I am at thy disposal, O prophet!' As he said this, the skies loured with thunder, and Omphram his Genius descended. At her approach, the tomb cracked and divided, and Haffan Affar again proftrated himfelf on the earth before the Genius of his kingdom.

'Happy, happy, happy caliph! happy art thou, O Haffan Affar!' cried out Omphram, 'who canft fubmit to the will of thy prophet; happy art thou in thy choice, and happy is Nakin Palata in exchanging a barbarous favage for a wife, prudent, and religious monarch. Nor fhall you find, O Haffan Affar,' continued the Genius Omphram, 'that the commands of Mahomet are grievous or heavy to be borne; for now look at her whom you defpifed, and examine the features of the once deteftable Nakin Palata.'

At her command the caliph arofe from the ground; but oh, how was his foul tranfported, when he beheld the countenance of his bride changed, and Nakin Palata glowing with every charm with which nature could inveft her.

'Ah, caliph!' continued Omphram, 'be not too much tranfported by the outward appearance of things; it is becaufe you love each other, that you feem thus beautifully changed; nor are you lefs amiable in the eyes of Nakin Palata, than fhe is in your fight. O caliph! this fhall continue, while your love continues: but when you, by caprice, by a refolute fuperiority, or by a vexatious ill-nature, put on the frown or difapprobation, then you fhall be divefted of this amiable comelinefs, and ftand like a cruel and infulting tyrant before your trembling bride; and when either her love or her obedience fails, then fhall fhe be again transformed, and wear the difgufting complexion of a tawny negro.

Having thus faid, fhe took Haffan Affar and his bride into her chariot, which was drawn by two majeftic lions, and wafted them in the air to the caliph's palace at Bagdat.

His fubjects, when they heard of his arrival, all flocked to the prefence of their royal mafter, and
welcomed

welcomed with the warmest affection his long-wished return. Hassan Assar presented to them his beauteous bride, and declared her the only sultana of his realms. The court rang with joyous acclamations, and all hailed the amiable Nakin Palata. Omphram declared to them the reasons of the caliph's choice, and promised in the name of the prophet, a royal successor. At this assurance, the palace again re-echoed with the voices of his subjects; and nothing was heard in his kingdom but the praises of Hassan Assar, the loving, obedient, and religious caliph, and Nakin Palata, the joy and consort of the best of princes.

Omphram having ended her tale, the sage Iracagem waved his wand, and commanding the race of the faithful to sit down on the carpets spread under their feet, he ordered a collation worthy of his race to be produced. A number of inferior Genii immediately brought in a service of milk and rice.

'Plain, like their instruction,' said he, 'is the diet of the faithful; their desires are not after the flesh, but after the immortal food of the mind. As the courser despiseth the pastures over which he engageth in the race, so doth the child of Heaven pass by the pleasures of the sons of earth. To satisfy the mind is the business of our race, and to liken it to the image of its original fountain: feed then, my children,' continued Iracagem, 'the necessary cravings of your earthly frames, but suffer not the clay-moulded case to weigh down the precious jewel it contains.'

The disciples of the Genii having finished their abstemious repast, Hassarack was ordered to recite the tale of Kelaun and Guzzarat.

TALE IV.

Kelaun and Guzzarat.

BENEATH the foot of a lofty rock, in the mountains of Gabel-el-ared, lived a homely peasant, whose business it was to lead a few sheep through the hollow passages of the mountains, from one fruitful valley to another, that they might feed on the herbs which grew plentifully near the rills and cascades, on every side descending from the craggy precipices.

Canfu had followed this pastoral life from a child, and his stock consisted of twelve sheep, which he attended, and four goats which his wife daily milked for the support of Canfu and her son.

If Canfu had harboured a wish beyond the present scene, it was, that Kelaun, his son, might hereafter become the husband of his neighbour Rauk's daughter. With this intent, the two children were made acquainted with each other from their infancy, and brought daily into the same spot of ground to play and gambol together.

But the haughty disposition of his comrade Guzzarat, soon grew offensive to the fiery temper of the impetuous Kelaun, and the young couple, instead of imbibing a love and friendship for each other in their infancy, broke out into mutual hatred and animosity. Canfu saw their growing dislike with the utmost grief and sorrow; he had asked of his prophet but one request, and that he perceived would be denied him.

The angry father could not conceal his vexation, but daily poured out his discontent against the gracious purposes of Heaven, which he imagined were for ever contrived to thwart and disappoint him.

As he was one day sitting on a stone, and watching his flock by the side of a cascade, which ran foaming from the rocks above, he perceived a naked body come tumbling down the torrent, and which having passed the fall, swam on the surface of the waters, and

seemed

TALES OF THE GENII.
Cansu the Shepherd saving the Genius
Ginarnha from being drownd in the river.

seemed to all appearance dead. He could not behold such a sight, without endeavouring to rescue the body from the current, which he effected with his crook, as the stream, though rapid, was very narrow. Having pulled it on the bank, he perceived it was the body of a beautiful women, which, as soon as the water dried from it, gave sings of life, and by degrees recovered its powers of action.

The modest Canfu had pulled from his shoulders the vest which he wore, and spread it on the stranger, when he drew her to the land, but he was greatly surprized to find that she was so soon recovered; nor was his amazement lessened, when he perceived a web like a wing expanded from each shoulder, and saw the fair stranger mount into the air, like an eagle soaring to the sun. Canfu watched her with his eyes; she flew toward the rock, from whence she was carried down by the torrent, and several times encircled the range of mountains in her flight, and seemed to be in quest of some prey.

On a sudden he perceived a second figure in the air; the winged female attacked it, and was repulsed, and fell again into the lake; and the shepherd again saw her carried down the cliff by the rapid stream. Canfu in amaze drew the body out again, which being dried, revived as before, and presented to his view a beautiful female.

'It is in vain, O Canfu, to strive against a race who are my superiors. But for your kindness I must have perished; for such is my nature, that the water, in the time that the sun runs his course round the earth, would dissolve my being. I am of the race of Genii, of those bold and free Genii, who dared disobey the seal of Solyman, and the commands of Mahomet. It is my delight to thwart the will of that prophet, you saw me this moment engaging with the Genius Nadoc, who was bearing a message from Mahomet. Nadoc knowing the imperfection of my nature, would not attack me till I flew directly over the lake; he then maliciously plunged me into the water, hoping to destroy me; but I knew one was near to help me, who was offended at the prophet, because he disregarded thy prayer. What Mahomet, therefore, denied thee, O Canfu, I will grant, provided thou consentest, for my power is limited; neither may I help or distress mankind, without their own approbation or concurrence.'

'O beautiful Genius,' answered Canfu, 'thou hast my consent; unite but my son Kelaun in the bonds of marriage with Guzzarat, and I will ever be obedient to thy commands.'

'Return then with joy to thine hut,' said Giuaraha, 'for already a part of thy wish is granted.' As she spake these words, she spread her airy pinions, and mounted from his sight.

Canfu was at a great distance from his hut, and did not arrive under his native rock, till the sun was hidden behind the mountains of Gabel-el-ared.

The twelve sheep and the four goats preceded him. His wife knew the bleat of the sheep, and ran out to meet her returning husband.

'Thy sheep,' said she, 'O Canfu, are compleat in number, thy goats also are four, even as they went out with thee so are they returned; but whare is Kelaun, thy son. 'Kelaun,' answered the astonished father, 'went not out with me; the way was tiresome and dangerous, and I would not suffer him to accompany me.'

'I know it well, O Canfu,' replied his wife, 'Kelaun went out, while the sun was yet in the vallies to seek thee——' At these words the countenance of Canfu fell, for he remembered at that time it was, that he had given Giuaraha his consent.

'Is he not,' replied the anxious father, 'with Guzzarat, the daughter of Raask?'

Their huts were not a furlong apart, Canfu hastened toward the dwelling of Raask, but Kelaun was not there. Tired as the shepherd was with the heat and labour of the preceding day, yet leaving the sheep to the care of his wife, he set out to seek among the mountains his wandering son. He laboured the whole night in a fruitless search, and returned to his hut in the morning, spent and overcome with grief, care, and remorse.'

'Alas,' said the unhappy father, 'I have consented to my own misery, and Guiaraha has stolen from me the only joy of my heart! O prophet—but,' said the wretched Canfu, 'I dare not call upon thee, for I have joined with thine enemies, and thou hast justly deserted me!' We must, however, leave the sorrowful hut of Canfu, and follow the steps of the little Kelaun among the mountains.

Kelaun was well acquainted with the vallies and rocks which stood near the habitation of his father; he knew the notches which Canfu, had cut as directions, and followed them faithfully till the day light decreased, every moment expecting to meet his father, and the sheep, and the goats, whose company he preferred to the imperious Guzzarat. But when night overtook him, his little knees knocked together with fear, and because his parent had forgotten to teach him to address any other power, he prayed to Canfu, and cried aloud that he would come and deliver him.

He was then on a barren spot, surrounded on all sides with rocks, except a small aperture through which he had crept. As he gained the middle of this vale, a small blue flame burst forth out of the ground, which increased in a pyramidical form, till it seemed like an hillock of fire.

The wind immediately arose, and bellowed on the cliffs and ragged tops of the surrounding mountains, but no storm could reach the bottom of the vale, where the infant Kelaun stood gazing at the rising flame which burned in the middle of the heath. Presently the air was filled with shrieks, and in a moment

ment the blue fire was surrounded with the Genii of the place.

The first in dignity stood the bold Giuaraha, she commanded silence among them, and ere they began their midnight rites, harangued them to the following effect.

'O ye invincible but by water! see among your ranks an infant devoted to the power of our art. His parent has consented to our dominion, and Kelaun, the son of Canfu, is committed into the care of the despisers of Mahomet. Let us see, therefore, O royal race, how far the human heart is capable of being tutored in the licentious maxims of our undaunted establishment: let us carry him to our palace, in the centre of the earth, and instruct him in such artifices and wiles, as may make him a scourge to the humble dependants on the prophet of Mecca.' To this exhortation the whole assembly muttered applause, and the valley sinking by degrees, descended with the Genii and their prize, and left the black heavy mountains above tottering with their powerful enchantments.

Kelaun, amazed and confounded at the sight, filled the air with his cries, but his fears were vain, Canfu had resigned his son, and Mahomet would not rescue those who mistrusted and hated his government. The valley having descended for some time, at length stopped, and with a shake like that of an earthquake, settled itself in the bowels of the globe. No sooner was the valley fixed, than the solid rocks which surrounded it, opened on every side, and formed rough and irregular arches and avenues leading from its centre.

Immediately an innumerable host of evil Genii issued from the rocks, and the place was filled with the restless spirits of those disturbers of mankind. But far above the rest was seen the proud Allahoara, the leader and encourager of that rebellious crew of Genii, whose voice was as the echoes of thunder on the mountains, and whose restless eye-balls shot flashes of lightning like the vengeful clouds.

The little Kelaun stood astonished at his presence, and Giuaraha led him trembling like the pendant aspin leaf that overshadows the flood. Allahoara, who knew the prize that his sister Giuaraha had brought, commended her care and fidelity to the cause of the restless Genii, and gave orders that the infant should be immediately put under proper tutors to educate him, and make him capable of the work they proposed to employ him in.

Giuaraha was appointed his nurse, and she it was whom Allahoara commanded to lead Kelaun through the schools of that abandoned race. These orders being issued, the tumultuous band dispersed through the caverns and the arched rocks, and left Giuaraha with her little prize.

At first the Genius led him through a range of vaulted rocks, into a long room of splendid garments, and endeavoured to fix his attention upon them; she made him try on several, and told him he looked like a little god. Kelaun was pleased withe finery of the place, and began to give credit to the words of Giuaraha. His little head was soon filled with vanity, and his thoughts centered in himself. Next she placed him on a soft sopha, at the extremity of the room, and while he lay entranced in sleep, she presented before his imagination a vision of the night.

Kelaun, as he slept, thought that he saw his father Canfu on the rocks of Ga-bel-el-ared; the form of his vilage was as the dark black precipice, and he spake as the angry waves when they rush into the hollow caverns; he chid the little Kelaun because he appeared so gay, and commanded him to put on his shepherd's coat, and follow the twelve sheep to the brook, Kelaun awaked with the terrors of the vision, and told his tale to the artful Giuaraha.

'Silly father!' said the Genius; 'silly Canfu, the shepherd! shall Kelaun, the favourite of the

Genii,

Genii, regard the dreams of a father, or think again of the poor shepherd Canfu? no, my son, despise the lessons which the base goat-herd has taught you, and think no more of the tale of thy unworthy parents, Kelaun, my son, was born to rule; how then shall he who is a king, regard the lessons of poverty and ignorance!'

She then took the vain son of Canfu by the hand, and led him, accoutred in tawdry robes, to a small field were a thousand little imps were playing together; at the sight of Kelaun, they all bowed, and began to praise the plumes, which adorned his head, and the robe which flowed from his shoulders. They entered into contests to divert him, and filled the place with tumult and disorder. Some brought before him divers little animals, which they contrived to torture by a variety of punishments. Others taught him to confound and destroy whatever he met with; while a little imp put in his hand several implements of cruelty, and encouraged him to exercise them on his comrades.

Kelaun entered with savage joy into the spirit of his instructor, and first began to wreak his wanton cruelty on the adviser of the sport: nor would aught but magic art have prevented him from goading the person of the Genius Giuaraha. Having a short time used him to these sports, she took him to a small hut, where dwelt an old hag, accoutred in rags and filth.

'Morad,' said the Genius 'I will leave this pupil with you for a time; instruct him in your arts, and make him a fit scourge for mankind.'

Morad immediately struck the little Kelaun to the ground with her crutch; after a time he arose with tears in his eyes, and found the Genius had left him.

'Strip, urchin,' said Morad, 'strip off these fool's feathers, and take that vessel to the brook for water.'

Kelaun recovering from the blow, refused to obey Morad, and enquired for his former instructor; but the old hag with curses drove him out of the house to
a muddy

a muddy ditch, where she commanded him to draw water for their support. Kelaun saw it was in vain to disobey; he brought the wretched produce of the ditch to the hut, and Morad set before him some carrion for his support.

'The lesson of poverty and necessity,' said the hag, 'is various; it makes men merciful, or it makes them cruel. It teacheth the mean spaniel to crouch, but it smeareth the mouth of the tyger with carnage and blood.'

'Be mine the tyger's lot,' said Kelaun, 'though Morad be the subject of my wrath.'

'The blessings of Morad, which are curses, attend thee,' replied the hag.

Morad then led the little urchin into a dark cave, filled with the bodies of the dead.

'There,' said she, 'learn to glut thyself with human gore; this is thy resting-place. Early in the morning must thou rise to some new work of misery.

Kelaun, though hardened in malice and stubbornness, yet shuddered at the thoughts of such a lodging, and followed Morad as she went forth from the cavern; but the hag seized him by the hair, and dragging him back, she muttered some enchantment over him, and left him without motion on the bodies of the slain. Custom soon reconciled the little imp to this scene of horrors, and Morad perceiving him sufficiently inured to the sight of wretchedness and poverty, carried him again to the Genius Giuaraha.

'Is Kelaun,' said the Genius, 'the favourite of Morad?' 'Yes,' answered the hag, 'Kelaun is now fit for the lessons of fraud and hypocrisy.'

Giuaraha then led him toward a dark gloomy wood, in the centre of which lived the old and decrepit Nervan. 'Nervan, the friend of our race,' said Giuaraha, 'receive this pupil into thy arms, and teach him the lessons of fraud and hypocrisy.'

Nervan

Nervan bowed humbly to the Genius, and taking Kelaun by the hand, he led him into a cell formed of bones and skulls.

'What doth the little imp of mortality,' said Nervan, 'think of my dwelling?' 'I think,' said Kelaun, 'that Morad has devoured the carcase, and left Nervan the bones.' 'So,' continued Nervan, 'think the sons of folly; as the eye believes, do they believe, and their minds are guided by the senses of their bodies. Such intellects will make thee inferior, and not above mankind; take then this sponge, and draw it over thine eyes.'

Kelaun took the sponge which Nervan drew forth from under his garments, and having applied it to his eyes, beheld not a cell of bones, but a noble mosque, adorned with the tombs of sultans and prophets. Nervan immediately prostrated himself before one of the tombs, and bid Kelaun do so likewise. The son of the shepherd knew not what worship he was to pay, but imitated the devout motions of Nervan.

As the old man arose, Kelaun enquired, why he, the servant of the race of Genii, who despise Mahomet, should worship in his temple.

'So,' said Nervan, 'think the sons of folly; as the eye believes do they believe, and their minds are guided by the senses of their bodies.

'Know then, thou feather, who swimmest upon the surface of the lake, but seest not what rocks it conceals, that the greatest irreligion is a mockery of Alla and his prophets, and that hypocrisy is the most dangerous vice of the evil-minded. Let the credulous followers of Mahomet believe thee devout, and let them see thee prostrate before this tomb, so shall thy vices be coloured by enthusiasm like unto virtues, and thy sins shall appear as the fulfilling of the dictates of religion. Weak minds are overpowered by superstitious fear; and he who believes without foundation, is as the quicksand in the sea.'

At

At these words Giuaraha appeared*: 'Enough,' said the evil Genius, 'enough is done: strong passions and desires thou hast by nature, O Kelaun! thy parents have suffered them to increase, and I have taught thee to indulge them. Thou art now a fit scourge for the faithful, and shalt this day see with me the realms of the Caliph of Bagdat.' As she spake, she seized the youth by the arm, and in a moment they were in the royal palace of Bagdat.

Kelaun found himself in a large apartment; a noble youth on a sopha was sleeping before him.

'Kelaun,' said the Genius, 'thou beholdest the heir of the Caliph of Bagdat.' 'But I have no weapon,' answered he, 'to eternize the sleep of this delicate heir.'

'That,' replied Giuaraha, 'is not permitted us. Could we carry our agents at pleasure to perpetrate what mischief we have conceived against the sons of the faithful, Kelaun should have a thousand darts, all charged with the poison of the scorpion; but, alas! our power is curbed by that Mahomet whom we detest! neither could I have brought Kelaun to this place, had not Raalcour, the heir of the Caliph of Bagdat, neglected to make his pilgrimage to the tomb of the prophet. But your hand must not be upon his life; therefore, I will secure Raalcour, and give to Kelaun the form of his person.

---

* In the original, Kelaun is led from one scene of villainy to another, which he learns from the several tutors Giuaraha appoints over him. But the descriptions are very horrid, and so full of the most abominable devices, that I thought it proper to suppress the account of the schools of vice, as bad hearts might be too far instructed by them, and good hearts could not read them without some uneasiness. I have therefore omitted these, and brought Kelaun out of the regions of darkness as soon as I could, though I am sensible the beauty of the tale will be lessened. The EDITOR.

So saying, Giuaraha breathed on the son of the shepherd, and touching the sleeping Raalcour with her finger, he became a bird.

Kelaun seeing the metamorphosis, ran eagerly to seize the bird, and Raalcour had died under his hands, but for the interposition of Guiaraha.

'What wretch!' said the Genius, art thou so abandoned in malice, that the commands of thy protectress can have no influence over thee! the curse then of blindness fall upon thee; and left you should betray by your malicious follies the secrets of our race, I will take from you the remembrance of the past.'

'And cursed,' returned Kelaun, cursed by the prophet whom thou hatest be thy detested race; may your toils and labours be ever attended with the execrations of those whom you pretend to serve! There is neither peace nor friendship, there is neither gratitude nor love in the workers of evil, and they shall be first to curse you, whom ye most seek to bless.' At these words, the Genius answered not, but fled howling away; for she perceived the spirit of the prophet of Mecca spake in Kelaun, and she sought with remorse the caverns of earth, the vallies of death.

And now the mutes and eunuchs opened the doors of the apartment, and prostrated themselves before the fictitious Raalcour. 'Death,' said they, 'hath closed the eyes of Zimprah, and the Caliph of Bagdat, thy father, is ascended into the ninth heaven! The Houri's bathe his precious body in rivers of milk, and everlasting virgins new weave, at his approach, the bowers of Paradise; he is gone unhurt over the burning grates, he is chief in honour among the race of the faithful?'

Kelaun heard the voices of the eunuchs, but saw them not, and they were amazed to find their supposed Caliph groping like unto one who searcheth for light.

'O,' said the chief of the eunuchs, 'what evil hath befallen my royal lord? Why doth he refuse to look upon his prostrate slaves? The whole city wait with
longing

longing eyes to behold their new Caliph, and Raalcour seeth not the slaves which acknowledge him for their lord.' 'Proclaim then,' said Kelaun, 'the mightiest rewards for him who shall restore to the powers of sight the Caliph of Bagdat.

Seven days went the heralds forth with trumpets and hautboys, and proclaimed the mightiest rewards for him who should restore to the powers of sight the Caliph of Bagdat. The tribe who gave ease to the sick came to the palace in throngs, all promising sight to the blind caliph; but their applications had no effect on the representative of Raalcour. The caliph, enraged by disappointment, commanded all those that failed to sudden execution. Every day was the axe of the executioner fed with blood, the city mourned the loss of its sages, but the eyes of the Caliph were still strangers to light.

After a time, came a young man in the habit of a physician, and required to be brought before the caliph, that he might try his skill. The attendants in the seraglio were sorry to see any more pretenders arrived; they cautioned the young physician not to undertake a cure which was so likely to end in his own destruction; nor add by his intrepidity to the blood which had been already spilled in the city.

To these remonstrances he answered nothing; but, with a smile, bid them not distrust his skill, but immediately admit him to the presence of the caliph. The slaves and eunuchs of Kelaun obeyed with reluctance, and led the young man into the chamber of the fictitious caliph, with the silence and sorrow that they would have carried out a friend to the inclosures of the dead.

The young physician made his obeisance before Kelaun; but the surly monarch bid him proceed to his work without delay, as the hand of the executioner waited for his head. The young man seemed not the least dismayed by his threats, but taking a quantity of powder from a bag which he held under his vest, he blew it in the face of the caliph, and the scales fell from his eyes, and Kelaun beheld the light.

The attendants in the seraglio beheld with joy the happy transformation, and the caliph surveyed with eyes of pleasure, the man who had blessed him with sight.

'Let this physician,' said he, 'be exalted in the land; let him be above every vizir and every noble in our realms; let honour attend him, and every new sun behold him more and more respected and beloved. Demand of me,' continued Kelaun, 'demand what reward your soul would wished to be possessed of, even to the half of my kingdom, and thou shalt enjoy it.

'O caliph,' answered the young physician, 'far be it from me to seek honour or riches; far be it from an humble cottager to mix in the tumults of the great; forgive me but one deceit, and the heart of thy servant shall rest satisfied for ever.'

As she spake these words, the young physician laid bare her bosom, and Kelaun beheld he was talking to a beauteous female.

'Happy am I,' said the Caliph Kelaun, 'that nature has pointed out a proper reward for my lovely physician: yes, fair stranger,' continued he, 'thou art the sultana of my heart, and shall divide with me the pleasures and the empire which I enjoy.

The fair stranger fell at the caliph's feet, and after a small silence, thus addressed the fictitious Raalcour.

'To be the meanest of thy slaves, is the wish of Guzzarat, the daughter of the peasant Raask, a base inhabitant of the mountains of Gabel-el-ared.'

'I know not,' answered Kelaun, 'the mountains you speak of, but Paradise itself would not be degraded by the birth of my lovely sultana. But why do I suffer such perfection to lie on the earth, like a jewel that is unfound, when it will add such lustre to my crown! Yes, lovely stranger, this day shall make thee mistress of the Caliph Raalcour.' 'Strange

'Strange it is, my lord,' said Guzzarat rising, 'that the Prince Raalcour should be ignorant of the mountains of Gabel-el ared, where you have so often chased the foaming tiger on the rocks that hung over the cottage of my father, and where I have, with wishful eyes, traced your divine steps; nay, doth not my lord remember, that once, when tired and fatigued with the chase, he prayed my mother to bring him a cup of water; and she sent your slave Guzzarat to you with the milk of her goats? Yes my lord, you smiled when I approached, and you bid me obey with cheerfulness the command of my parent.'

The son of Canfu understood not this conversation; his memory of the past was taken from him; neither otherwise could he have known what the true Raalcour had done before his transformation.

'Alas, my princess!' answered Kelaun, 'I lost with my sight all the memory of the past; neither knew I my state, when my slaves came around me, till my faithful eunuch declared to me my titles; but whether thou art descended from a throne or a cottage, whether thou camest like the sapphire, from the entrails of the earth, or like the morning star from the chambers of the sun, thy worth are in thyself, and can receive no additional lustre from that which surrounds it. But by what art, my fair stranger, did you work this miracle in my behalf? Who did open the treasures of physic before thee, and where did the young virgin of the mountains obtain a knowledge surpassing the sages who have long studied in the city?'

'My lord,' answered Guzzarat, 'shall hear his slave unfold all her knowledge before him. Several moons had passed, since I had seen my prince Raalcour hunting in the mountains, when I heard from the caravans which travelled over our rocks, that the Caliph Zimprah was no more, and that Raalcour, his son, was proclaimed Caliph of Bagdat; the travellers also informed me, that the caliph's sight was departed from him, and that high rewards were published for those who should restore him to his sight. Hearing these things, my mind was with my lord the caliph, and I wished for the power of giving light to the eyes of my prince; and I said to my mother, "O that Guzzarat was capable of restoring sight to the blind!"

"Wherefore," said the wife of Raask, "doth Guzzarat long to occupy the business of the sages? Then made I answer, "Knoweth not my mother, that the caliph languisheth in darkness, and the sight of his eyes are passed from him?" And she answered, "Vain Guzzarat! how doth the pomp of greatness bewilder the thoughts and wishes of the poor? Alas, my daughter hath forgotten contentment, since she saw the richness of the garments of the prince Raalcour! Vain Guzzarat, return to thy charge, and feed the goats in the pastures of Gabel-el-ared."

'So saying my angry parent drove me before her, and ordered me to keep my father's goats from straying on the mountains. My feet obeyed the voice of my mother, but my heart fled like a leopard over the rocks, and was fixed on my lord the caliph.

'I went discontented with my goats to the mountains, and ridiculed the poverty and humility of my parents. "Why," said I sighing, "hath nature put aspiring minds under the fetters of age and authority! why must the quick pulse of gaiety and youth be deadened by the torturing precepts of infirmity! doth not the young lion rush more furiously on its prey, than the aged sovereign of the woods? doth not the colt outstrip its mother in the chace. Why then should the bloom of Guzzarat be hidden and buried with the wrinkles of the wife of Raask?"

'As I spake thus to the rocks and caverns, I beheld a young shepherdess entering the pastures; her hair was interwoven with the pride of the fields, and chaplets of flowers hung around her garments; she lightly tripped with her feet to the music of a flute which she breathed upon, and her voice, like the voice

of

of melody, was intermingled with the wild notes of her inftrument. As fhe advanced with her flocks, I arofe to meet her in the dance. She fmiled at my approach, and thus fhe began her pleafant raillery.

"O elegant companion of the goats and fheep, how doft thou love to revel here in the luxurious bofom of thy parent mountain! Happy Guzzarat, whofe pleafure is obedience; and happier wife of Raafk, who is bleffed with the eldeft daughter of duty and fubmiffion!"

'As fhe thus fpake, fhe caft a fmile of ridicule upon me, and turning, cried out, "Follow, dear Guzzarat, yon adventurous goat; behold thy companion is clambering among the precipices!"

'I looked, indeed, and faw the goat was ftraying, but ftung with her feverities, I cried out, "O fair ftranger, rather leffen my misfortunes by your pity and advice, than increafe them by your cruel reflections?"

"Is Guzzarat, then," faid the fhepherdefs, "willing to follow the advice of her friend?" "Yes," anfwered I "deliver me but from this diftreffed fituation and I will for ever acknowledge your kindnefs."

"Then," anfwered the fhepherdefs, "return to your cottage, and whatever you are ordered to perform, be difobedient; and if I find you faithful, meet me here in three days." As fhe faid thus, fhe again began her fong, and winding with her flock among the rocks, foon ftole from my fight.

'At night I returned to the cottage, and the wife of Raafk ordered me to prepare a kid for our fuppers; but her commands were to me of lefs confequence than the promife which I had made the fhepherdefs of the mountains. The wife of Raafk was enraged at my difobedience; and my father being abfent, fhe called her neighbour Canfu, to help in fubduing her refractory daughter.

'The

'The monster Canfu was rejoiced to torment me; he dragged me by the hair to the cottage, and tied me to a post that is fixed before the door.'

'Who,' said the caliph enraged, and interrupting Guzzarat's tale, 'who is this wretch Canfu, who dared violate the beauties of my lovely Guzzarat?'

'Prince of my life,' answered Guzzarat, 'you have not yet heard the cruelties of this base shepherd; my ignominious situation did not satisfy the malice that he had conceived against me. My father returned home at night, and hearing my obstinacy, commended his wife for calling in the assistance of Canfu to subdue me. But I told him, I was tired of a peasant's life, and would not controuled.

'Raask put on frowns as I spoke, and his countenance was turned against me. "What!" said he, with fury and rage, "dost thou despise the parents that have nourished thee, and thy friends that would reclaim thee? Then let the blessings of them that would bless thee, turn into curses on thy disobedient head, and let the friendship of Canfu be fury and controul over thee." "Yes, answered the cruel Canfu, "I, my friend, will subdue this wicked Guzzarat for thee. The heart of the parent bleedeth for the tears of its offspring, but correction cometh best from a friend."

'My father then delivered me into the hands of the monster Canfu, who forced me from the sight of my parents to his odious cottage. As soon as we arrived there, I was given over to the correction of his wife.'

"There," said the wretch Canfu, "revenge the loss of thy son on this proud disobedient female." The eyes of the wife of Canfu glistened as she beheld me, and her rage and revenge broke out in blows and imprecations; nor did the merciless woman forbear, till, overcome with her cruelty, I sunk to the ground.

'By

' By the powers of desolation,' said the fictitious Caliph Kelaun, ' the wretch Canfu and his cursed wife, shall experience the most exquisite tortures! Let them,' continued he, ' turning to his eunuchs, let the wretches be brought ere the morning to the divan, and let a scaffold be erected so that the whole city may be witness to their punishment.'

'Yea,' answered Guzzarat, prostrating herself before the caliph: ' so let the enemies of the righteous perish !'

' Proceed,' said the caliph, raising her up, ' proceed, lovely Guzzarat, in your tale; I am in terrors to think how you escaped the malice of your accursed enemies.'

' For two days, answered Guzzaret, ' I was confined and tortured by Canfu and his wife; and the third day, as she dragged me forth to inflict her daily stripes upon me, (her husband being with his flock) I rose up against her, and contended with her. She called for help, but no one was near; at length I prevailed, and leaving her stretched on the ground in a swoon, I hastened to the rocks, where I had before seen the shepherdess of the mountains, still in terrors lest Canfu should stray in the same paths. At the decline of the sun, my fair instructress appeared, but her flock followed her not; she held in one hand a bag, and in the other a bundle of raiment.

' As she advanced forward, she held forth the bag, to me, saying, " My spirited pupil, take this powder, and put on this raiment, the garb of a sage of Bagdat, and I will convey you to that city, where you must demand admittance to the caliph, and throwing some of this powder in his eyes, he shall receive his sight."

' She then arrayed me in the vestments she had brought and giving me the bag, she blew upon me and in a moment I found myself in the streets of Bagdat before the royal palace. A crowd soon gathered around me.'

" What

" What!" said they, art thou alone left of our sages, or art thou a stranger? which if thou art and cannot give sight to the blind, depart this city." "Yes," answered I, " I am come to restore Raalcour to his sight." " Then may the prophet bless thy work," answered they.

' Immediately I entered the palace, and thy eunuchs brought me before my lord the caliph.'

' This day,' said the fictitious Raalcour, ' shall be for ever remembered with joy, for I have not only received the sight of my eyes, but also an object worthy of their utmost contemplation.' The caliph then took the ambitious fair-one by the hand, and that day she was proclaimed sultaness of Bagdat.

In the mean time the messengers of the caliph ordered the scaffold to be prepared, and sent out an armed body to apprehend Canfu and his wife. The soldiers arrived at the cottage in the night, and beating against the door, demanded Canfu to come forth. Canfu looked through the lattice, and saw the soldiers of the caliph; and being terrified at the sight, he cried out, ' O Genii of the air, where is Kelaun, my son? where are the promises which you made to the wretched Canfu? now, if ever, O help my distress.'

As he spoke, the evil Genius Giuaraha appeared. ' What,' said she, ' does my subject Canfu require?' ' O,' answered Canfu, ' the soldiers of the caliph beset me; thou knowest, good Genius, that they are the instruments of death.'

' Fear not, shepherd,' answered Giuaraha; ' have not I said it, and who shall make vain my words? Even yet shalt thou see Kelaun thy son, in the arms of the imperious Guzzarat. Nay,' continued she, ' ask me no more, thy wish alone was to see thy son Kelaun, the husband of thy neighbour Raask's daughter; the Genii of the air are contented to fulfil their promises. If we grant your wish, what more
have

have you to require? Whether the blind wish of mortality proceedeth from wisdom or folly, concerneth but little our immortal race.' Thus saying, Giuaraha turned from Canfu with a smile of contempt, and spreading her airy pinions, disappeared from his sight, and the soldiers rushing into the cottage, bound the wretched parents of Kelaun, and led them away to the city of Bagdat.

Before the sun was awakened from the dream of night, Canfu and his wife were led in chains to the outer court of the palace, and the first salutation which the eunuchs gave the fictitious Raalcour and his new sultana, was, that Canfu and his wife were confined in chains in the outer court of the seraglio.

The eyes of Guzzarat swam in malice at the eunuch's report, and the metamorphosed caliph arose with indignation to see the enemies of his sultaness tortured before his face. A throne was prepared at a distance from the scaffold, whither the pretended Raalcour and Guzzarat ascended, with all the nobles of the court of Bagdat. The streets were filled with expecting eyes, and the whole city with eagerness strove which should be the nearest spectators of the bloody tragedy:

The caliph had commanded that no terrifying ceremony should be omitted. His short reign had already been a reign of cruelty, and in this execution he was willing greatly to exceed the former measures of his tyrannic disposition. Twenty officers in black, their heads bald, and their legs and feet naked, proceeded to the scaffold, bearing a skull in their right hands, and a torch burning with fœtid odours in their left. These were followed by six dressed in white, on whose close garments bones were painted, in imitation of skeletons and other fearful ghastly forms. These spectres had each a raw piece of flesh in their mouths, dropping with gore and clotted blood.

Next twelve of a gigantic stature came stalking forward; their faces were painted of a fiery red, a fictitious

titious smoke seemed to issue from their nostrils, and each bore in his arms a naked infant, on whom they inflicted real torments; for such was the cruelty of the Caliph Kelaun, that rather than lose that addition to the fatal tragedy he meant to represent, he had commanded twelve infants to be furnished out of the city for that inhuman scenery. The cries of these poor infants struck the hearts of the populace with the most lively terrors, and multiplied, beyond thought, the distress of Canfu and his wife, who followed the twelve of gigantic stature.

First came the wife of Canfu. Two naked figures, smeared with blood and carnage, drew her along with red-hot pincers. Her cries pierced every heart, but those of the cursed Kelaun, and his imperious sultaness. The malice of Guzzarat was unsatisfied with the performance of the tormentors, and she called out from the throne, and commanded them to strike their instruments still deeper into the flesh of her enemy. The last in this melancholy scene was the shepherd Canfu; he was borne by eight slaves, arrayed in the bloody skins of as many tigers. Each slave held a jagged hook in his hand, which being plunged into he flesh of the wretched shepherd served as handles to suspend him in torment. The cries, the groans, and lamentations of this miserable couple, were such as the enemies of Mahomet only could utter, and the hearts of the evil Genii hear, without remorse and horror; the whole city groaned to see the tyranny of the caliph, and the savage joy of his haughty sultaness.

As this hated possession was moving from the seraglio to the scaffold, the shouts of a multitude, and the instruments of war, were heard at a distant part of the city. The fictitious caliph, in terrors, commanded the bloody tragedy to stop, and enquired what noise in the city disturbed his ears. The whole populace were amazed, no one knew the cause, nor could imagine where the distant tumult could proceed.

The

The caliph's uncertainty was ſhort, for in a moment the Genius Haſſarack appeared. She was clad in a refulgent armour of gold, a thouſand feathers nodded on her creſt, on her left hand ſat perched a little bird, and in her right hand ſhe held a wand of adamant. An hundred thouſand armed troops followed behind; the guards of Kelaun were confounded at the ſight, and the tyrant was ſo univerſally hated, that no one ſtrove to arm in his behalf.

As the Genius came forward, ſhe waved her adamantine wand, and the fictitious caliph and his cruel ſultaneſs became fixed on their thrones. She then turned to the wretched ſhepherd Canfu, who was ſtill upheld by the jagged hooks of the cruel tormentors. 'Curſed alike,' ſaid ſhe, 'are the agents and the inſtruments of cruelty.' As ſhe ſpake, the whole proceſſion ſeemed in flames, and in a moment all but Canfu and his wife were reduced to aſhes.

The ſinews of Canfu were almoſt benumbed with death, and the viſion of day was fading from his eyes; when Haſſarack appeared, ſufficient life only remained, for him to ſee and underſtand the ſcene before him.

'The law of his prophet was grievous unto Canfu,' ſaid the genius Haſſarac, 'and the unſearchable ways of the great Alla ſeemed unto him crooked and unjuſt. Shall then the thoughts of the righteous Alla be likened unto his thoughts? Or ſhall the hand of him who made the ſtars and ſun, be guided by the vain decrees of a reptile's heart?

'O Canfu! thou ſhort-ſighted unbelieving wretch, what haſt thou gained by leaving the worſhip of Mahomet, to follow the wicked ſteps of the Apoſtate Genii. It was becauſe the prophet of the faithful knew, that only evil could ariſe from the loves of Guzzarat and Kelaun, that he had intended ever to ſeparate them, thereby to bleſs and prolong the life of Canfu, his votary; but ſince you have denied Mahomet, your guardian, and ſought fellowſhip with his enemies,

enemies, therefore he hath suffered them to repay your impious services with such exquisite miseries, by granting you the foolish wishes of your heart. Behold then, thou worshipper of the evil Genii, thou infamous renegade, thou blasphemer of our holy prophet, the desires of thy heart compleated.' As Hassarack spake thus, she again waved her wand, and the robes of the caliph fell from the fictitious Raalcour, and the form of his face was as the form of Kelaun, the son of the shepherd Canfu.

The tortured Canfu looked with amaze on his metamorphosed son; nor was Kelaun less astonished, when recovering his former shape and memory, he perceived that his cruelties had been directed against his father and mother. 'O cursed Giuaraha,' said the faultering Canfu, 'thou hast indeed joined Kelaun with the haughty Guzzarat. Thy promise is fulfilled, and Canfu falls a prey to the follies of his own short-sighted desires.' As he thus spake, the wretched shepherd expired with his eyes fixed on Kelaun and his imperious mistress; nor did the spirit of his wife survive her husband's melancholy fate.

Guzzarat beheld these strange interviews with displeasure; instead of the caliph Raalcour, she found herself tied to her neighbour Kelaun, and herself no longer Sulaness of Bagdat, but again a mean shepherdess of Gabel-el-ared. Her tongue was charged with malice, and her eyes with resentment, but Hassarack had by her magic power stopped all further utterance of her passions.

The Continuation of the Tale of Kelaun and Guzzarat.

THE multitude of Bagdat, who were gathered around the scaffold, which the fictitious caliph had erected for the execution of Canfu and his wife, were hardly less astonished at the amazing changes which the Genius Hassarack had caused, than the principal actors themselves. They saw with pleasure

one

one tyrant depofed, but they knew not how the shepherd Kelaun could perfonate their caliph.

Haffarack knew their thoughts, and turning to the populace, 'Where,' faid fhe, O inhabitants of Bagdat, 'where is your caliph Raalcour? Behold him,' proceeded fhe, ' here in the form of this bird, fuffering the malice of the evil Genii. But do not think, O inhabitants of Bagdat,' continued fhe, ' that Mahomet had permitted this transformation, unlefs Raalcour, by neglecting to attend the mofques of the prophet, had fubjected himfelf to the difpleafure of Alla. But his fufferings are at an end, and to me it is given to reftore your loft caliph to his fubjects.' Thus faying, fhe gently ftroked the bird with her wand, and by degrees Raalcour was reftored to his former fhape.

The inhabitants of Bagdat faw with the utmoft joy the pleafing transformation, and fent up their public thankfgivings to Mahomet and Haffarack, who had delivered them from the bondage of the tyrant Kelaun, and reftored to them their lawful caliph Raalcour. Raalcour was no fooner fenfible of his transformation, than he afcended the fcaffold, and kneeling in the fight of all his fubjects, 'Thus,' faid he, 'O my people, do I petition our prophet for pardon and peace. To Alla, the All-powerful, belongeth glory and worfhip; and bafe are we his creatures, if we neglect to pay our religious fervices unto him. For what is the moft perfect mode of life, or uprightnefs, free from guile, if we neglect to praife and blefs the Author of our exiftence?' 'Well pleafed am I,' faid Haffarack, ' to fee thefe early acknowledgments of your gratitude, O caliph; and now having humbled yourfelf before Alla, afcend your throne, and begin your reign of juftice upon thefe offenders againft Alla and his people.'

'Let then,' faid Raalcour, ' let the wretches, Kelaun and Guzzarat, afcended the fcaffold which themfelves have prepared for a different execution. But
let

let their deaths shew the humanity of their judge, though not the heinousness of their own offences.'

'May the rest of your judgments, O righteous caliph,' returned Hassarack, 'be ever like the first; then will your subjects obey you with joy, and Mahomet, the rewarder of the faithful, will hereafter receive you into the blissful seats of ever-living paradise.' At these words, the Genius Hassarack disappeared, and the executioners led the haughty Guzzarat and Kelaun, the son of the shepherd Canfu, to the scaffold.

Kelaun ascended with a sullen reluctance, and Guzzarat seemed more wishful to avoid her companion than the fate which she met. Ere the axe had severed the head of the malicious shepherd, Kelaun turned his eyes toward the earth, and stamping with his feet, thus uttered his last rageful imprecations.

'Slave have I been to evil all the days of my life; I have toiled and earned nothing; I have sown in care, and reaped not in meriment; I have poisoned the comfort of others, but no blessing hath fallen into mine own lap; hated am I among the sons of men, blasted are the paths whereon I tread; my past actions are ravenous vultures gnawing on my bowels, and the sharpened claws of malicious spirits await my arrival among the regions of the cursed. Strike then, O axe, since the lightning of Alla delays to blast me; and let my baneful body be trampled under the feet of the faithful, as the traveller crusheth with his heel the venomous adder!'

'The words of Hassarack,' said the sage Iracagem, arising, are laden with the dew of instruction; nor are our labours needless for the benefit of the children of men, since those accursed Genii, the rebellious mockers of our holy prophet, are incessantly beguiling the footsteps of the reptiles of earth; but praised be the prophet whom we serve, that impious race have no power over the faithful and obedient disciples

of

of Mahomet. Such as have refused his sacred laws, or what is more dreadful, such as have known, and yet disregarded his commandments, are left a prey to those disobedient spirits.'

'But, O my sister,! continued the sage Chief, to the Genius next to speak, the eye of day grows dim, and these tabernacles of earth whom we are instructing, will shortly sink with nature into the sleep of night; nor shall we break through the laws of the creation, or detain them from the blessings of rest. Alla hath made the day for labour and care, and the night for peace; and the works of Alla are wonderful and good.'

At these words the bright assembly arose, and left the children of earth to their attendant Genii, who were led into apartments, and refreshed with plain and simple diet: and early the next morning, after their ablutions and attendance in the mosque, where the race of immortals do frequent homage to their prophet, they returned with their guardian Genii to the magnificent saloon; where after the assembly were seated, the sage Iracagem arose and said—

'The lessons of my brethren yesterday were first designed to inculcate a regular search after happiness, which religion alone can teach us, as the merchant Abudah experienced in his various researches.

'Our first and greatest duty is to obey the all-powerful Alla, and to serve him in truth and humility; not to mistake, like Alfouran, the creature for the Creator; nor, like Sanballad, to leave the duties of our respective stations unfulfilled, to follow after an idle phantom in cells and caverns of the earth; much less to mix hypocrisy with devotion, and to offend Alla, in order to deceive mankind. But to love and prefer his will and his law above all things, even above the pleasure and temptations of the world; lest, like the Sultan Hassan Assar, we add presumption to our crimes, and having been instructed in our duty, refuse to practise it. Obedience to Alla will make all things easy to us, it will give bloom to Nakin Palata, and joy and comfort to the sons of the faithful, while we readily submit to our allotted task, and call not in question, like Canfu, either the wisdom or mercy of Alla, who doth often withhold what might be esteemed blessings from us, in order to prevent us from the storm which we neither can foresee nor dissipate. To trust therefore in him, to love him, to exalt him, to obey, and to give him praise, is the chief end and creation of man.

'But as mutual weakness requires mutual support, so the great Alla has given to his children, the laws and the duties of social morality, which will be explained to their tender minds by example, fraught with the blessings of instruction—Therefore, O sister,' said the sage Iracagem, to her whose throne was placed by Hassarack's, 'let this favoured assembly partake of your entertaining advice.' The Genius immediately arose, and began the adventures of Urad, or the Fair Wanderer.

TALE V.

The Adventures of Urad; or, the Fair Wanderer.

ON the banks of the river Tigris, far above where it washes the lofty city of the faithful, lived Nouri in poverty and widowhood, whose employment it was to tend the worm who cloaths the richest and the fairest with its beautiful web. Her husband, who was a guard to the caravans of the merchants, lost his life in an engagement with the wild Arabs, and left the poor woman no other means of subsisting herself, or her infant daughter Urad, but by her labours among the silk-worms, which were little more than sufficient to support nature, although her labours began ere the sun-beams played on the waters of the Tigris, and ended not till the stars were reflected from its surface. Such was the business of the disconsolate Nouri, when the voluptuous Almurah was proclaimed sultan throughout his extensive dominions; nor was

it

it long before his subjects felt the power of their sultan; for Almurah resolving to inclose a large tract of land for hunting and sporting, commanded the inhabitants of fourteen hundred villages to be expelled from the limits of his intended inclosure.

A piteous train of helpless and ruined families were in one day driven from their country and livelihood, and obliged to seek for shelter amidst the forests, the caves and desarts, which surround the more uncultivated banks of the Tigris. Many passed by the cottage of Nouri, the widow, among whom she distributed what little remains of provision she had saved from the earnings of her labours the day before; and her little stock being exhausted, she had nothing but wishes and prayers left for the rest.

It happened, among the numerous throngs that travelled by her cottage, that a young man came with wearied steps, bearing on his shoulders an old and feeble woman, whom setting down on the ground before the door of Nouri, he besought her to give him a drop of water to wash the sand and the dust from his parched mouth. Nouri having already distributed the contents of her pitcher, hastened to the river to fill it for the wearied young man; and as she went, she begged a morsel of provisions from a neighbour, whose cottage stood on a rock which overlooked the flood.

With this, and her pitcher filled with water, she returned; and found the feeble old woman on the ground, but the young man was not with her. 'Where,' said Nouri, 'O afflicted stranger, is the pious young man that dutifully bore the burden of age on his shoulders?'

'Alas!' answered the stranger, 'my son has brought me hither from the tyranny of Almurah, and leaves me to perish in the deserts of the Tigris: no sooner were you gone for the water, than a crowd of young damsels came this way, and led my cruel son from his perishing mother: but, courteous stranger,' said she to Nouri, 'give me of that water to drink,

that

that my life fail not with me; for thirst, and hunger, and trouble, are hastening to put an end to the unhappy Houadir.'

The tender and benevolent Nouri invited Houadir into the cottage, and there placed her on a straw-bed, and gave her the provisions and a cup of water to drink. Houadir being somewhat refreshed by the care of Nouri, acquainted her with the cruel decree of Almurah, who had turned her son out of his little patrimony, where, by the labour of his hands, he had for many years supported her, and that till that day she had ever found him a most dutiful and obedient son; and concluded with a wish, that he would shortly return to his poor helpless parent.

Nouri did all she could to comfort the wretched Houadir, and having persuaded her to rest a while on the bed, returned to the labours of the day. When her work was finished, Nouri, with the wages of the day, purchased some provisions, and brought them home to feed herself and the little Urad, whose portion of food, as well as her own, had been distributed to the unhappy wanderers. As Nouri was giving a small morsel to Urad, Houadir awaked, and begged that Nouri would be so kind as to spare her a bit of provisions. Immediately, before Nouri could rise, the little Urad ran nimbly to the bed, and offered her supper to the afflicted Houadir, who received it with great pleasure from her hands, being assured her mother would not let Urad be a loser by her benevolence.

Houadir continued several days with the widow Nouri, expecting the return of her son, till giving over all hopes of seeing him, and observing that she was burdensome to the charitable widow, she one evening, after the labours of the day, thus addressed her hospitable friend.

'I perceive, benevolent Nouri, that my son has forsaken me, and that I do but rob you and your poor infant of the scanty provision which you by your
hourly

hourly toil are earning: wherefore, listen to my proposal, and judge whether I offer you a suitable return; there are many parts of your business, that, old as I am, I can help you in, as the winding your silk, and feeding your worms. Employ me, therefore, in such business in the day as you think me capable of performing; and at night, while your necessary cares busy you about the house, give me leave (as I see your labour allows you no spare time) to instruct the innocent Urad how to behave herself, when your death shall leave her unsheltered from the storms and deceits of a troublesome world.'

Nouri listened with pleasure to the words of Houadir. 'Yes,' said she, 'benevolent stranger, you well advise me how to portion my poor infant Urad, whom I could neither provide for by my industry, nor instruct, without losing the daily bread I earn for her: I perceive a little is sufficient for your support; nay, I know not how, I seem to have greater plenty since you have been with me than before;—whether it be owing to the blessing of Heaven on you, I know not. Far be it from me,' said Houadir, ' to see my generous benefactress deceived; but the thinness of inhabitants, occasioned by the tyranny of Almurah, is the cause that your provisions are more plentiful; but yet' I insist upon bearing my part in the burden of the day, and Urad shall share my evening's labour. From this time Houadir commenced an useful member in the family of Nouri, and Urad was daily instructed by the good old stranger in the pleasures and benefits of a virtuous, and the horrors and curses of an evil life. Little Urad was greatly rejoiced at the lessons of Houadir, and was never better pleased than when she was listening to the mild and pleasing instructions of her affable mistress.

It was the custom of Houadir whenever she taught Urad any new rule or caution, to give her a peppercorn; requiring of her, as often as she looked at them, to remember the lessons which she learnt at the time

she

she received them. In this manner Urad continued to be instructed, greatly improving, as well in virtue and religion, as in comeliness and beauty, till she was near woman's estate, so that Nouri could scarce believe she was the mother of a daughter so amiable and graceful in person and manners. Neither was Urad unskilled in the labours of the family, or the silkworm; for Nouri growing old and sickly, she almost constantly, by her industry, supported the whole cottage.

One evening as Houadir was lecturing her attentive pupil, Nouri, who lay sick on the straw bed, called Urad to her. 'My dear daughter,' said Nouri, 'I feel, alas! more for you than myself; while Houadir lives, you will have indeed a better instructor than your poor mother was capable of being unto you; but what will my innocent lamb, my lovely Urad do, when she is left alone, the helpless prey of craft, or lust, or power? Consider, my dear child, that Alla would not send you into the world to be necessarily and unavoidably wicked: therefore always depend upon the assistance of our holy prophet when you do right, and let no circumstance of life, nor any persuasion, ever bias you to live otherwise, than according to the chaste and virtuous precepts of the religious Houadir. May Alla and the prophet of the faithful ever bless and preserve the innocence and chastity of my dutiful and affectionate Urad!' The widow Nouri spoke not again, her breath for ever fled from its confinement, and her body was delivered to the waters of the Tigris.

The inconsolable Urad had now her most difficult lesson to learn from the patient Houadir, nor did she think it scarcely dutiful to moderate the violence of her grief.

'Sorrows,' said Houadir, 'O duteous Urad, which arise from sin, or evil actions, cannot be assuaged without contrition or amendment of life; there the soul is deservedly afflicted, and must feel before it can be cured;

cured; such sorrows may my amiable pupil never experience; but the afflictions of morality are like the portions of piety or iniquity; it is necessary that we should be taught to part with the desirable things of this life by degrees, and that by the frequency of such losses, our affections should be loosened from their early attachments. While you continue good, be not dejected, O my obedient Urad; and remember, it is one part of virtue to bear with patience and resignation the unalterable decrees of Heaven; not but that I esteem your sorrow, which arises from gratitude, duty, and affection. I do not teach my pupil to part with her dearest friends without reluctance, or wish her to be unconcerned at the loss of those, who, by a marvellous love, have sheltered her from all those storms which must have in a moment overwhelmed helpless innocence. Only remember that your tears be the tears of resignation, and that your sighs confess an heart humbly yielding to his will, who ordereth all things according to his infinite knowledge and goodness.'

'O pious Houadir, replied Urad, 'just are thy precepts; it was Alla that created my best of parents, and Alla is pleased to take her from me; far be it from me, though an infinite sufferer, to dispute his will; the loss indeed wounds me sorely, yet will I endeavour to bear the blow with patience and resignation!'

Houadir still continued her kind lessons and instructions, and Urad with a decent solemnity attended both her labours and her teacher, who was so pleased with the fruits which she saw spring forth from the seeds of virtue that she had sown in the breast of her pupil, that she now began to leave her more to herself, and exhorted her to set apart some portion of each day to pray to her prophet, and frequent meditation and recollection of the rules she had given her, that so her mind might never be suffered to grow forgetful of the truths she had treasured up: 'For,' said the provident Houadir, 'when it shall please the prophet to snatch me also from you, my dear Urad will then have only the pepper-corns to assist her.'

'And how, my kind governess,' said Urad, 'will these corns assist me?' 'They will,' answered Houadir, 'each of them, if you remember the precepts I gave you with them, but not otherwise, be serviceable in the times of your necessities.'

Urad, with great reluctance, from that time, was obliged to go without her evening lectures, which loss affected her much; for she knew no greater pleasure in life, than hanging over Houadir's persuasive tongue, and hearing, with fixed attention, the sweet doctrines of prudence, chastity and virtue. As Urad, according to her usual custom, (after having spent some few early hours at her employment) advanced toward the bed to call her kind instructor, whose infirmities would not admit her to rise betimes, she perceived that Houadir was risen from her bed.

The young virgin was amazed at the novelty of her instructor's behaviour, especially as she seldom moved without assistance, and hastened into a little inclosure to look after her; but not finding Houadir there, she went to the neighbouring cottages, none of whom could give any account of the good old matron; nevertheless the anxious Urad continued her search, looking all around the woods and forest, and often peeping over the rocks of the Tigris, as fearful that some accident might have befallen her. In this fruitless labour the poor virgin fatigued herself, till the sun, as tired of her toils, refused any longer to assist her search, when returning to her lonely cot, she spent the night in tears and lamentations. The helpless Urad gave herself up entirely to grief; and the remembrance of her affectionate mother added a double portion of sorrows to her heart; she neglected to open her lonely cottage, and went not forth to the labours of the silkworm; but, day after day, with little or no nourishment, she continued weeping the loss of

Houadir,

Houadir, her mild instructor, and Nouri, her affectionate mother.

The neighbouring cottages observing that Urad came no longer to the silk-works, and that her dwelling was daily shut up, after some time knocked at her cottage, and demanded if Urad the daughter of Nouri was living. Urad seeing the concourse of people, came weeping and trembling toward the door, and asked them the cause of their coming.

'O Urad,' said her neighbours, 'we saw you, not long ago, seeking your friend Houadir, and we feared that you also were missing, as you have neither appeared among us, nor attended your daily labours among the worms, who feed and provide for us by their subtle spinning.' 'O, my friends,' answered Urad, suffer a wretched maid to deplore the loss of her dearest friends! Nouri, from whose breasts I sucked my natural life, is now a prey to the vultures on the banks of the Tigris; and Houadir, from whom I derive my better life, is passed away from me like a vision in the night.

Her rustic acquaintance laughed at these sorrows of the virgin Urad. 'Alas,' said one, 'Urad grieves, that now she has to work for one, instead of three.' 'Nay,' cried another, 'I wish my old folks were as well bestowed.' 'And I,' said a third, 'were our house rid of the old-fashion lumber that fills it at present; my superannuated father and mother, would soon bring an healthy young swain to supply their places with love and affection.' 'Aye, true,' answered two or three more, 'we must look out a clever young fellow for Urad: who shall she have?'

'O, if that be all,' said a crooked old maid, who was famous for match-making, 'I will send Darandu to comfort her, before night; and, if I mistake not, he very well knows his business.' 'Well, pretty Urad,' cried they all, 'Darandu will soon be here; he is fishing on the Tigris; and it is but just, that the river, which has robbed you of one comfort, should give you a better.'

a better.' At this speech the rest laughed very heartily, and they all ran away crying out, 'O, she will do very well when Darandu approaches.'

Urad, though she could despise the trifling of her country neighbours, yet felt an oppression on her heart at the name of Darandu, who was a youth of incomparable beauty, and added to the charms of his person an engaging air, which was far above the reach of the rest of the country swains, who lived on those remote banks of the Tigris. 'But, O Houadir, O Nouri,' said the afflicted virgin to herself, 'never shall Urad seek in the arms of a lover, to forget the bounties and precepts of so kind a mistress, and so indulgent a parent.' These reflections hurried the wretched Urad into her usual sorrowful train of thoughts, and she spent the rest of the day in tears and weeping, calling for ever on Nouri and Houadir, and wishing that the prophet would permit her to follow them out of a world, where she foresaw neither comfort nor peace.

In the midst of these melancholy meditations, she was disturbed by a knocking at the door; Urad arose with trembling, and asked who was there. 'It is one,' answered a voice in the softest tone, 'who seeketh comfort and cannot find it; who desires peace, and it is far from him.'

'Alas!' answered Urad, 'few are the comforts of this cottage, and peace is a stranger to this mournful roof; depart, O traveller, whosoever thou art, and suffer the disconsolate Urad to indulge in sorrows greater than those from which you wish to be relieved. 'Alas!' answered the voice without, 'the griefs of the beautiful Urad are my griefs; and the sorrows which afflict her, rend the soul of the wretched Darandu!'

'Whatever may be the motive for this charitable visit, Darandu,' answered Urad, 'let me beseech you to depart; for ill does it become a forlorn virgin to admit the conversation of the youths that sorround her;

her: leave me, therefore, O swain, ere want of decency make you appear odious in the sight of the virgins who inhabit the rocky banks of the rapid Tigris.'

'To convince the lovely Urad,' answered Darandu, 'that I came to soothe her cares, and condole with her in her losses, (which I heard but this evening) I now will quit this dear spot, which contains the treasure of my heart, as, however terrible the parting is] to me, I rest satisfied that it pleases the fair conqueror of my heart, whose peace to Darandu is more precious than the pomegranate in the sultry noon, or the silver scales of ten thousand fishes inclosed in the nets of my skilful comrades,' Darandu then left the door of the cottage, and Urad reclined on the bed, till sleep finished her toils, and for a time released her from the severe afflictions of her unguarded situation.

Early in the morning the fair Urad arose, and directed her steps to the rocks of the Tigris, either invited thither by the melancholy reflections which her departed mother occasioned, or willing to take a nearer and more unobserved view of the gentle Darandu.

Darandu, who was just about to launch his vessel into the river, perceived the beauteous mourner on the rocks; but he was too well versed in love affairs to take any notice of her; he rather turned from Urad, and endeavoured, by his behaviour, to persuade her that he had not observed her; for it was enough for him to know that he was not indifferent to her. Urad, though she hardly knew the cause of her morning walk, yet continued on the rocks till Darandu had taken in his nets, and with his companions was steering up the stream, in quest of the fishes of the Tigris. She then returned to her cottage more irresolute in her thoughts, but less than ever inclined to the labours of her profession.

At the return of the evening, she was anxious lest Darandu should renew his an visit; an anxiety, which though it arose from fear, was yet near allied to hope; nor was she less solicitous about provisions, as all her little stock was entirely exhausted, and she had no other prospect before her than to return to her labours, which her sorrows had rendered irksome and disagreeable to her.

While she was meditating on these things, she heard a knocking at the door, which fluttered her little less than the fears of hunger, or the sorrows of her lonely life. For some time she had not courage to answer, till the knocking being repeated, she faintly asked who was at the door?

'It is Lahnar,' answered a female: 'Lahnar, your neighbour, seeks to give Urad comfort, and to condole with the distressed mourner of a mother and a friend. Lahnar,' answered Urad, 'is then a friend to the afflicted, and kindly seeks to alleviate the sorrows of the wretched Urad.' She then opened the door, and Lahnar entered with a basket on her head.

'Kind Lahnar,' said the fair mourner, 'leave your burden at the door, and enter into this cottage of affliction. Alas! alas! there once sat Nouri, my ever-affectionate mother, and there Houadir, my kind counsellor and director; but now are their seats vacant, and sorrow and grief are the only companions of the miserable Urad!'

'Your losses are certainly great,' answered Lahnar, but you must endeavour to bear them with patience, especially as they are the common changes and alterations of life; your good mother Nouri lived to a great age; and Houadir, though a kind friend, may yet be succeeded by one as amiable; but what I am most alarmed at, O Urad, is your manner of life; we no longer see you busied among the leaves of the mulberries, or gathering the bags of silk, or preparing them for the wheels; you purchase no provision
among

among us, you seek no comfort in society, you live like the mole, buried under the earth, who neither sees nor is seen.' 'My sorrows indeed, hitherto,' replied Urad, 'have prevented my labour, but to-morrow I shall again rise to my wonted employment.'

'But even to night,' said Lahnar, 'let my friend take some little nourishment, that she may rise refreshed, for fasting will deject you as well as grief, and suffer me to partake with you; and see, in his basket I have brought my provisions, some boiled rice, and a few fish, which my kind brother Darandu brought me this evening from the river Tigris.'

'Excuse me, kind Lahnar,' answered Urad, 'but I must refuse your offer; grief has given away appetite to aught but itself, far from me, and I am not solicitous to take provisions which I cannot use.' 'At least,' replied Lahnar, permit me to sit beside you, and eat of what is here before us.'

Upon which, without other excuses, Lahnar emptied her basket, and set a bowl of rice and fish before Urad, and began to feed heartily on that which she brought for herself. Urad was tempted by hunger, and the example of Lahnar, to begin; but she was anxious about tasting the fish of Darandu, wherefore she first attempted the boiled rice; but her appetite was most inclined to the fish, of which she at last eat very heartily, when she recollected, that as she had partaken with Lahnar; it was equal whatever part she accepted.

Lahnar having finished her meal, and advised Urad to think of some methods of social life, took her leave, and left the unsettled virgin to meditate on her strange visitor. Urad, though confused, could not help expressing some pleasure at this visit; for such is the blessing of society, that it will always give comfort to those who have been disused to its sweet effects.

But Urad, though pleased with the friendship of Lahnar, yet was confounded, when some few minutes after she perceived her again returning. 'What,' said

said Urad, 'brings back Lahnar to the sorrows of this cottage?' 'Urad,' says Lahnar, 'I will rest with my friend to night, for the shades of night cast horrors around, and I dare not disturb my father's cottage by my late approach.'

As they prepared for their homely bed, Urad turning round, beheld Lahnar's breast uncovered, and saw, by the appearance, it was no female she was preparing to receive into her bed. She immediately shrieked out, and Darandu, the fictitious Lahnar, leaped eagerly forward, and caught her in his arms. 'O, delicious Urad,' said he, 'I die, I die without you: your tears, your calls are vain, the cottage is lonely, and no traveller walks by night to meet the wild beasts of the forest; therefore let us take our fill of love, for Darandu will not otherwise be satisfied.'

Urad, full of trembling, confusion, horror, and despair, raved in his arms, but could not get free. He still pressed her close, and endeavoured to pull her toward the bed, when she recollecting her lost friend Houadir, felt for a pepper corn, and let it fall to the ground. A violent rapping was in a moment heard at the cottage, at which Urad redoubled her outcries, and Darandu with shame and confusion, quitted his mistress, and looked trembling toward the door.

Urad ran forward and opened the door, when the son of Houadir entered, and asked Urad the reason of her cries. 'O thou blessed angel,' said Urad, 'but for you, that wicked wretch, disguised in his sister's cloaths, had ruined the too credulous Urad.' But Darandu was fled, as guilt is ever fearful, mean, and base. 'Now Urad,' said the son of Houadir, 'before you close your doors upon another man, let me resume my former features.' Upon which Urad looked, and beheld her old friend Houadir.

At the sight of Houadir, Urad was equally astonished and abashed. 'Why blushes Urad?' said Houadir; 'and her blushes are the blushes of guilt.'

'How,

'How, O Genius,' said Urad, ' for such I perceive thou art, how is Urad guilty? I invited not Darandu hither, I wished not for him.'

'Take care,' answered Houadir, ' what you say: if you wished not for him, you hardly wished him away; and but for your imprudence he had not attacked you. Consider, how have your days been employed since I left you? Have you continued to watch the labours of the silk-worm? Have you repeated the lessons I gave you? Or, has the time of Urad been consumed in idleness and disobedience? Has she shaken off her dependance on Mahomet, and indulged the unavailing sorrows of her heart?'

'Alas!' answered the fair Urad,' ' repeat no more, my ever-honoured Houadir; I have indeed been guilty under the mask of love and affection, and I now plainly see the force of your first rule, that idleness is the beginning of all evil and vice. Yes, my dearest Houadir, had I attended to your instructions, I had given no handle to Darandu's wicked intentions; but yet methinks some sorrows were allowable for the loss of such a mother and such a friend.'

'Sorrows,' answered Houadir,' ' proceed from the heart, and totally indulged, soon require a change and vicissitude in our minds; wherefore, in the midst of your griefs, your feet involuntarily wandered after Darandu, and your soul, softened by idle sighs, was the more easily impressed by the deceits of his tongue.

'But this remember, O Urad; for I must, I find, repeat an old instruction to you, that of all things in the world, nothing should so much engage a woman's attention as the avenues which lead to her heart. Such are the wiles, the deceits of men, that they are rarely to be trusted with the most advanced post: give them but footing, though that footing be innocent, and they will work night and day till their wishes are accomplished.

'Trust not, therefore, to yourself alone, nor suffer your heart to plead in their favour, lest it become as much your enemy as the tempter man. Place your security in flight, and avoid every evil, every gay desire, left it lead you into danger; for hard it is to turn the head, and look backward, when a beautiful or agreeable object is before you. Remember my instructions, O Urad, make a prudent use of your pepper-corns, and leave this place, which holds a man sensible of your softness, and resolute in his own dark and subtle intention.'

Urad was about to thank Houadir, but the Genius was fled, and the eye-lids of the morning were opening in the east. Urad, in a little wallet, packed up her small stock of necessaries, and full of terror, and full of uncertainty, struck into the forest, and, without reflection, took the widest path that offered.

And first it was her care to repeat over deliberately the lessons of Houadir. She then travelled slowly forward, often looking and fearing to behold the wicked Darandu at her heels. After walking through the forest for the greater part of the day, she came to a steep descent, on each side overshadowed with lofty trees; this she walked down, and came to a small spot of ground, surrounded by hills, woods, and rocks. Here she found a spring of water, and sat down on the grass to refresh herself after the travels of the day.

As her meal was almost at an end, she heard various voices issuing from the woods, on the hills opposite to that which she came down. Her little heart beat quick at this alarm, and Urad, recollecting the advice of Houadir, began to repeat the lessons of her instructor, and ere long she perceived through the trees, several men coming down the hill, who at the sight of Urad gave a loud halloo, and ran forward, each being eager who should first seize the prize.

Urad, trembling and sighing at her danger, forgot not to drop one of her pepper-corns, and immediately she found herself changed into a pismire, and with great pleasure she looked for a hole in the ground,

and

and crept into it. The robbers coming down to the bottom of the vale, were surprised to find their prize eloped, but they divided into separate bodies, resolved to hunt till night, and then appointed that little vale as the place of rendezvous. Urad, perceiving that they were gone, wished herself into her original form; but, alas! her wish was not granted, and the once beautiful Urad still continued an ugly pismire.

Late at night the robbers returned, and the moon shining bright, reflected a gloomy horror upon their despairing faces: Urad shuddered at the sight of them, though so well concealed, and dared hardly peep out of her hole, so difficult is it to forget our former fears. The gang resolved to spend the rest of the night in that place, and therefore unloaded their wallets, and spread their wine and provisions on the banks of the spring grumbling and cursing each other all the time for their unfortunate search.

'I would to Alla,' says one, 'I had taken hold of her, and I would soon have kissed her into a good humour.' 'You ugly wretch,' said another, 'she would have died at the thoughts of you: but if I had caught her'—'Yes,' said a third, 'with those bloody hands, that have butchered two maidens already to day.' 'Aye,' returned he, 'and she should have suffered the same sauce.' 'Well,' answered the captain of the gang, 'if I had first secured her, she should have gone fairly round among you all.' Urad heard this with the utmost horror and indignation; and praised continually the gracious Alla, who had rescued her from such inhuman wretches.

While they with singing and drinking spent the greatest part of the night, and wishing that their comrades in the other part of the forest had been with them; at length falling into drunkenness and sleep, they left the world to silence and peace. Urad finding them fast asleep, crawled out of her hole, and going to the first, she stung him in each eye: and thus she went round to them all. The poison of the

little

little pismire working in their eyes, in a short time occasioned them to awake in the utmost tortures; and perceiving they were blind, and feeling the pain, they each supposed his neighbour had blinded him, in order to get away with the booty. This so enraged them, that feeling about, they fell upon one another, and in a short time almost the whole gang was demolished.

Urad beheld with astonishment the effect of her stings, and at a wish resumed her pristine form, saying at the same time to herself, 'I now perceive that Providence is able, by the most insignificant means, to work the greatest purposes.'

Continuing her journey through the forest, she was terribly afraid of meeting with the second band of robbers, and therefore she directed her steps with the greatest caution and circumspection. As she walked forward, and cast her eyes all around, and stopped at every motion of the wind, she saw the son of Houadir coming to meet her in the path in which she was travelling.

At this sight Urad ran toward him, and with joy begged her old governess would unmask herself, and entertain her with instruction and persuasion.

'No, my dear child,' answered the son of Houadir, 'that I cannot do at present, the time is not as yet come. I will first, as you have been tried, lead you to the palace of the Genii of the forest, and present your unspotted innocence before them; for, O my sweet Urad, my heavenly pupil,' said he, kissing and taking her in his arms, 'your virtue is tried, I have found you worthy of the lessons which I gave you. I foresaw evils might befal you, and therefore I took pity on your innocence, and lived with Nouri your mother, that I might train up my beloved Urad in the paths of virtue; and now your trial is passed, Urad shall enjoy the happiness of a Genii.'

Urad, though somewhat confounded at Houadir's embrace under the appearance of a man, yet with great humility thanked her benefactor. And the son of of Houadir turning to the left, led Urad into a little bye path, so concealed, that few, if any, might ever find its beginning. After a long walk through various turnings and intricate windings, they came to a small mean cottage, where the son of Houadir leading the way, Urad followed.

The son of Houadir, striking fire with his stick, a bright flame arose from the centre of the floor, in which he cast divers herbs, and repeating some inchantments, the back side of the cottage opened, and presented to the view of Urad a beautiful dome, where she saw sitting round a table a numerous assembly of gay persons of both sexes.

The son of Houadir leading in Urad, said, 'This, my dear pupil, is the assembly of the Genii of the forest:' and presenting her to the company, 'Behold,' said he, 'the beautiful and well-tried Urad—but here you may cast off your reserve, fair maid, and indulge in the innocent pleasures of the Genii of the forest.'

The son of Houadir then led her to the table, and seated her on the same sopha with himself. The remainder of the day was spent in mirth and pleasure; nor did the female Genii refuse the gay advances of their partners. Urad having never beheld any thing splendid or magnificent, was greatly delighted at the gay company and beautiful saloon, nor did she seem to receive the caresses of the son of Houadir so reluctantly as before.

At night Urad was shewn a glorious apartment to rest in, and the son of Houadir attended her. 'My dear Houadir,' said Urad, 'when shall I behold your proper shape, when shall I see you as my tutelary Genius?'

'That,' answered the son of Houadir, 'I shall be in every shape, but call neither one nor the other my *proper* shape, for to a Genius all shapes are assumed; neither is this my proper shape, nor the wrinkles of an old woman; but to confess the truth, O beautiful
Urad,

Urad, from the firſt moment of your birth, I reſolved to make you my bride, and therefore did I ſo patiently watch your growing years, and inſtructed you in the fear of vice and the love of virtue. Come, therefore, O beautiful virgin, and let me, in thoſe precious arms, reap the fruit of my long labour and toil.'

Urad, aſtoniſhed at the words of the ſon of Houadir, knew not what anſwer to make; but the natural timidity of her ſex, and the ſtrangeneſs of the propoſal, filled her with ſtrange apprehenſions; however, ſhe begged at leaſt that the Genius would for a time leave her to herſelf, that the bluſhes of her cheeks might be covered in ſolitude.

' No, my lovely Urad,' anſwered the ſon of Houadir, ' never, never, will thy faithful Genius leave thee, till thou haſt bleſſed me with the poſſeſſion of what I hold dearer than even my ſpiritual nature. Why, then,' ſaid Urad, ' didſt thou beſtow ſo many pepper-corns upon me, as they now will become uſeleſs?'

' Not uſeleſs,' ſaid the ſon of Houadir, ' they are indeed little preſervatives againſt danger; but I have the ſeeds of ſome melons which will not only reſcue you, but always preſerve you from harm. Here, faithful Urad, continued he, take theſe ſeeds, and whenever you are fearful, ſwallow one of theſe, and no dangers ſhall ſurround you.

Urad thankfully received the ſeeds: ' And what,' ſaid ſhe, ' muſt I do with the pepper corns? Give them,' ſaid the ſon of Houadir, ' to me, and I will endue them with ſtronger virtues, and thou ſhalt by them have power alſo over others, as well as to defend thyſelf.'

Urad pulled the pepper-corns out of her bag, and preſented them to the ſon of Houadir, whoſe eyes flaſhed with joy at the ſight, and he immediately thruſt them into the folds of his garments.

' O ſon of Houadir, what haſt thou done?" ſaid Urad. ' I have,' anſwered the falſe ſon of Houadir,

' gained

'gained the full possession of my lovely Urad, and now may address her in my proper shape;' so saying, he resumed his natural figure, and became like a satyr of the wood. 'I am,' said he, 'O beautiful Urad, the enchanter Repah, who range in the solitude of the forest of the Tigris, and live and solace myself upon the beauties who venture into my haunts. You I saw surrounded by the influence of the Genius Houadir, and therefore was obliged to use artifice to gain my dear, dear charmer. But why waste I time in words, when the fulness of thy ripe beauties tempt my closest embrace!' So saying, he rushed on Urad, and stifled her with his nauseous salutes.

The poor deluded victim, with tears in her eyes, implored his mercy and forbearance; but he laughed at her tears, and told her, her eyes glittered the brighter for them.

'What,' cried the enchanter, 'shall I wish your sorrows at an end, which so tumultuously heave those worlds of bliss, or stop by kindness those sighs which send forth more than Arabian perfumes! No, no, I love to enjoy nature in her fullest workings, and think it an higher bliss to ride on the stormy tempest than through the gentle breeze.' As he spake thus, he again clasped the wretched Urad in his arms, and mad with furious lust, forced her to the sopha; while she, shrieking and crying, filled the apartment with vain lamentations.

As the enchanter was dragging the disconsolate virgin Urad to the sopha, she, in a fit of despair, again put her hands into the bag, from whence she had fatally resigned the pepper-corns; and felt about in agonies for the lost treasure. And now finding none, and perceiving that the Genius Houadir attended not to her cries, she was drawing out her hand, when in a corner of the bag she felt one pepper-corn, which had before escaped her search. She instantly drew it out, and throwing it on the ground, the enchanter quitted his hold, and stood motionless before her; the apartments vanished, and she found herself with him in a dark hut, with various kinds of necromantic instruments about her.

Urad, though fearful, yet was so much overcome with fatigue and struggling, that she sunk on the ground, and happily for her the enchanter was no longer in a condition to persecute her.

'Curse on my folly,' said he, as he stood fixed to the ground, 'that I neglected to ask for the bag itself, which held the gifts of the Genius Houadir; her pretty pupil had then been sacrificed to my desires, in spite of the many fine lessons she had been taught by that pitiful and enthusiastic Genius! but now by chance, and not by the merit of thy virtues or thy education, art thou delivered from my seraglio, where vice reigns triumphant, cold modesty and colder chastity are excluded, to make room for the mixed revels of what pious cheats call lustful rioters. But it grieves me not so much to lose a sickly girl, as that I find a superior power condemns me to declare to you the causes of your error.

'Know then, Urad, (I speak not from myself, but he speaks, who from casual evil can work out certain good) he forces me to declare, that no specious appearance, no false colours, should incline the virtuous heart to listen to the wiles of deceit; for evil then comes most terrible, when it is cloaked under friendship. Why then had Urad so great an opinion of her own judgment, as to confide in the false appearance of the son of Houadir, when she might have consulted her faithful monitors! The falling of a pepper-corn would have taught her to trust to no appearances, nor would she have parted with her pepper-corns, which were to refresh in her memory the sentiments of virtue, chastity, and honour, no, not to Houadir herself. No adviser can be good, who would destroy what he himself has first inculcated, and no appearance ought to bias us to receive as truths, those things which are contrary to virtue

and

and religion. How then did Urad keep to the instructions of Houadir? But if Houadir really had bred her up for the purposes of lust, and taught her only the paths of virtue to keep her from others; of all persons they are most to be guarded against, who, having the power of educating the female mind, too often presume upon the influence which such intimate connections give them; they, therefore, as the most base and ungrateful, should be most cautiously watched and resolutely repulsed.'

Thus spake the enchanter, and no more; his mouth closed up, and he stood fixed and motionless; and Urad finding her spirits somewhat recovered, hastened out of the hut, and perceived that it was morning.

She had now no more pepper corns to depend upon, wherefore she cried to Houadir to succour her, but the Genius was deaf to her intreaties. ' Poor, miserable wretch,' said Urad to herself, ' what will become of thee, inclosed in a forest through which thou knowest no path! But,' continued she, ' why should I not examine the enchanter, who perhaps is yet immoveable in the cottage: I saw him fold them in the plaits of his garments, and they may yet become mine.'

So saying, she returned to the hut, where entering, the very sight of the dumb enchanter affrighted her so much, that it was a long time before she could venture near him. At length she put out her hand, and pulled forth her beloved pepper-corns, the enchanter still standing motionless.

Away flew Urad like lightning from the hut, and ran till she had again reached the road from which she had been decoyed. She continued her journeying for seven days, feeding on the fruits of the forest, and sleeping in the most covert thickets. The eighth day, as she was endeavouring to pass a ford, where a small rivulet had been swelled by the rains, she perceived a large body of horsemen riding through the woods, and doubted not but it was the remainder of the gang of robbers whom she had before met with.

Urad was now in some measure reconciled to danger, and therefore, without much fear, dropped a pepper-corn, and expected relief.

The pepper-corn had been dropped some time, the horsemen advanced, and no one appeared to her succour.

'Alas!' said Urad, 'why has Houadir deceived me; neither her advice, nor her magical pepper-corns, can relieve me from these lustful and cruel robbers. Better had I fallen a prey to Darandu, better had I sated the lust of one enchanter, than undergo the various curses of so many monsters. O Genius, Genius, why hast thou forsaken me in my severest trials?'

By this time the robbers were come up, and were highly rejoiced to find such a beautiful prize.

'This only,' said the leader, 'was what we wanted, a fair one to regale with, and this dainty morsel will serve us all. Here is luxury, my friends, such as Almurah cannot find in his whole seraglio; let him be dissatisfied with an hundred females, while we, my friends, will be satisfied with one! She shall serve us all, and me first.' 'But first,' said one, 'let us all embrace her, for I never yet had the pleasure to embrace a virgin, except one that I stabbed first.'

At this he leaped from his horse, and the trembling Urad gave a loud shriek, which was answered from the woods by the roaring of an hundred lions.

'O Alla,' said the chief, 'the lions are upon us.' 'That may be,' said he, who was dismounted, 'but were the whole world set against me, I would secure my prize;' so saying, he took Urad in his arms to place her on his horse.

The roaring of the lions continued, and many of them came howling out of the woods; the robbers fled in dismay, all but the ruffian who had seized on the fair Urad, who was striving in vain to fix her on his horse.

A lion

A lion furiously made at him, and tore him limb from limb, while Urad expected the same fate from several others, who came roaring around. 'But,' said she, 'better is death than infamy; and the paw of the hungry lion, than the rude hands of the lustful robber.'

The noble beast having devoured his prey, came fawning at the feet of Urad, who was surprized at his behaviour and gentleness, but much more was her astonishment increased when she heard him speak.

'O virgin, for none other can experience the assistance of our race, or stand unhurt before us, I am the king and sovereign of these mighty forests, and am sent by the Genius Houadir to thy protection; but why did the distrustful Urad despair, or why did she accuse Providence of deserting her? Should not the relieved wait with patience on the hand that supports him, and not cry out with impatience, and charge its benefactor with neglect?'

'True, O royal lion,' answered the fair Urad, 'but fear is irresistible, and the children of men are but weakness and ingratitude, but blessed be Alla, who, though justly provoked at my discontent, yet sent to my assistance the guardian of the fair: yet how cometh it to pass, O royal protector, that you who are so bold, and so fierce in your nature, should yet behave with such tenderness and kindness to an helpless virgin, whom you might, with pleasure to yourself, in a moment devour?'

'The truly great and noble spirit,' answered the lion, 'takes a pride in protecting innocence; neither can he wish to oppress it. From hence learn, fair virgin, that of all mankind, he only is noble, generous, and truly virtuous, who can withhold his desires from oppressing or ruining the virgin that is in his power. What then must you think of those mean wretches, who endeavour to undermine your virtues and pious dispositions, who cajole you under the appearance of affection, and yet tell you, if they succeed not, that it was only to try you. He that is fuspicious, is mean; he that is mean, is unworthy of the chaste affection of the virtuous maid. Wherefore, O Urad, shun him, however honoured by mankind, or covered by the specious characters of virtue, whoever attempts the honour of your chastity, for he cannot be just; to deceive you he must himself swear falsely, and therefore cannot be good; or if he tell the truth, he must be weak and ungenerous, and unworthy of you, as he invites you to sin.'

In such conversation they passed along the forest, till after a few days they were alarmed at the noise of the hunters, and the music of the chace.

'Alas,' said the beautiful Urad, 'what is this that I hear?'—'It is answered the royal beast, 'the noise of the hunters, and thou shalt escape, but me will they in sport destroy. The lion you call cruel, who kills to devour. What then is he who wantons in the deaths of those who advantage him not? But man is lord of all; let him look to it how he governs!'

'Nay, but,' answered Urad, 'leave me, gentle protector, and provide for your safety; nor fear but Houadir will prevent the storms that hover over, from breaking upon me.'—'No,' answered the royal beast, 'she has commanded me to follow you till I see her presence; and where can I better sacrifice my life than in the service of chastity and virtue!'

The hunters were now in sight, but advanced not toward the lion; they turned their coursers aside, and only one, of superior mien, with several attendants, rode toward Urad. The lion erecting his mane, his eyes glowing with vivid lightnings, drew up the wide sinews of his broad back, and with wrathful front leaped toward him who seemed to have the command.

The horseman perceiving his intention, poised his spear in his right hand, and spurred his courser to meet him. Ere the royal beast had reached the horseman

man, the rider threw his spear, which, entering between the fore paws of the lion, nailed him to the ground. The enraged animal tore his paw from the ground, but the spear still remained in his foot, and the anguish of the wound made him shake the forest with his lordly roarings.

The stranger then rode up to the fair Urad, whom viewing, he cried out—' By Alla, thou art worthy of the embraces of the Vizir Mussapulta; take her, my eunuchs, behind you, and bear her through the forest of Bagdat, to the seraglio of my ancestors. The eunuchs obeyed, and bore her away, though Urad dropped her corn upon the ground; but still she trusted in the help of Houadir.

The Vizir Mussapulta then ordered that one of his slaves should stay behind and destroy and bury the lion, which he commanded to be done with the utmost caution, as Almurah had made a decree, that if any subject should wound, maim, or destroy, any lion, in his forests, the same should be put to death. The eunuchs bore away Urad to the seraglio, taking her through bye-ways to the palace of the vizir, lest her shrieks should be heard. Mussapulta followed at a distance, and the slave was left with the tortured and faithful lion. In a few hours they reached the palace, and Urad being conducted to the seraglio, was ordered to be dressed, as the vizir intended visiting her that night.

Urad was thunderstruck at the news, and now began to fear Houadir had forgotten her, and resolved, as soon as the eunuchs had left her, to drop a second pepper-corn. But poor Urad had forgotten to take her bag from her old garments, which the eunuch who dressed her had carried away. She dissolved in fresh tears at this piece of carelessness—' Well,' said she, ' surely Houadir will neglect me, if I so easily neglect myself.' She waited that night with fear and trembling, but no vizir appeared.

The

This eased her greatly; and the next day, when the eunuchs came, they informed her, that Mussapulta had that evening been sent by the sultan to quell an insurrection, and that they did not expect him home under twenty days. During this time, no pains were spared with Urad to teach her the accomplishments of the country; all which, in spite of her unwillingness to learn in such a detestable place, she nevertheless acquired with the utmost ease and facility.

The insurrection being quelled, the vizir returned, and, not unmindful of his fair captive, ordered that she might be prepared for his reception in the evening.

Accordingly Urad was sumptuously adorned with jewels and brocades, and looked more beautifully than the fairest Circassian; and the dignity of her virtue added such a grace to her charms, that even her keepers, the eunuchs, dared not to look upon her.

Mussapulta, in the evening, came to the seraglio, where he found his beautiful captive in tears. 'What,' said he, 'cannot a fortnight's pleasure in this palace efface the remembrance of your sorrows! But be gay and chearful, for know, that the vizir Mussapulta esteems you even beyond his wives.'—'The esteem of a robber, the esteem of a lawless ranger,' answered Urad, 'charms not the ears of virtue. Heaven, I trust, will not suffer you to plunder my body; but no power can make me look with pleasure on the murderer of my friend, or on the lustful wretch.'

'What,' said Mussapulta, sternly, 'do you refuse my proffered love! Then will I, having first deflowered thee, cast thee forth among my slaves, and them shalt thou lie down before; thy body I have, and I will make such full use of it, as shall sting thy squeamish virtue to the soul; I will also have witnesses of my triumph, my whole seraglio shall be present, and my female slaves shall be ordered to laugh at

thy

thy cries, as thou lieſt on the bed of my deſires; and I too will enjoy thy ſcreams, and take a pride in the ſorrows and throbs of thy departing chaſtity, nor ſhalt thou riſe till many have followed the example of their maſter. Here eunuchs,' continued he, 'bind that ſtubborn piece of virtue, and ſtretch her on the bed; call all my females here, and bid my ſlaves attend. Take off thoſe trappings from her, and let us ſee the whole of her virtuous compoſition.'

The eunuchs advanced to Urad, and began their maſter's commands, while ſhe, with the moſt fearful outcries, pierced the air, calling on Alla, on Mahomet, and on Houadir, to relieve her. The females arriving, Muſſapulta gave them their leſſon, who, going to the beauteous victim, began laughing at her ſorrow, and talking to her in the moſt ungrateful terms.

The ſlaves alſo attended, and beheld the lovely Urad now almoſt expoſed in all her uncovered charms to the eyes of the brutal company. 'Why,' ſaid the proud vizir, 'do ye delay my wiſhes? Haſte, ſlaves, and lay bare this delicate piece of virtue to public view.' As he ſaid this, an eunuch came running in haſte, crying, 'The ſultan, the ſultan Almurah approaches!'

All was inſtant confuſion; Muſſapulta turned pale and trembled; he ordered the eunuch to releaſe and cover the fair Urad, and ere ſhe was well adorned again, the faithful lion entered with the Sultan Almurah. The lion inſtantly ſeized on the Vizir Muſſapulta, and tore him limb from limb, in the ſight of thoſe very ſervants whom he called together to behold his cruelty and luſt. Yet the generous animal would not defile himſelf with the carcaſe, but with great wrath toſſed the bloody remains among the females of the ſeraglio.

Almurah commanded Urad to advance; and at the ſight of her, 'O royal beaſt,' ſaid he to the lion, 'I wonder not that thou wert unable to deſcribe the

beauties

beauties of this lovely maid, since they are almost too dazzling to behold.

'O virtuous maid,' continued Almurah, 'whose excellencies I have heard from this faithful animal, if thou canst deign to accept of the heart of Almurah, thy sultan will be the happiest of mankind; but I swear, by my unalterable will, that no power on earth shall force or distress you.'—'O,' sighed Urad, 'royal sultan, you honour your poor slave too much; yet happy should I be were Houadir here!'

As she spoke, the Genius Houadir entered the room; the face of the sage instructor still remained, but a glowing splendour surrounded her, and her walk was majestic and commanding. Almurah bowed to the ground, Urad made obeisance, and the rest fell prostrate before her.

'My advice,' said Houadir, 'is necessary now, O Urad, nor ought young virgins to enter into such engagements without counsel, and the approbation of those above them, how splendid and lucrative soever the union may appear. I, who know the heart of Almurah, the servant of Mahomet, know him to be virtuous; some excesses he has been guilty of, but they were chiefly owing to his villainous Vizir, Mussapulta.' Here the lion gave a dreadful roar. 'Against your command, Almurah, did he wound this animal, which I endued with speech for the service of Urad, to teach her that strength and nobleness of soul would always support the innocent.

Mussapulta having wounded him, commanded his slave to put the royal beast to death; but I gave the slave bowels of mercy, and he carried him home to his cottage, till the wound was healed. When the lion, faithful to his trust, came toward you as you were hunting, and being endued with speech, declared the iniquity of Mussapulta. But he is no more.

'Now, Urad, if thy mind incline to Almurah, receive his vows; but give not thine hand where thy

heart

heart is eftranged, for no fplendour can compenfate the want of affection'—' If Almurah, my gracious lord,' anfwered Urad, ' will fwear in three things to do my defire, his handmaid will be happy to ferve him.' ' I fwear,' anfwered the fond Almurah, ' hadft thou three thoufand defires, Almurah would fatisfy them, or die.'

' What ftrange things,' faid Houadir, ' has Urad to afk of the Sultan Almurah?'—' Whatever they are, gracious Genius,' faid Almurah, Urad, the lovely Urad, may command me.'

' Then,' faid Urad, ' firft I require that the poor inhabitants of the foreft be reftored to their native lands, from whence thou haft driven them.'—' By the great Alla, and Mahomet the prophet of the juft,' anfwered Almurah, ' the deed was propofed and executed by the villain Muffapulta! Yes, my lovely Urad, they fhall be obeyed.

' But now, Urad,' continued the fultan, ' ere you proceed in your requefts, let me make one facrifice to chaftity and juftice, by vowing in the prefence of the good Genius Houadir, to difmifs my feraglio, and take thee only to my arms.'

' So noble a facrifice,' anfwered Urad, ' demands my utmoft returns; wherefore, beneficent fultan, I releafe thee from any farther compliance with my requefts.'

' Lovely Urad,' faid Almurah, ' permit me then to dive into your thoughts: yes, by your kind glances on that noble beaft, I perceive you meditated to afk fome bounty for your deliverer. He fhall,' fair virgin, be honoured as Urad's guardian, and the friend of Almurah; he fhall live in my royal palace with flaves to attend him; and that his reft may not be inglorious, or his life ufelefs, once every year fhall thofe who have ravifhed or deflowered the innocent, be delivered up to his honeft rage.'

' The lovely Urad fell at the feet of her fultan, and bleffed him for his favours; and the fage Houadir ap-

proved

proved of Urad's request, and the promises of Almurah. The lion came and licked the feet of his benefactors, and the Genius Houadir, at parting, poured her blessings on the royal pair.

'To guard the soft female heart, from the delusions of a faithless sex, said Iracagem, 'is worthy of our race, and the sage Houadir has wisely blended chastity and prudence in her delightful instructions! but female delicacy makes an unequal opposition to brutal cunning, unless the protection of the Just One overshadow the footsteps of the virtuous maid; wherefore, Alla is the first and chief supporter of the female sex, who will assuredly, when requested, confound the vain artifices of man, and exalt the prudent counsels of the modest fair. But, most illustrious,' said the sage Iracagem to one of the Genii of a superior mien, 'let me not any longer delay the noble lessons of thy tongue; from thee we expect to hear the adventures of Misnar, the beloved of Alla and Mahomet his prophet.

'Chief of our race,' answered the Genius, 'whose praises rise earliest and most frequent in the presence of Alla, I am ready to obey thee.' So saying, the Genius thus began her much instructive tale.

TALE VI.

The Enchanters; or, Misnar, the Sultan of India.

AT the death of the mighty Dabulcombar, the lord of the east, Misnar, the first-born of the sultan, ascended the throne of India; but though the hand of time had scarcely spread the fruits of manhood on his cheeks, yet neither the splendour of his court, nor the flatteries of the east, could steal from the youthful Sultan the knowledge of himself. His first royal command was, to assemble together the wise men throughout his extensive dominions, from Cabul and Attok, which are the evening boundaries of the fun, to Kehoa and Thoanoa, the heads of whose mosques are tipt with the earliest beams.

Then came the Faquir Ciumpso, from Bansac; and Balihu, the hermit of the faithful, from Queda; the sage Bouta hastened from Bisnagar: and Candusa, the Iman of Lahor, was not inobedient to the royal decree. Sallasalsor also, from Necbal, was there; and Carnakan, a faithful worshipper from the banks of Ava; the prophet Mangelo, from the hollow rocks of Caxol; and Garab, a silver-bearded sage, from the mountains Coharsi; from Azo came a wise interpreter of dreams; and from Narvan, the star-read philosopher Nexmaked. Zeuramaund, the father of the prophets of Naugraccut, led his visionary tribe from their native mountains, and the wisest of their community were deputed to represent the bramins of Lactora.

The Sultan Misnar ordered the illustrious assembly to meet in the divan, where, being placed on the throne of his forefathers, he thus opened unto them the desires of his heart.

'O ye sources of light, and fountains of knowledge,' said Misnar, 'more precious are your counsels to me than the mines of Raalconda, or the big emerald from Gani; wisdom is the true support of honour, and the sultan is established by the counsel of his sages. Say, then, ye treasures of experience, what shall Misnar devise, that may secure him in the throne of the mighty Dabulcombar?'

The sages in the divan were struck with astonishment at the condescension of their young sultan, and one and all fell prostrate before his throne. 'May wisdom,' said they, 'guide the footsteps of the illustrious Misnar; may the mind of our sultan be as the eye of the day!'

Then arose the prophet Zeuramaund, and said,

'I perceive, O mighty sultan, the dark clouds of evil are gathering to disturb the hours of futurity; the spirits of the wicked are preparing the storm and the tempest against thee; but—the volumes of fate are torn from my sight, and the end of thy troubles is unknown!'

The venerable sages looked aghast as Zeuramaund uttered these ominous predictions in the spirit of prophecy; for they perceived he spake as he was moved; the whole council were dismayed at his words, and all fell again prostrate on the earth.

Misnar alone appeared unconcerned at his fate.

'O my friends,' said the youthful sultan, 'the rose cannot blossom without the thorn, nor life be unchequered by the frowns of fate; the clouds of the air must lower before the rice springs forth, and the mother feel the pangs of child-birth ere she knows the pleasure of a parent. Grieve not, my friends, that trials attend me, since the spirit of prudence and virtue blossoms fairest in a ruggid soil.' The sages arose as their royal master spake, and beheld with wonder the youthful countenance of their prudent sultan.

Silence and amazement for a time prevailed, till one of the sages advancing before the rest, thus counselled the intrepid prince.

'O light of the earth,' said the trembling sage 'whose virtue and innocence have not been vexed by frauds and deceit, whose pure mind seeth not the foul devices of man's heart, trust not to the fickle interpositions of chance, where thine own arm can work security, and establish a permanent foundation to thy father's throne. Thou hast a brother, O my sultan, whose veins are filled with royal blood, and whose heart is by descent above controul. Ahubal, therefore, ere the bud of his youth unfolds in the fulness of manhood, should be cut off, as the husbandman destroyeth the deadly lacar* in the field.' 'What,'

* Lacar is a kind of poisonous weed, found in great plenty in the inland parts of India, but little, if at all, known to the Europeans.

'What,' said the young sultan Misnar, 'what do thy base suspicious fears advise? Is there no way to build up the seat of justice and mercy but in murder and fraticide? Caution, when besmeared in blood, is no longer virtue, or wisdom, but wretched and degenerate cowardice: no, never let him that was born to execute judgment, secure his honours by cruelty and oppression; the righteous Alla planted me not here to spread a poisonous shade over the offspring of his prophet Mahomet; though fear and submission is a subject's tribute, yet is mercy the attribute of Alla, and the most pleasing endowment of the vicegerents of earth. But as thou, weak man, hast dared to advise the extirpation of one of the race of the mighty Dabulcombar, the vengeance of my injured brother's blood fasten upon thy life.'

The guards of the divan hearing the sentence of the sultan, approached with their drawn sabres towards the decrepit sage, but Misnar arising, cried out—

'Who of my subjects shall dare to violate with blood the sanctity of this refuge for the oppressed; let the divan of justice be sacred: nevertheless, lead that author of malice from my sight, and let his own blood make a satisfaction for the cruelty of his desires.' As he spake thus, the guards attempted to seize the sage; but as they advanced towards him, flames of fire burst from his mouth, and his whole form appeared as the form of a fiery dragon.

The rest of the sages fled from the dreadful monster, but Misnar, with an intrepid countenance, stood before his throne, with his drawn sabre, pointing towards the dragon: when through the flames he perceived an hoary magician, on the back of the monster.

'Vain, O silly child of Mahomet,' said the enchanter, 'was thy sabre against the power of my art, did not a superior force uphold thee; but tremble at thy doom, twice four of my race are determined against thee, and the throne of Dabulcombar noddeth over thy head; fear hath now preserved thee, and the weakness of thy heart, which the credulous believers of Mahomet will call prudence and moderation; but the fiend of darkness is let loose, and the powers of enchantment shall prevail!' As the hoary magician spake thus, his fiery dragon with tremendous hissings arose, and cleaving the dome of the divan, disappeared from their sight.

'Thus,' said the illustrious Misnar, let the enemies of Mahomet be dismayed; but inform me, O ye sages, under the semblance of which of your brethren did that foul enchanter gain admittance here?'

'May the lord of my heart,' answered Balihu, the hermit of the faithful from Queda, 'triumph over all his foes. As I travelled on the mountains from Queda, and saw neither the footsteps of beasts, nor the flights of birds, behold I chanced to pass through a cavern, in whose hollow sides I found this accursed sage, to whom I unfolded the invitation of the Sultan of India, and we joining, journeyed toward the divan; but ere we entered, he said unto me, "Put thy hand forth, and pull me toward thee into the divan, calling on the name of Mahomet, for the evil spirits are on me, and vex me."

The Continuation of the Tale of the Enchanters; or, Misnar, the Sultan of the East.

AFTER the hermit Balihu had spoken, Mangel arose.

'May the power of the sultan of the east be multiplied!' said he; 'but know, O sultan, that neither evil Genius, nor enchanter, can enter this seat of justice, unless he be invited in the name of Mahomet.'

'If it be so,' answered the Sultan Misnar, 'then neither can they be masqued against the voice of justice; for thou, O righteous Alla, wilt uphold the tribunal which thou hast founded upon earth, and make

make the visions of fraud to depart from him who seeketh truth. Therefore, continued the sultan, 'lest this assembly be still tainted with malice and infidelity, as the poisonous herb groweth most luxuriantly beside the plants of health, I command the evil spirits to stand confessed before me.'

At his word, sulphureous smoke arose, and from the thronged assembly seven hideous forms broke forth.

First, on a vulture's pinions the fell enchanter Tasnar soared aloft, whose skin was as the parched Indian's when he writhes impaled upon the bloody stake. Next, on the back of an enormous scorpion, whose tail dropped deadly poison, Ahaback appeared, and with his eyes darted malignant flashes on the youthful sultan. Him followed Happuck, a subtle magician, on the shoulders of a tyger, whose mane was shagged with snakes, and whose tail was covered with twining adders.

Hupacusan also, that decrepit hag, who personated the righteous Sallalalsor, from Necbal, now stripped of the garments of hypocrisy, filled the eyes of the sages with terror and amazement. Her lean bones, wrapped round with yellow skin, appeared like the superstitious mummies of the western Egypt. She was mounted on a monster more dreadful and uncouth than the fever-parched wretch beholds, when in restless slumbers he sinks from woe to woe upon his bed of sickness. Its form was like the deadly spider, but in bulk like the elephant of the woods; hairs like cobwebs covered its long bony legs, and from behind, a bag of venom of a whitish hue spurted forth its malignant influence.

Here followed her malicious sister Ulin, squatting on the back of a broad-bellied toad, whose mouth opened like the pestilence that swalloweth up the fainting inhabitants of Delly. Then, with a loud hiss, started forth in many a fold, a black serpent, in length and bulk like the cedars of the forest, bearing the powerful enchantress Defera, whose wide-extended ears covered an head of iniquity, and whose long shrivelled dugs weakly panted over an heart of adamant.

Last, with majestic horror, the giant Kifri swelled into his full proportion; and, like a tottering mountain, reared himself aloft; the long immeasurable alligator that bore him, groaned with his load, and opening all his mouths, for every scale appeared a mouth, vomited forth streams of grumous blood. In his hand the giant brandished a stately pine blasted with lightning, which, shaking at the dauntless Misnar—

' Tremble, vile reptile,' said he, in a thundering voice; ' tremble, vile reptile, at a giant's wrath! tremble at the magic powers of all my brethren; if such a name becomes our race, unbound, unfettered by the ties of nature: tremble, vile reptile, for thy doom is fixed! At these words the infernal brood joined their voices with Kifri's, and all at once pronounced in harsh discordant sounds, ' Tremble, vile reptile, for thy doom is fixed!'

The enchanters were then involved in a thick cloud of smoke, from which issued broad flashes of red lightning, which ascending to the roof of the divan, in a moment disappeared.

' There is neither wisdom nor prudence,' said Misnar, as he prostrated himself on the ground, after the enchantments were at an end, ' but what are derived from Alla, and are the gift of the prophet of the faithful. If thou dost vouchsafe to direct my steps, O protector of Mussulmen, the fear of evil shall not come upon me. ' Happy,' said Candufa, the iman of Lahor, with his breast on the earth, ' happy is the prince whose trust is in Alla, and whose wisdom cometh from the thirteenth heaven.'—' Happy, said all the sages, humbling themselves before the sultan Misnar, ' happy is our sultan, the favourite of Alla!'

' That,'

'That,' replied Misnar, 'O sages, is too much even for the sultan of the east to hear. But may the all-righteous Alla approve of my thoughts and actions! so shall the infernal powers destroy the wretches that employ them, and the dark poisoned arrow recoil upon him that blew it forth*. But, O sages, though your numbers are reduced, your integrity is more tried and approved: therefore let Misnar, your sultan, partake of the sweetness of your counsels, and learn from aged experience the wisdom of the sons of earth. Say, then, what doth the peace and sincerity of my throne require from me concerning my brother Ahubal, the issue of the mighty Dabulcombar?'

'Far be it from me,' said the sage Carnakan, 'to presume to utter my words as oracles before the prince; but may not the security of the east require, that the prince, thy brother, be not enlarged as my sultan is, to do whatsoever seemeth good in his heart: should not the younger be as servant to the first-born of his father, and are not all the princes the vassals of the sultans of the east. Let, therefore, the prince Ahubal enjoy the pleasures of life, but let him be removed from giving pain and uneasiness to my royal sultan Misnar. At the resources of the springs of Ava, on the craggy rocks of Aboulfakem, is a royal castle, built by the sage of Illfakircki, to which there is no passage but through a narrow vale, which may be ever guarded by the slaves of Misnar. Hither let the prince be sent, and let him live there, and enjoy life, without having any power to molest the glories of thy reign.'

The counsel of Carnakan seemed agreeable unto the sultan and his sages, and Misnar gave immediate orders,

---

* *Blew it forth.* This may need explanation. In many parts of Asia, the inhabitants use small poisonous arrows, which they blow from an hollow cane upon their adversaries.

orders, that the mutes of his seraglio should attend the prince to the royal castle at Aboulfakem; and then dismissing, for the present, the assembled sages, he commanded them every week to attend the divan. In a few days the mutes and guards were sent with the prince Ahubal, and being admitted into the presence of their sultan, they fell on their faces, and cried out,

'O let not the displeasure of the sultan fall upon his slaves; thy slaves, in obedience to thy royal word, journeyed toward the castle of Aboulfakem, and as they passed along through the desarts, a party of five thousand horse appeared, who, setting upon us, ordered us either to deliver up the prince Ahubal, or defend him with our lives. Thy slaves would willingly have chosen the latter fate. Yet, alas! what were four hundred guards and twenty mutes to the army that opposed us. But our consultation was vain; for while we debated how to defend ourselves, the prince drew his sabre, and killing three of our number, cut his way through the guards to his friends. The horsemen then would have set upon us, and hewed us in pieces; but their chief forbade them, saying, "No, let them live, and be the messengers of the prince's escape.—Go," continued he, "dastard slaves, and let your sultan know, that Ahubal has friends who will shortly punish him for his designs on the prince."

At these words of his guards, Misnar gave a deep sigh, and said,

'Human prudence alone is far too weak to fight against the wiles of the deceitful; but Alla is more powerful than man! I will therefore send for the prophets, and enquire of them, where I may seek for the assistance of Mahomet.' The sultan then commanded Zeuramaund and his tribe, and Mangelo, the prophet, from the hollow rocks of Caxol, to be brought before him; and when they were come into

his

his presence, he demanded of them, where he might seek for the assistance of Mahomet and the countenance of Alla.

Then answered Zeuramaund, the sultan, in these words:

'In the tomb of the prophet of Mecca is the signet of Mahomet, which no human power may remove; but if the prophet will hear the prayer of the sultan, it may easily be taken from thence.' 'Yes,' replied Mangelo, the prophet, from the hollow rocks of Caxol, 'the seal of Mahomet will indeed preserve the prince from enchantment; but it is also necessary that he put on the girdle of Opakka, which is worn by the Giant Kifri, the sworn enemy of the eastern throne. For although the signet of Mahomet will preserve the sultan from evil, yet will the girdle of Opakka only save him from deceit.'

The sultan Misnar was moved at the discourse of his prophets, and spent the night in thought and perplexity. He had little hope that the signet of Mahomet, which had for ages remained immoveable, should yield to him; or that, with all his numerous armies, he should be able to force the girdle of Opakka from the loins of an enchanter, who could in a moment overwhelm his troops by the power of his art. However, he determined the next morning to go with his court a public pilgrimage to Mecca, and to offer up the most solemn petitions to the prophet of his faith. Early in the morning the sultan arose from his seraglio, and commanded his courtiers to prepare the procession, as he intended immediately to make a public pilgrimage to Mecca. But as Misnar was making known his intentions, a messenger arrived in haste at the entrance of the seraglio, who brought advice, that one of the southern kingdoms had revolted, and was led on by a sage heroine, who declared her intentions of placing Ahubal, the brother of the sultan, on the throne of India.

Misnar

Misnar was conscious that this revolt was brought about through the contrivances of the enchanters, and therefore despaired of conquering them by means of his armies; but left the other kingdoms, seeing no troops were sent to repel the rebels, should also join the adverse party, the sultan commanded the rough music of war to sound; and sending for his grand Vizir Horam in private, he ordered him to lead out the armies of Delly against the rebels, and to dispatch daily messengers to the capital to bring advice of his success.

The Vizir Horam received the sultan's commission with reverence, and said,—' Let not my sultan be angry at his slave. If my lord should require ten thousand messengers, his slave Horam would dispatch them. But if my lord will accept of this tablet, he shall know in a moment the success of his servant, though numberless leagues between us.'

' What,' said Misnar, taking the tablet from his vizir, by what means is this tablet endued with these rare virtues?' ' My lord,' answered Horam, ' when my father, through the malice of his enemies, was banished from the presence of the mighty Dabulcombar, (whom the Houris of Paradise do serve) he called me to him, and said, ' O Horam, the evil-minded have prevailed, and thy father is fallen a sacrifice to the enemies of truth: no more, my son, shall I behold the children of my strength, nor the splendour of my sultan's court; whither I go, I know not! but do you my son, take this tablet; and whatever befalleth thy parent, shall at times be made known to you in the leaves of this book; and to whomsoever thou givest it, that friend shall, after my death, read therein whatever Horam my son shall wish to make known unto him."

' Faithful Horam,' answered the sultan, ' thy present is of such exquisite value, that thy prince shall, in confidence, honour thee with the first place in his

esteem

esteem. Know then, my faithful vizir, that the powers of enchantment are let loose against my throne, and the prophets have said, " Thou shalt not prevail but with the signet of Mahomet, and the girdle of Opakka;"—' therefore it is expedient that I first go to Mecca to obtain this valuable gift of the prophet: my purpose but this morning was to go surrounded by the nobles of my court; but while rebellion stalketh abroad, pageants are idle, and the parade of a sultan's pilgrimage will give my enemies time to increase in their numbers and strength. No, Horam, I myself will in secret approach the tomb of my prophet, for Alla requireth the service of the heart, and searcheth out the purity of his servants' intentions; I shall go with greater humility as a peasant than as a prince. In the mean time, my royal tent shall be pitched, and Horam only shall be suffered to approach it. So shall my slaves imagine their sultan goeth forth with them to the field, and the hearts of my subjects shall be strengthened.'

'Be the desires of the sultan fulfilled,' said Horam, with reverence: ' but will not my lord take with him a guard in his pilgrimage; for the dangers of the journey are great over the mountains and desarts, and the voyage by the seas is perilous!' ' No,' answered the sultan, ' those who are my slaves here, may at a distance become my masters, and sell me to my foes: where the trust is great, great is the danger also. Shall I set guards over my person in the heart of my kingdom, amidst my faithful subjects, and trust my life in a slave's hand, where I am neither known nor respected? When the diamond lieth concealed in the mine, it is free and unmolested, but when it shireth abroad on the earth, all covet its possession.' The vizir Horam was struck with the prudence of his youthful sultan, and bowed in assent to the words of his lord.

In a few days the armies of India assembled; the royal tent was pitched, and the vizir was declared the leader of his sultan's forces. Misnar entered his
tent

tent in great state, and Horam alone followed the sultan into the retirements of the moveable pavilion. The vizir had, according to the sultan's instructions, prepared a disguise for his master; and at midnight led him, like a peasant, through the encampments into a wood, where, falling at his feet, he besought him to consider well the dangers he was about to encounter.

'Horam,' answered the sultan, 'I well know the goodness of thy heart, and that thy fears are the daughters of thy love. Sensible am I, that the dangers of my pilgrimage are great; but what resource have I left? More than man is risen up against me, and more than man must assist me, or I perish. To whom then can I fly but to the prophet of the faithful? For I am well assured that no enchantment shall prevail against me while I journey toward Mecca; for such is the faith of all true believers, though they may oppress and fatigue me, yet in the end shall I triumph. Besides, Horam, there is no other resource.'

'True, my sultan,' answered the vizir, 'without Alla, vain is the counsel of man; but is not Alla every where present to aid and defend the sons of the faithful?'

'Though Alla be all-powerful,' answered Misnar, 'yet is not the slave of his hand to direct the lord of all things. If we would gain the help and assistance of Alla, we must obey his commands; and well are we assured in the law of our prophet, that at Mecca shall the prayer of the faithful be heard. Wherefore, O Horam, no longer my slave, but my friend, lead forth my armies with confidence and trust, and doubt not but that he, who daily refresheth the sun with light, will shortly restore Misnar to the throne of his forefathers.' As he spake thus, the sultan broke from his Vizir Horam, who was fallen upon his master's feet and weeping at his fixed resolves, and penetrated into the gloomy recesses of the forest.

All was silence and darkness, save where through broken fragments of fleeting clouds, the sultaness of night

night sometimes threw a feeble light on the horrors of the forest.

'This gloomy recess,' said Misnar, as he passed on, 'which hides me from the world, makes me better known to myself. In the court of my forefathers, I am called the light of the world, the glory of the east, and the eye of day; but in the wild forests of Tarapajan, I am a poor helpless reptile, on whom the cedars drop unwholesome dews, and whose steps are hidden from the light of the moon by the branches of the palm. What then is the pride of man but deceit! and the glories of the earth, but the shadows of illusion! surely more had I to fear from enchantment on the throne of Dabulcombar, than in the bosom of this forest. Here the wild beasts will not flatter me, nor will the lordly lion acknowledge me the sultan of his wild domains. On what prop then must that weak tendril, man, entwine himself, on what rock must the son of earth build his security! Thanks be to the faith delivered unto me by Mahomet, the holy prophet of Arabia, in Alla shall be my trust, who ruleth over all the children of his hand, and is lord over the haunts of wild beasts, as well as the dwellings of mankind.

With such thoughts Misnar passed along for many days, till one night at a distance he perceived the skies looked red with light and various fires; and by the noise, which increased in his ears, found that some Indians were carousing in the woods before him. The disguised sultan endeavoured to avoid them, striking into a path which led round their fires; but some of the Indians observing him by the light of their fires, called to their brother peasant, and desired him to partake of their mirth.

Misnar thought it would be in vain to refuse the request, as they all seemed disposed to insist on their demands, and therefore hastened to the scene of their festivity. Here he found ten or twelve fires, with a mixed number of males and females, some sitting and some dancing around them; the uncouth rustic music enlivened their dance, and the mask of care was not on their faces.

Misnar inquired the cause of their mirth. 'What!' said an ancient female, 'though you are a stranger in Tarapajan, and know not that the feast of Tigris is celebrated by these nightly fires, yet must you now learn, that no stranger comes but to partake of our joy, nor departs till the fires are extinct.'

'And how long,' said Misnar, 'doth this feast last?' 'This,' answered the old woman, 'is the third night, and these fires must blaze yet eleven nights and days more, during which time the axe is not seen in the hand of the forester, nor doth the bow twang in the woods of Tarapajan; neither may he which seeth these rites depart till they be fulfilled.'

Misnar was thunderstruck at this relation; and ere he could answer, the crowd gathered around him. 'Come,' said he that appeared to be the chief, 'let us initiate this stranger in our rites; bring hither the skin of the tyger, and the paw of the lion, and the lance, and the bow that twangs not in the woods of Tarapajan during these nightly festivals.'

Then did one bring the skin of a tyger, and threw it over the shoulders of Misnar; and another came with the paw of a lion, and hung it before him; and a third brought a lance, and put it into Misnar's right hand; and a fourth flung a bow on his breast. Then did all the crowd make a loud howling, and danced around the astonished sultan.

'Now,' said the chief, when the dance was finished,' 'sound the hollow instruments of brass, which give notice to the moon and the stars, that this stranger is about to swear not to reveal our rites. Lay thine hand on thy head,' said the chief to the disguised sultan, 'and put thy fingers on thy mouth, and say—' As the starless night is dark, as the cave of death is dark, so shall my thoughts and words continue in darkness concerning the festival of tygers.'

'And

'And wherefore,' said Mifnar, 'is this filence impofed? and what fhall befal him that fweareth not unto you? Is not the mind of man free; and who fhall offend him who feeketh not to offend others?'—' Whofoever,' anfwered the chief, ' travelleth, fhould become obedient to the cuftoms of thofe people among whom he tarrieth.'

'Right,' continued Mifnar, ' and I am willing, upon two conditions, to fulfil your will: firft, you fhall all fwear that I be at liberty to purfue my journey on the eleventh day; and next, that I fhall not be bound to perform aught contrary to the law of Mahomet.'

'Stranger,' replied the chief, ' when we are at liberty to depart, thou fhalt depart likewife; but during this feftival, which is held in honour of our noble anceftor, who remained fourteen days in this foreft, till he had fubdued a ravenous race of tygers, no man that is entered here may ftir from hence till the fires be extinguifhed; for by fire did our anceftor drive away and deftroy the tygers and beafts of the forefts, and by fire do we commemorate his mighty deeds. Neither,' continued the chief, ' may we reveal thefe rites to any one but thofe who by accident efpy them; for fuch as are prefent with us we are bound to receive into our fociety; wherefore we compel thofe who come among us, to keep in filence the knowledge of our rites.'—' If fuch is your cuftom,' anfwered Mifnar, 'I fhall willingly comply; and fwear to you, that as the ftarlefs night is dark, as the cave of death is dark, fo fhall my thoughts and words continue in darknefs concerning the feftival of tygers.' As he uttered thefe words, the whole affembly again danced around him, till the hollow brazen inftruments were ordered to found, and all the inhabitants of the foreft were commanded to receive the difguifed fultan as their brother.

Then the men one by one paffed by Mifnar, each as he paffed laying the hand of the fultan on his breaft.

After they were paſſed by, came the females alſo, who embraced their new brother. Theſe Miſnar ſuffered to paſs by without much reflection, till among the youngeſt, who laſt approached, he beheld a beauteous virgin with downcaſt looks drawing near him, and who ſeemed aſhamed of that freedom the cuſtom of the place obliged her to uſe.

At the ſight of this amiable figure, Miſnar at once forgot his purpoſe and his crown, and was impatient till the ceremony brought her into his arms, where he would willingly have held her for ever. The reſt of the females perceived his emotion; and the chief of the feſtival approaching, aſked Noradin, the beauteous fair one, 'Whether ſhe would at length fix her choice—for in this place,' continued the chief, addreſſing himſelf to Miſnar, 'every ſex hath freedom, and none are compelled to take the hand they do not love: Noradin hath for theſe three days been courted by all our tribe, but the coy maid hath refuſed every advance; if ſhe refuſe not you, our joy will be the more complete, as then none of our company will be without his mate.'

Miſnar, forgetting the great deſigns of his heart, waited for the fair one's anſwer, and felt more fear at her ſilence, than at the dreadful enchantments of his monſtrous enemies. At length, with bluſhes, and half-ſmothered words, Noradin anſwered, 'May the joy of my comrades be complete!'

Miſnar, in raptures at the fair Noradin's preference, took her by the hand, and led up the dance, while the hollow inſtruments of braſs a third time ſounded, to proclaim the choice of Noradin, the beauteous fair one.

At the appearance of day, each repaired to the cottage around, and Miſnar and Noradin were led by the chief to a ſpot, where ſhortly the whole aſſembly built them a cottage of bamboo and the leaves of the plantain. As ſoon as they were retired, Noradin taking Miſnar in her hand, aſked him,

whether

whether she deserved his constant love, for the choice she had made.

Misnar, somewhat startled at her question, asked what were the customs of her tribe.

'For ten days,' answered the amiable Noradin, 'I shall be with thee, and on the eleventh, if our choice be fixed, the chief will lead us to him who readeth the Koran, that our vows may be pledged in his presence; during this interval, my father's friends will attend us, that in case you refuse me, I may return a virgin to their arms; nay, even now are they building their huts around us.'

Misnar was much chagrined at these words, as in his heart he expected the full enjoyment of his beautiful mistress, and his mind now turned upon the great business he had to perform. 'But,' said he to himself, 'to what purpose is it to think of my kingdom or my pilgrimage, since I am here detained and watched by a set of savage foresters, who acknowledge no law but their own will: it is the part of prudence, then, to bear with patience and ease the misfortunes of life. I will indulge myself with this amiable female till the days of my confinement are at an end.' Then turning to the fair Noradin, the sultan said, 'O thou joy of life, I will wait with patience; nevertheless, I would that the hours of anxiety were shorter, and that the dawn of my happiness would this moment arise. 'Say, then,' answered Noradin, 'thou on whom my thoughts hang, shall the compliance of thy beloved, fix my lovely wanderer for ever in these arms?'

Misnar was confounded at the request of his fair companion, and his heart recoiled at her words. 'What,' said the sultan to himself, shall I, for the casual gratifications of my passion, give up the glories of my father's kingdom, and the viceregency of Mahomet! Or shall I basely betray that love which is proffered me, and for a few day's pleasure, imbitter fair Noradin's future cup of life! 'No,' said he aloud, turning to his amiable mistress, 'never let the man of integrity deceive the soft heart that means him happiness. Forgive me, all-beauteous Noradin! but the volumes of my fate are open, and the prophet of the faithful will not permit me to indulge here the secret affections of my mind: though the soul of thy slave will be torn and divided, yet must he depart with the expiring fires of your festival.'

'Base, cold, and senseless wretch,' said the false Noradin (as the beauteous vision vanished from the eyes of the sultan, and he beheld the enchantress Ulin before him), 'call not thy frozen purpose virtue, but the green fruits of unripened manhood; beauty is ever superior to prudence, and the extasies of love are triumphant over the powers of reason; but thou art susceptible of neither love nor beauty, and therefore not thy prudence but my folly have saved thee, who threw a tasteless bait in the paths of thy pilgrimage. However, what nature would permit, I have obtained? and though thou art escaped, puny animal as thou art, from the power of my enchantments, yet shall the southern kingdoms of India feel my scourge. Proceed then, superstitious reptile, on thy tame pilgrimage to Mecca, while Horam feels the vengeance of my arm in the sultry desarts of Ahajah.'

As she spake thus she stretched out her wand, and the fires and the foresters, and the enchantress Ulin, disappeared from the sight of the astonished sultan. The sultan immediately prostrated himself on the ground, and gave glory to Mahomet for his wonderful escape; and pursuing his journey, continued his course for two moons through the wide extended forest of Tarapajan.

During this time, he daily examined the tablets which the Vizir Horam had given him, but was very uneasy at finding the leaves always fair. 'Alas,' said he to himself, 'I have trusted to a base man, who perhaps has taken this advantage of my credulity, and intends

tends to set the crown of India on my brother's head! there needed not the powers of enchantment to overthrow me, since I have betrayed at once my folly and my cause.'

Misnar, therefore, resolved to travel back to Delly, and learn the cause of Horam's silence; but, however, as he neglected not to look on the tablets every day, he at length, as he was examining them under a palm tree, found the following inscription therein:—

'*Horam the Faithful Slave of the Sultan of the East, to Misnar, the Lord of his Heart.*

'SOME time after I left my royal sultan in the forest, while my heart was sad within my breast, and my eye-lids were heavy with the tears of separation, came an hasty messenger from the outskirts of the rebel army, and declared their approach, and that the southern provinces had revolted, and were added to the opposers of the sultan of the earth. When thy slave was certain of this intelligence from the mouths of many, who hastened to the camp with these bad tidings, I commanded the armies of India to be increased, and a more exact discipline to be observed in my master's camp, and perceiving that the enemy hastened to meet my sultan's forces, I shortened the march of my slaves, that the fatigues of the desarts might not prevail more against them than the face and the sword of their enemies. Moreover, I led thy troops through the most cultivated countries, that the necessaries of life might be procured for the multitudes that followed thy tent with the greater ease. But, alas! the presence of my lord is not with his people, and the army murmur that they are led by a sultan who cheers not their labours by the light of his person, so that the hearts of thy people are withdrawn from Horam thy slave, and the captains of thousands demand admittance to thy tent, and accuse thy vizir with evil devices against thee, my lord, the sultan.'

As

As the sultan read this intelligence in the tablet of Horam, his heart failed within him, and the sight of his eyes was as a mist before him.

'O Misnar, Misnar!' said he, falling to the ground, 'the fiend of darkness is let loose upon thee! and the powers of enchantment still prevail!' 'Yes,' said Ulin, the enchantress, who immediately appeared, 'the powers of enchantment shall prevail! Misnar, the faithful servant of Mahomet, hath at length yielded to my power, and Alla hath given to my vengeance the wretch that doubts his protection. 'Crawl, therefore,' continued she, 'vile reptile, on the earth, and become a toad that sucketh the poisonous vapour, and that draweth from the sun-beam a venomous fire.'

At the powerful voice of her enchantment, the sultan shrunk from his native figure, and became a reptile on the earth. He opened his pestiferous jaws, and the black venom fell from his tongue, and he trailed his broad, yellow, speckled belly in the dust. His change of form did not take from Misnar his memory or recollection: he was sensible of his disgrace, and of the justness of his sentence; and though he could not fly from himself, yet he hastened into the thicket, that he might hide his filthy corse from the light of Heaven.

But the hungry calls of nature soon drove him from his recess to seek his proper food in the desart. He crawled forth, and found himself led on by a scent that pleased him; his spirits seemed enlivened by the sweet odour, and his cold feeble limbs were endued with a brisker motion.

'Surely,' said he, in his heart, 'the bounteous Alla hath not left the meanest of his creatures without comfort and joy. The smell is as the smell of roses, and life and vigour are in these attractive paths."

With these thoughts he crawled forwards into the thickest covert; and though his body was drawn with

a secret

a secret impulse, yet his mind was filled with horror, when he came in sight of a mangled and corrupted body, which lay hid among the bushes. One of his own deformed kind sat squatting beside it; and, like himself, seemed to desire, and yet detest, the loathsome feast.

Misnar, at the sight of one of his hideous kind, was filled with scorn and rage; and, forgetting his present transformation, was about to drive him from the mangled body: when the reptile, opening his mouth, addressed him in the language of Delly. 'Whether art thou really what thy form bespeaks thee,' said the reptile, ' or, like me, the victim of enchantment answer?'

The sultan, surprised at this address, and perceiving that misery was not his portion alone, desired to know by what means his fellow-creature suffered such a wretched change.

' Since I perceive by your speech,' said the reptile, ' that one event has happened to us both, I shall not be averse to declare to you the cause of my transformation; but I shall expect that my confidence will not be misplaced, and that after I have made you acquainted with my history, you will not refuse to reveal your own.' ' A similitude in our fates,' replied Misnar, ' has already made us brethren; and I should be unreasonable to ask a favour I meant not to return.'

' Well then,' said he, ' we will depart from this wretched sight, into a different thicket, where we may unmolested bewail our uncommon fates; for although the enchantress Ulin, to disgrace our former natures, and to make us the more sensible of our present deformity, obliges us, by a miserable attraction, to meet daily before this horrid spectacle, yet our food is of the fruits of the earth; for the wicked enchantress has not the power to make us, even in this deformed habit, do that which is contrary to our human nature.'

As

As he was speaking, came another toad to the corse, 'Here,' continued the first, 'is another of our brethren, and another will soon be here; we were three before you came among us.—Where, O princess, is the last victim of Ulin's rage?' said he to the second. 'He was basking,' answered the second, 'in the sand, but I arouzed him, and he is now on his way.'

In a few minutes the third arrived, and as soon as he beheld the mangled body, the attraction ceased; when, the first leading the way, they departed into another thicket. 'Here,' said the first, 'O stranger, we may rest securely, and the serpent cannot annoy us, for we are seated under the shade of the fragrant cinnamon. We are obliged to you for your care of us,' said Misnar, 'but I am eager to hear the cause of your transformation.'

TALE VII.

The History of Mahoud.

'I AM,' replied the toad, 'the son of a jeweller in Delly, and my name is Mahoud; my father, after a life of industry and parsimony, finding himself declining, sent for me, and on his death-bed said, " O Mahoud, my days have been the days of care, but success hath attended them; I have toiled, that thou mayest reap; sown, that thou mayest gather; and laboured, that my son may enjoy the fruits of my industry. My peace and comfort have been sacrificed to thine, and now do I die, assured that my beloved Mahoud will not be pinched by poverty, or oppressed by penury and want. Happy are those prudent parents, who, like me, can smile at death, and leave their offspring independent of the world!"

'Thus, said my aged father and expired, and my tears accompanied his departing spirit; but these soon gave place to that ardent curiosity, which drove me me to explore those riches he had left me. I opened box after box with a silent rapture, and was pleased to find wealth sufficient to satisfy even the appetite of youth; many diamonds appeared among my father's wealth, which never could have passed the royal sieve*, and many others of infinite value, besides large quantities of gold and silver; so that in my youthful judgment, there appeared no end to my riches.

'It was not wonderful, that being so suddenly put in possession of these riches, I should seek every pleasure and diversion which wealth could purchase. All who were the companions of my childhood, all who would court an unexperienced heart, were admitted to my table, and the strict laws of Mahomet were less regarded at my house than the rich wines which sparkled at my feasts. Nor were the charms of the fair forgot: we endeavoured to procure Houris, if not as pure, at least as beautiful, as those of Mahomet; and, while our goblets were filled with wine, we envied not the deceased their rivers of milk.

'Thus passed I my life, among those who jest with religion, and make a mock at the rules of prudence and sobriety. But the time soon came when my hours of revelry were to be changed for those of sorrow, and when I was first to learn, that a father's prudence will not secure a wicked son from the shafts and arrows of bitterness and grief. My possessions, though ample, were nearly exhausted by ignorance and extortion; my jewels were gone; unacquainted with their value, I had rather flung them away than sold them; my silver and gold was become the property of my friends; who, when I applied to them in return, were much more assiduous, if possible, in
preserving

---

* The mogul is paid, by way of duty, all jewels which are found in the mines too large to pass through a sieve of a particular size.

preserving it from me, than I had been in squandering it on them; so that in a few days, even the merchants who had been such gainers by me, came now to demand some trifling sums that I had borrowed of them; and, being unable to pay them, they seized my furniture, and stripped me of my cloaths to satisfy their cruel demands.

' In this situation, I was turned out of my own doors, by those whom I had received a thousand times in my arms, and spurned at, like a dog, by those whom I had pressed to my bosom. Stung by reflections on my former follies, and ignorant where to fly for shelter, I covered myself with some few rags that had been cast to me, and sat down before the house of a rich young man, who, like myself, seemed to be squandering his wealth on the scum of the earth.

' Bennaskar, for that was his name, soon came forth, with his minstrels and singers at his heels, and seeing a miserable figure before his doors, he asked what I wanted. I told him, that once, like himself, I gave life to the dance, and mirth to my friends; but that want of caution had been the cause of my ruin, and too much confidence on those who least deserved my favour.

' Several of his friends hearing this, would have driven me from his presence, saying it was unfit such a wretch should even enjoy the blessings of the air. But Bennaskar would not suffer it, and asked me whether the insincerity of my friends had learned me to be sincere to others. I answered him, that I had ever been sincere, even to those who were undeserving, and that I had rather die than betray my friend.

" If what you say is true," said Bennaskar, " I will try you: go in, and my servant shall cloath you, and you shall live with me; I only ask in return, that you never disclose to any one what you hear or fee tranfacted in my houfe." ' Sir,' anfwered I, ' your offer is gracious, and befpeaks your generous intentions: but I do not chufe to live on another's bounty, without I can make myfelf ufeful."

"That," anfwered Bennafkar, "you may do, if I find I can truft you. I have long been in fearch of one I could truft. I want fuch a one but cannot find him." The friends of Bennafkar then furrounded their lord, and each confufedly offered his fervices to him. "No," faid the young man, "though I appear unthoughtful in your eyes, O fervile race of flatterers! yet know, to all your confufions, that I have tried you all, and find you trifling and infincere: this man alone refufes my proffered love, unlefs he can return it; and this man alone is worthy of my efteem."

' The friends of Bennafkar were thunderftruck at his words, and renewed their proteftations; but he commanded his fervants to drive them from his houfe, and, taking me by the hand, he led me into an inner, but fumptuous apartment. As foon as we arrived there, I proftrated myfelf at his feet, and faid, Let not my lord be angry with his fervant! but thou haft not told me what fervice thou wilt expect from me.'

"All that I require," anfwered Bennafkar, " is, that you difclofe not to any one what you hear or fee tranfacted in my houfe."—"My lord," anfwered I, " of what fervice can I be to you by fuch compliance? If I am filent thy flaves may fpeak, and I fhall be blamed for their infincerity. I pray thee, let me return to my rags, and fet me not in a place where thy vaffals will be tempted to ruin me in thy favour."

"Your anfwer," faid Bennafkar, " is the anfwer of a prudent man: but fear not; I cannot do without you, and I hope you will not refufe my proffered love. What you will fee none will fee befides you, therefore none but yourfelf will be unfaithful to

VOL. I. Q me."

me."—" On this assurance, I accepted the bounteous offer of Bennaskar, and the slaves led me to the bath, and I washed, and was perfumed, and arrayed in a vestment of my lord's.

'Bennaskar was impatient to see me, and as I was led into his presence, the young man hastened to meet me, and, folding me in his arms, he said," "May I at length meet a friend I can trust!" 'And I answered, May Mahoud be the friend of thy bosom!" Bennaskar then led me into another apartment, and meats were set before us, and he ordered the females that dance to come and entertain us.'

" Women," said Bennaskar, as we were eating, " are the sweeteners of life."—" Rather, answered I," " they are the curses of life. But for these, Mahoud had still slept secure, and the will of his father had prospered."

" What," answered Bennaskar, " is my friend able to withstand the charms of beauty, and the lovely invitations of the charmer! Then, (continued he) thou mayest indeed become my friend, for he who can conquer love is master of the earth." " Not so," answered I, " I do not say I have conquered; far otherwise, I have been conquered, and the wounded dread and loath the spear and the sword."

" But," said Bennaskar, " these are common forms; to slight these is easy, but I will lead thee where thou must be subdued." " Lead me not," answered I, ' O Bennaskar! I shall receive no pleasure, though thou set before me the sultanas of Delly, and the female thou lovest may be disgusted at my indifference.'

" Rest satisfied," said Bennaskar, with a smile, " I meant but to try thee; these dances suffice me; I covet not the trouble nor the parade of more costly females. But I see thou art moved; let us walk into the orange grove, and enjoy the breeze." Thus, for some time, I spent my time with the agreeable Bennaskar;

Bennaſkar; every day we varied our enjoyments, and were mutually ſatisfied with each other.

' I had now been with my friend eighteen days, and no interruption was given to our friendſhip; when, on the nineteenth morning, Bennaſkar appeared with a clouded viſage. "What," ſaid I, my lord, "is the cauſe of your grief? Shall not Mahoud ſhare alike with you the ſmiles and the frowns of Alla?"

"Is it not," ſaid Bennaſkar, "O Mahoud, the full of the moon?" "It is," replied I, with a ſmile; "but doth Bennaſkar intend to change with that fluctuating planet?"

"O Mahoud," ſaid Bennaſkar, " the fate of thy friend is dependant on the caprice of the ſtars; to-night muſt I put thy utmoſt friendſhip to the trial! If Mahoud prove inſincere, then is Bennaſkar curſed among men. If thy heart is not firm now, while there is time, depart. But why ſhould I doubt thee; ſurely Mahoud is of the ſons of the faithful. What muſt I ſay! Leave me, Mahoud, leave me: nay, if thou departeſt, where ſhall I find thy fellow! and the preſence of a friend is neceſſary to my quiet." "Then," anſwered I, "fear not, Bennaſkar; Mahoud may be unhappy, but he cannot be unjuſt. But what is this dreadful trial that obliges Bennaſkar to ſuſpect his friend?" "True," ſaid Bennaſkar, "Mahoud is undeſerving of ſuſpicion; let us wait till the ſun ſink from the ſkies, and the ſtars return with their glimmering light."

' Bennaſkar then proceeded to the bath, and arrayed himſelf in a coſtly robe, and deſired me to do the ſame. I obeyed my friend, and we met in the ſaloon together. "Alas," ſaid Bennaſkar, as we met, " how can I requeſt my friend to wear the image of deformity?" "What image of deformity," ſaid I, " muſt Mahoud wear? All appearances are to Mahoud alike, and the ſeverer the trial, the more ſhall I commend thy friendſhip."

"Then,"

"Then," said Bennaskar, pulling out a pot of black ointment, "thou must suffer me to disguise thy face with this ointment; Mahoud to-night must personate a black slave." "Is such a trifle," said I, "the test of friendship! give me the ointment, and furnish me with the habit of a slave."

"The habit," answered Bennaskar, "is ready, and all is ready; but you must not as yet disguise yourself, lest my slaves observe us. Come, let us for the present enjoy ourselves, and when night approaches Bennaskar will rely on the friendship of Mahoud." The slaves then brought us the costly viands of Delly, but Bennaskar remained pensive, and seemed not to relish the dainties before him.

'I endeavoured all I could to divert his melancholy; I smiled; I sang before him; the dancers were introduced, and the music attempted to dissipate his gloom; but Bennaskar still remained mute, and his thoughts could not be recalled by the entertainment of his slaves. The music continued till night, when Bennaskar commanded the slaves to withdraw, and, taking a lamp in his hand, he led me through a long variety of apartments.'

"Mahoud," said he, as we went along, "has never yet seen the wonders of my palace." "Mahoud," answered I, "is happy, my lord, to see the wealth of his friend; but he is not inquisitive to explore, unbidden, the secrets of another. 'As I said this, we arrived at a small vaulted room, from the centre of which hung a lamp, which Bennaskar trimmed, and put out that which he held in his hand.'

"Now," said he, "Mahoud, enter that closet which is opposite us, and put on the slave's dress which you will find there, and anoint thy face and thy hands with this black ointment."—"I immediately obeyed Bennaskar, and in a short time I came forth arrayed like a slave."

"Kind Mahoud," said Bennaskar, "thou art excellently disguised; now obey with silence, and stand as a mute before his lord." I folded my arms, and nodded assent, at which Bennaskar smiled.

"Take hold, Mahoud," said he, "of that ring of iron, which is fastened to the middle of the floor, and pull." I obeyed, and a little trap-door came up. I looked down, and perceived a woman in rich vestments, half buried in the earth. I shuddered at the sight, and was falling backward, when Bennaskar struck me with a chabouc*, which he drew from his bosom, and said—" Villain, if thou fail me I shall use thee as my slave." Although I was enraged at the blow, yet I remembered my promise, and returned to the trap door. "Slave," said Bennaskar, "dig that female out of the ground, the spade and the mattock are hidden under the floor."

'I immediately jumped down, and found the tools, and began to work; but neither my fear nor my labour could prevent my fixing my eyes on the lovely female, who seemed as one dead. As soon as I had removed the earth from the female, which I did with great care, Bennaskar commanded me to lift the body into the apartment, gave me a phial of clear blue liquor, and ordered me to pour it into her mouth, while he retired into the closet.

'I willingly obeyed Bennaskar, and hastened to pour down the liquor, while Bennaskar retired. As soon as the liquor was down, the lovely female began to move, and in a short time she opened her languishing eyes, and, casting them upon me, she shrieked out, and, clapping her hands together, she cried—" O Alla, defend me!"

'Bennaskar at the same time spoke as follows, from the closet where he was concealed—

"Hemjunah," said he, "are you as yet disposed to yield yourself to the will of Bennaskar, or must we still experience the evils of opposite enchantment;

* A chabouc is a large whip.

for although Macoma will not permit me to see you without depriving you of sensation, and me of desire, yet will Ulin still subject you to her imperial will."

"Wretch!" answered the fair stranger, "I fear not the powers of your accursed magic, for Macoma has assured me, that you shall not be able to overpower me without my own consent; and Mahomet, though for a time he permits this enchantment, will at length assuredly deliver me."

"Then," answered Bennaskar, "must the lash of compulsion issue forth.—Here," continued he, "slave Mahoud, inflict fifty lashes on that obdurate female."

'I took the chabouc from Bennaskar, and began, with trembling, my ill-fated task, cursing inwardly my own blind compliance, in promising to obey a monster, and not a friend.

'As the lash touched the beauteous Hemjunah, she made the vaulted roof re-echo with her cries; nor did my heart feel less sensibly the strokes I gave than her own: the tears trickled down my cheeks, and I prayed inwardly to be delivered from the cursed task, and was never more happy than when it was completed.

"What," said Bennaskar, from the closet, "what doth Hemjunah now say to my desires?" "The hardhearted and the cruel," said Hemjunah, faintly, "are the last to win the soft affections of a female heart; rather let me die than be the property of the vile Bennaskar." "If so," said he, coming from the closet, "die; for the present I resign my power; let Macoma hide thee again in the dust of the earth."

'Bennaskar did no sooner appear, than the beautiful Hemjunah again seemed to die away; and immediately a hissing noise was heard, and an ugly dwarf arose from the trap-door, and took the body of Hemjunah, replacing it in the earth, and the trap-door was closed with a roaring noise.

'Bennaskar

'Bennaskar then beckoned me to follow him; and he led me to the bath, and bid me wash, and after return to the saloon in my proper vestments.

'I was so surprised at the wonders which I had seen, that I hardly knew what I did. However, in the bath I had time to recollect myself; but recollection was of little service, for reflection rather increased than cleared my confusion. One moment I resolved to apply to the cadi, and declare every circumstance of the horrid adventure. The next, I was awed by the thoughts of my rash and imprudent vows of secresy. "Bennaskar," said I, "has for a month appeared as an angel before me; but one base action has deformed all his former purity. How can I reconcile these inconsistencies? Can he, who is the tenderest, the best of friends, be also the vilest and most cruel of mankind? Is there not enchantment employed against him, and may not this phantom be employed to destroy him? What," said I again, recollecting myself, "can aught excuse such horrid barbarity, exercised upon the most perfect of her sex! What cruelties have I not seen; nay, and been forced, through my own imprudence, to transact! How did my heart bleed within me at her piercing cries? how did it curse the hands which were the base ministers of such unmanly cruelty! I have been accessary to the torture of a most beautiful female; one too, who called on the perfect Alla to deliver her. I have been the instrument of a mean revenge on an helpless woman, and now I yet delay to inform the cadi of the villainies of this house of enchantment."

'I resolved immediately to repair to the cadi, and give him a full information of the sorceries of Bennaskar. I hastened out of the bath, threw my vestments over me, and advanced to the door. "But," said I, as I went along, "what am I about to do! I shall forfeit my faith, without serving the distressed. Bennaskar expects me in the saloon; and when he
finds,

finds that I am gone forth, he will, by the power of his art, secrete the beautiful female from the eyes of the cadi. I have been the guest of Bennaskar a month, and never, till this day, did I perceive the rooms through which I was led to that detestable act of cruelty : nay, Bennaskar himself was obliged to wait; he was impatient till the full of the moon, and oppressed with sorrow and care when it arose. I will, therefore, for the present, return to Bennaskar, will put on the face of chearfulness, and make my countenance to shine before him."

' Bennaskar met me on my return. " From whence cometh Mahoud?" said he, " I am just," answered I, " risen from the bath, and I come to meet my friend Bennaskar." " Mahoud," answered Bennaskar, " art thou faithful, and wilt thou ever remain faithful to thy friend?"

' The words of Bennaskar embarrassed me, and not daring to answer otherwise, I said—" Why doth my lord doubt the sincerity of my heart?"

" Mahoud then," returned he, " is faithful?" " He is," answered I, " but with an unwilling heart." " I doubt not," continued Bennaskar, " but my friend is amazed at the scene he lately beheld ; but ask no explanations, let thy mouth be ever closed to seek or reveal."

" Then," answered I, " you doubt the faithfulness of Mahoud, else why may not I know the meaning of the wonders I have seen?"

" The age of thy friendship," said Bennaskar, " is a month, and wouldst thou be admitted in so short a time to all the secrets of my heart? Forbear, rash youth! and soar not at the sun, while thy fluttering pinions will not lift thee over the tops of the mountains. A well-tried friend is Bennaskar's joy ; but woes and death are in the paths of his enemies."

' As he said this, he frowned and left me ; and I retired to my chamber, irresolute in my mind. As I entered my chamber, I perceived a small book open on a desk before the burning lamps. I went up to it, and found it was the Koran of our holy law. Being little desirous of sleep, I sat down; and as I read concerning the holy cow, methought I saw the name of Mahoud in the book.

'Startled at the vision, I looked again, and read distinctly these words—

"Mahoud! Mahoud! Mahoud! There is much good in the world; but there is more evil: the good is the gift of Alla, but the evil is the choice of his creatures. Because of man's sin, and because of the darkness of his heart, do the evil Genii and the enchantments of wickedness prevail. Even now is Mahoud in the house of a magician, to whom he is imprudently bound by the ties of honour: to draw back is meanness, but to persist is sin. When men act wrong, they subject themselves to the power of a wicked race; and we, who are the guardians of morality, cannot interpose, but in proportion to their remorse. Taken by the crafty dissimulation of Bennaskar, thy easy soul gave into his snares, and thy prudence was decoyed by the voice of his mouth. Thou hast promised, at all events, not to reveal the secrets of his house, and thou hast unknowingly joined thyself in the fellowship of the wicked. But can man, who is bound to the service of Alla by an unalterable law, dispose of himself against the will of his Maker? or, can the worm of earth, the property of Heaven, set up itself against the hand that formed it? Had Mahoud engaged to conceal every thing but what the law of Mahomet obliged him to reveal, he had behaved wisely; but he who walketh in darkness, will undoubtedly fall into the pit. Past errors cannot be recalled, and Mahoud must learn the wisdom of experience. Under the resemblance of the Koran behold the Genius Macoma instructs thine heart. I perceive evil will attend thee, if thou dost attempt the enlargement of the princess of Cassimir; and yet without it, thou must still continue the servant

vant of cruelty and oppression. Choose, therefore, for yourself: if injured innocence can move thee, boldly suffer in the cause of truth, and take this book in thy bosom, which shall at all times admit thee to a sight of the princess; if not, be still the slave of the enemy of thy prophet."

'After this, I looked again on the book, but found I could read no more; however, I doubted not to engage in the service of the princess; and therefore, taking the book in my bosom, and the lamp in my hand, I went toward the saloon, supposing that Bennaskar was asleep. I searched for the rooms through which I had passed before, and soon perceived the vaulted apartment at the end of them.

'I hastened to take up the trap-door, and touching the princess Hemjunah with the book, I essayed to deliver her from her miserable confinement. The princess awakened at the touch of the book; but, at the sight of me, shrieked aloud, and I feared lest her cries should awaken Bennaskar. I assured her that I was sent by the Genius Macoma to effect her deliverance, and that I abhorred every kind of crulty which I had practised upon her.

"Alas!" said she, still shrieking at intervals, "your story betrays your wickedness; I never before saw you, unless you are, as I suspect, the magician Bennaskar, under some feigned appearance: but rest assured, vile man! that no deceit or cruelty shall ever make me the creature of Bennaskar. I will ever persist in my hatred of you, and I am assured that you cannot defile or destroy me."

"Most adorable Princess Hemjunah!" said I, prostrating myself before her, "let me beseech you to hear me: I am not Bennaskar, nor a creature of Bennaskar's, but the servant of the Genius Macoma, who has instructed me, by means of this holy book (which I then pulled out), to attempt your rescue, and I am willing to lay down my life for your safety. You have not indeed seen me in my present character, but this very

very night was I brought hither by Bennaskar, under the similitude of a slave, and forced, through a most accursed oath, to inflict the severest tortures on the most delicate of her sex."

"Wretch!" said the princess, "I am now convinced of thy perfidy, allowing thine own account to be true; for what promise could bind thee to a cruel action, or why wast thou afraid to suffer thyself, rather than make an innocent virgin the subject of thy cruelties? But if thou art truly the servant of Macoma, and ashamed of thy late inhuman deeds, quit the house of the vile Bennaskar, and inform the cadi of his cruelties and sorceries."

"Rather," said I, "my princess, let me dig around you, and release you from this miserable confinement."
"That," said the princess, "you cannot do, unless you are indeed, as I suspect, the wretch Bennaskar; for by his command alone can I be released. O fool that I was," continued she, with tears, "to listen for a moment to the falsities of man!"

"If my information," said I, "O lovely Hemjunah, will avail, this moment will I fly to the cadi, and acquaint him with your distress." I then hastened to go; but O, judge my terror and amazement, when I saw Bennaskar moving through the apartments which led to the vaulted chamber!

'As he advanced, Hemjunah shrieked, and I was ready to sink: though my intentions were just and good, yet was I terrified by his appearance; so much was I sunk by the rash promise which I had made; and I every moment expected the dreadful effects of his powerful malice.

'As Bennaskar entered the vaulted chamber, I shrunk back with fear, and dared not lift up my eyes; but my terror was soon quieted, when I saw him fall prostrate at my feet. I then no longer doubted but that the Genius Macoma supported me, and attributed his behaviour to her supernatural power.

"O Mahoud,"

"O Mahoud," said Bennaskar, "the friend of my bosom, the partner of my secrets; although the power of love has not the rule in thine heart, yet pity those who are the slaves of its dominion; if the lovely Princess of Cassimir did but know the purity of my heart, the————."

"Hear not the villain!" said Hemjunah, "O servant of Macoma, unless he release me from this detested place; me he hath already deceived, and you will be subjected likewise to his power, unless the prudent spirit of Macoma direct thee."

"Then," said Bennaskar, rising up, and laying bare his bosom—"Here, Mahoud, strike, and end my miseries, and the miseries of Hemjunah; but never will Bennaskar consent to lose the treasure of his heart."

"I will not," answered I, "lift up my private arm against thy life, but I shall deliver thee to the power of the cadi, who is the deputy of the great Alla's vicegerent."

"Give me then," said the Princess of Cassimir, "the book of the Genius Macoma, that I may be defended from the insults and contrivances of the base Bennaskar." The request of the princess appeared so reasonable, that I obeyed her, and put the book into her hands.

'Bennaskar, when I was leaving the vaulted chamber, besought me not to destroy the friend that had supported me; but I told him that Alla was to be obeyed rather than man. I hastened to the cadi; but, as it was night, his officers told me I could not be heard, till I informed them that I had in my power a wicked magician, who by his sorceries had stolen the Princess Cassimir. When they heard this, they acquainted the cadi, and that vigilant magistrate arose, and followed me to the house of Bennaskar with his guard. As I entered the house of Bennaskar, I was amazed to see him standing in the entrance with a lamp in his hand: but my astonishment increased,

increased, when I saw him fall down before the cadi, and confess his guilt.

'The cadi commanded the guards to seize him, and then ordered him to lead us to the place where he had concealed the Princess of Cassimir. Bennaskar obeyed; but as he went through the apartments, he said to me—"Mahoud, you are sensible, that the Princess Hemjunah's body is half buried in the earth, and uncovered, therefore prevail upon the cadi, that he suffer us to go before and release her; for my part, my sins oppress me, and I wish to restore to her dignity a much-injured princess."

"If," said I, "you will promise to release the princess, I will endeavour to prevail on the cadi to permit what you propose; but otherwise, let the whole world be a witness of your accursed malice." "O my friend," said Bennaskar," accuse me not, my own heart persecutes me sufficiently; yes, Mahoud," continued he, "I will, as you require me, release the princess, and trust to the mercy of the cadi; for the service of the evil Genii will neither bring me profit nor peace."

'I was pleased at this repentance of Bennaskar, and besought the cadi that he would suffer us to enter the first vaulted chamber, and recover the princess from her enchantment. The cadi acquiesced in my proposal, but ordered the guards to surround the entrance, while Bennaskar and myself entered the chamber.

'As soon as we were entered, Bennaskar seized me suddenly by the throat, and before I could speak or recollect myself, he dragged me into the closet, and shut the door after us.

"Now," said he, "villain! receive the just rewards of a perjured heart." Saying this, he spit in my face, and threw me on the ground, and then flew out of the closet, shutting the door forcibly after him. I remained for some moments stupified by my fall; but after a time arose, and opening the closet, I was surprized to see neither the Princess of Cassimir, nor the magician Bennaskar.

'While I was in this confusion, the cadi and his guards being impatient at our stay, entered the chamber, and the cadi commanded his guards to seize me, saying—"Villain, where is the Princess of Cassimir, and the man who revealed thy unrighteous actions?"

'At this I began to answer; when, O accursed fortune! I perceived my voice was as the voice of Bennaskar. I immediately looked on my cloaths, and found them changed. In short, I doubted not but that my malicious foe had transformed me into his own appearance.

'I fell at the feet of the cadi, and besought him one moment to hear me: I acquainted him with every circumstance of my adventures, from my entrance into the house of Bennaskar, till that present moment. But he and his guards laughed at my tale; however, in a few moments he grew more cool, and commanded me to deliver up my friend and the Princess of Cassimir. In vain did I call Alla to witness the truth of my story. The cadi was enraged at my persisting in the tale, and ordered his guards to give me an hundred strokes with the chabouc.

'To add to my misfortune, Bennaskar appeared at one end of the room, and when I cried out, and pointed to him, the cadi, who saw him not, thinking that I meant to mock him, ordered me another hundred lashes with the chabouc. Vexed with myself, and subdued by the pains of my punishment, I fell on the ground, and my guards were ordered to carry me to the prison, where I was thrown into a deep dungeon, loaded with chains.

'The next morning I was brought out again before the cadi, and carried into the public hall of justice. The cadi there passed judgment upon me, that I should be burnt alive the next day, unless I delivered up Mahoud and the Princess of Cassimir. Finding it in vain to repeat my declarations, that I was the real Mahoud,

Mahoud, and that I suffered through the vile enchantments of Bennaskar, I remained silent; but this was construed into surliness, and I was ordered five hundred bastinadoes to make me speak. I therefore begged the cadi to conceive what I could possibly answer; supposing my tale to be true, I had, I said, suffered severely for my rash promise to Bennaskar, and I must submit to my fate.

'The cadi then commanded me to be carried back to the dungeon, and that a large pile of wood should be raised in the market place, whereon I might be burnt the next morning, before all the people. I spent the night in the utmost horror, and earnestly wished that the sun might never more behold my sorrows. But yet the night passed away as usual, and the stars fled from the face of day, and I beheld the dreadful morning of my execution.

'A tumultuous crowd were gathered together before the door of the dungeon, to see me pass to my execution; and I was dragged along, the common people nearly overwhelming me with stones. As I advanced to the pile, I perceived the cadi and his officers were seated before it, and that magistrate commanded me to be brought again before him ere I was bound to the pile.'

"Art thou," said he, as I approached him, "art thou, wretched magician, willing to bring forth the princess, or thy friend, who are concealed by thy wicked arts, or must the sentence of our law be executed upon thee?"

"O judge," said I, "since my tale will not gain credit with thee, at least let me know by whose accusation it is that I am brought before thee, and who is it that that accuses me of magic or sorcery? Am not I Bennaskar, the wealthy merchant of Delly, and where are my accusers? Who dare say aught against my fame? You came into my house by night, you seized my person, you inflicted on me the punishment of a slave, you cast me into a dungeon, and condemned me to the flames, and all this without the appearance of a single witness against me: wherefore, O cadi, I appeal unto the righteous sultan of the east, and I hope my fellow-citizens will not suffer me to be executed, while no proofs of guilt are brought against me."

"Young man," answered the cadi, "your appeal is unnecessary, for I am not desirous of destroying my fellow-creatures without a cause. Your plea were just and proper, did not your own confession contradict your present assertion. Yesterday you declared that you was not Bennaskar, and to-day you say you are; wherefore, out of your own lips I have convicted you of falsity; whereas, had you really been Bennaskar the merchant, and not a magician, there had been no need of two different accounts of yourself."

' The people hearing this distinction of the cadi, applauded their judge; and one and all cried out, that I was a magician, and deserved the flames. The guards were then ordered to bind me on the pile, and I was led up and fixed to a post by the chains which had been fastened on my body the day before; and now amidst the acclamations of the people was the pile kindled, and the smoke and the flame surrounded the unfortunate Mahoud.

' In a moment the crowd and the heavens disappeared from my sight, and I found myself in the body of a toad, at the bottom of the pile. I hopped forward out of the flames, and with difficulty hid myself beneath a stone in the street. The crowd having waited till the pile was consumed, carried the ashes out of the city, and scattered them in the air, and I remained till night beneath the stone.

' It was my intention as soon as it was dark, to creep out of the city into the woods, but sleep overtook me at the time when animals retire to their rest; and when I awaked in the morning, I found myself in this forest, where I remained, during the space of a moon, alone, till these two, the miserable companions of my solitude, were joined unto me.'

'Your adventures, O Mahoud,' said the sultan of India, 'are wonderful, and an excellent lesson of caution and prudence to us who are joined in one common fate; and since I perceive both your misfortunes, and my own, have been brought about by want of trust and prudence, I shall, with the utmost resignation, acknowledge, that the all perfect Alla is ever willing to assist those who are not wanting to themselves.

'But, O Mahoud, suffer me, ere I declare my own griefs, to ask what is become of the lovely Hemjunah, the Princess of Cassimir; nor wonder at my solicitude, for the mention of her name brings to my memory the ideas of the past. How was it possible, that lovely fair-one should be betrayed into the power of those wicked enchanters! but why should I be surprized at her weakness, who am myself the object of their malice? Surely,' continued the sultan, 'this our companion, whom you called princess, cannot be the daughter of Zebenezer, the Sultan of Cassimir?''

'You are right, indeed, in your conjectures,' answered Mahoud: 'the Princess of Cassimir is a fellow-sufferer with us? and he who is on my right-hand is Horam, the favourite of Misnar, the Lord of Delly.'

'What,' said Misnar, transported, and yet at the same time recoiling with surprize, 'is my faithful Horam, also, the unfortunate partner of my griefs? Then is Misnar indeed, as the leaf of autumn, as a feather in the winds of oppression.' Horam understanding that his lord was before him, made such acknowledgements of his respect as his hideous form would permit: and Mahoud, when he perceived that he had been speaking to the Sultan of India, followed the example of the Vizir Horam.

Misnar then, turning to the Princess of Cassimir, said—

'O princess, whom a severe enchantment has deprived of the most exquisite of all forms, to load thee with the most wretched, permit me to request an account of your unfortunate labours, since you left the court of your father Zebenezer; that at least I may indulge my wishes for your recovery, though my arm is too weak to work either my own or your enlargement.'

'Most illustrious sultan,' answered the Princess Hemjunah. 'I shall obey your commands, although the remembrance of my misfortune is grievous, and the confession of my indiscretion must fill me with shame.'

'It is enough, O princess,' said the sultan, 'to confess our faults to Heaven, and he is the weakest of the sons of earth, who takes pleasure to hear the failings of others.'—'I thank Alla,' returned the princess, 'that my indiscretions are not such as my sultan suspects; they were indeed the causes of my misfortunes, but such as the youth of our sex are very likely to commit.'

'The brighter the jewel,' answered Misnar, 'the more conspicuous is the speck that deforms it; and the slenderer the twig, the more easily is it shaken by the motion of the air. There is a delicacy and a splendour in the female sex, which makes every error more glaring and hurtful. But I doubt not the prudence of the Princess of Cassimir; her own humility may esteem that a crime which all the world beside will rank among her perfections.'

'O sultan,' replied Hemjunah, 'your politeness cannot extenuate, though it may gloss over my imprudence; and while I am delaying to unfold my little history to you, my crime may seem more black, while hidden, than when it shall be revealed.' As the princess uttered these words, a dervise, worn with age,

age, and bowed down by the years of infirmity, appeared among the thickets of the forest. Horam immediately recollected the features of the good old saint, and said—'My royal master, yonder is Shemshelnar, the most pious worshipper of Alla among all the sons of Asia.'—'I do not recollect his features,' answered Misnar: 'came he not to the council of our divan?' 'No, my royal lord,' said Horam, 'the oppressions of age were upon him.'

By this time Shemshelnar arrived at the place where the transformed company were seated; and falling prostrate before Misnar, he said—

'Wonder not, O prince of India, that Shemshelnar, thy slave, doth thus acknowledge his prince, though deformed by the enchantments of the wicked. Yes, prince,' continued Shemshelnar, 'I knew the evils that surrounded thee; and although I was unable to attend thy council, yet I prayed in secret to Him who bestoweth at the noon-day, that he would avert from my royal master the misfortunes which threatened to overpower him. Alla heard my prayer, as I lay prostrate in my cell, and the Genius Bahoudi appearing, commanded me to seek thee in the forest of Tarapajan, whither thy wayward fortune should lead thee.'—"O Genius," replied I, "how shall age and infirmity comply with thy commands?"

"Go," said Bahoudi, touching me with his finger, "for strength is given thee from above. The Enchantress Ulin hath transformed thy prince into the most hideous reptile of the earth. But wonder not at the deformity of his appearance, nor at the malice of her who has overpowered him; for such is the fate of those who are most exalted in their virtues, that their enemies, whenever occasion is given them, will strive to render them most odious. Thy prince will be, ere you arrive in the forest, surrounded by three others in equal affliction; it is permitted thee to rescue the Sultan of India, but the rest must wear the chains of the enchantress, till Ulin is no more."

'But

'But ere I restore thee, O sultan of my heart,' continued Shemshelnar, such are the words which the Genius hath commanded me to utter before thee—

'Religion, O Misnar, is the first and the greatest duty of life, and the service of Alla and his prophet the sweetest offering of a grateful heart. But he who appointed the ceremonies and services of piety and devotion, hath also given to all their respective stations in the warfare of life. How then shall we pay honour to Alla, if by complying with the fantastical pilgrimages of the devotees, we neglect and desert the peculiar duties of that post wherein Alla hath placed us! the signet of Mahomet, O prince, of which Mangelo the prophet did prophesy, is it not that seal which the faithful bear on their frontlets, when they obey the voice of reason and religion? and the girdle of Opakka, with which Kifri the enchanter is endued, what is it but foresight and prudence, the best allies of the sultans of the earth! To save his people, my prince hath deserted them, and given away what he sought to keep. When Alla placed thee on the throne of India, from thence he expected to hear thy petitions; but as faults which proceed from goodness, though uninstructed, are beheld with Heaven's piteous eye, therefore rise, O sultan,' said Shemshelnar, and touched him, 'rise from the filth of the earth, and become again endued with the glories with which Alla hath endued thee; and know, that such is the care of Mahomet over thee, that he hath curbed the hands of thine enemies, and bids thee go forth against them, assured of this, that they shall not be able by their enchantments to foresee thy designs, nor to overpower thee by the help of their magical deceits, unless thou yield to their snares. Be prudent and vigilant, and fear them not. Only this is permitted against thee, if thou canst not overpower and destroy them unawares, they may use their art to conceal their escape, and avoid thy arm; therefore be

bold

bold and quick, and yet cautious and discerning, lest when force avail not, they employ fraud to destroy thee.'

The Continuation of the Tale of the Enchanters; or, Misnar the Sultan of the East.

AS Shemshelnar finished these words, Misnar arose in his just proportion: but ere he spake to the holy dervise who had released him, he fell prostrate, and adored the goodness of Alla, and of Mahomet his prophet, who had thus rescued him from the power of Ulin. Then rising, he took Shemshelnar by the hand, and thanked him for his release and advice.

'Thou hast done right, O Misnar,' said the dervise, 'to give the greatest honour to Alla: for to him alone belongs all honour, and Shemshelnar is the slave of Mahomet, thy prophet.'—'And what,' continued the sultan, must I not hope that it will please the great prophet of the faithful to release also these my fellow-sufferers?'

'Misnar alone can release them,' answered the dervise. 'Let Ulin perish, and these unfortunate persons shall be restored to thee and themselves: but in the mean time they must learn to bear their misfortunes with patience, and offer their prayers for thy safety. The road to Delly is through this desart forest, and to the left is situated the palace of Ulin. She is already acquainted of thy transformation, and is studying to deceive thee a second time: but beware, O Misnar! for if she prevail, death and destruction await thee.' Misnar having received the instructions of the dervise, took leave of his companions; assuring them that he was desirous of meeting the crafty Ulin as soon as possible, that he might either give up all pretensions to his kingdom, or deliver his subjects and his friends from the hands of the enchantress.

The sultan of the Indies having left the dervise and his friends, advanced into the forest, chewing
some

some leaves which Shemshelnar had given him to support him till he should arrive at his palace. He had not advanced more than two days' journey in the forest, before he heard the violent shrieks of a distressed woman; and at a distance saw four ruffians stripping a lady, and beating her inhumanly.

Misnar was enraged at what he saw, and flying to the lady's assistance, he bid the ruffians defend themselves. The ruffians, leaving the lady, chose not to encounter the arm of Misnar, but fled; and the prince stepping up to the lady, desired to know by what accident she fell thus alone into the hands of the robbers.

' O, noble Sir,' said the lady, in tears, ' for I perceive by your mien I speak to no common friend, it was my fate to be beloved by the handsomest of the sons of the faithful. I lived in Delly, the daughter of an emir; and Hazar, the captain of a thousand in the armies of Misnar, the sultan of the east, was my admirer; but, alas! his love has proved my destruction. The second son of the great Dabulcombar, being assisted by Ulin the enchantress, aspired to his brother's throne; and the soldiers, who loved the hazardous chance of war, deserted frequently from Misnar our sultan: among the rest, Hazar, in spite of my utmost endeavours, revolted with his thousand men.'

" There is no preferment," said he, " in the peaceful reign of Misnar. I will follow the fortunes of his brother, whose throne must be gained and supported by arms."—' In vain I remonstrated and urged both love and duty.'—" My love," said Hazar, " is still unalterable: thou wilt soon see me return the favourite of the new monarch; and it will then be in my power to raise thee to higher dignities than those which thy father now possesses."

' Hazar then left me by night, and soon I heard that he had joined the rebel army: but, O generous stranger! what was my grief, when I understood that

Ulin,

Ulin, the detestable enchantress, was stricken with his appearance, and had invited him to her bed! I set out without delay for the camp, and studying to avoid the army of Misnar, travelled through this wood with four attendants; but ere the second day of my journey was past, I was seized by two satyrs of the wood, and my retinue were left behind me. The satyrs hurried me along till the night overshadowed us, and then brought me, through many dark and intricate windings, to a palace which was illuminated with ten thousand lamps. "Now," said they, "aspiring mistress of Hazar, enter, and behold thy paramour."

' Immediately I was led into a magnificent hall, and from that into a second; where, on a throne of silver, sat Hazar, the perfidious Hazar, with the hideous Ulin by his side. My rage was so great, that I forgot my situation; and calling aloud, I said—" O cursed Hazar, thou rebel both to love and duty, canst thou prefer that detested wretch to these arms, which have received thee and thy plighted faith?"

' Ulin hearing my rage, burst into a loud fit of laughing. "It is well done, O sweet mistress of Hazar," said she; "I sent for you to divert me, and you well answer my expectation: the possession of this lovely youth were nothing, was not I assured that he preferred my substantial pleasures to your empty and imaginary joys; yes, sweet creature," continued she, " satiate thine eyes with the lovely prospect of him you so much admire."—' So saying, the ugly wretch threw her arms round Hazar; and that deceitful and dishonourable rebel returned her caresses.

' This cruel treatment made me swoon. When I recovered, I found myself alone in a filthy apartment; where, I suppose, I had been ordered by the cruel enchantress. The next day I was dragged into the same hall, to hear the taunts of the enchantress, and to see the most faithless of a faithless sex. Being desirous of knowing by what method I was conveyed
away,

away, I pretended again to fwoon, and fell again on the ground; when Ulin commanded that none fhould approach to recover me. "Let her continue there," faid the enchantrefs, "till my lovely Hazar and I quit the hall, and then drag her into the mean apartments which are beneath the palace."—' Still feigning my fwoon, the flaves, foon after Ulin and Hazar were departed, drew me forth, and cafting me into my hole, they left me to my fate.

' As foon as they were gone, I endeavoured to find out fome paffage that might lead to day-light; and after much trouble and fear, and paffing through feveral dark entries, I arrived at the foot of a ftair-cafe, which led up into a yard belonging to the palace. On the top of this ftair-cafe I fat till night, and then ventured forth, refolving rather to die than continue in that detefted place. Having croffed the yard, I this morning came to a deep ditch, or canal, which I perceived wound round the palace; and I make no doubt but that all accefs or recefs from this palace muft be over a bridge which was guarded, as I perceived when I was led by the fatyrs of the wood.

' As I had learned to fwim in the women's baths which were in my father's palace, I refolved rather to run the rifque of my life, than to be kept a prifoner in Ulin's palace; and therefore boldly threw myfelf into the canal, and, fear giving me ftrength, I croffed the water in a fhort time. Being now arrived at the farther fide, I ftruck into the thickeft part of the foreft, and wandered about for fome time till morning, when on a fudden I heard feveral voices among the trees. In an inftant four ruffians furrounded me, and had not your powerful alarm interpofed, I had fuffered the vileft of deaths, or what is worfe than death itfelf.'

Mifnar endeavoured to comfort the afflicted ftranger; and afked her whether fhe thought it poffible for any man to enter the palace of Ulin undifcovered. ' If,' anfwered fhe, ' I was able to get out without moleftation,

moleftation, doubtlefs the fame method will give you an opportunity of entering it.'

The Sultan Mifnar feemed in doubt as fhe fpoke.

'O fultan,' faid fhe, 'let me prevail upon you to follow me, and I will enfure your fuccefs.'

Mifnar recovering from his mufing pofture, befought her to walk before, and fhew him the path which led to the palace. 'We fhall reach it by night,' faid the ftranger, 'when the darknefs fhall protect thee.' The beautiful ftranger then went forward, and Mifnar followed at her heels.

Ere they had proceeded twenty paces, Mifnar faid,—'It will be proper, O fair ftranger, to draw my fcymitar, left we be fet upon fuddenly by the robbers.'—'You are right,' anfwered the fair ftranger: 'and your precaution is juft.'

The Sultan Mifnar having drawn his fabre, followed clofe behind the beautiful ftranger, and fuddenly with a blow fmote her on the fhoulder, and felled her to the ground.

The fair ftranger was no fooner fallen, than her countenance changed; her foft, plump cheeks, fell in two bags from the bones, the forehead and the temples were contracted with wrinkles, and the jaws, parting as with age and infirmity, difcovered to Mifnar the features of the malicious Enchantrefs Ulin; who, though nearly fpent and exhaufted by the blow, yet lived to utter the following imprecations—

'May the curfe of our fex light upon thee, thou traitor to manhood! fince neither the charms, nor the afflictions of the fair, have been able to foften thine heart. Thou haft, indeed, avoided my fnares, by doing violence to the nobleft of paffions, and by trampling on the moft facred laws of humanity and hofpitality. Idiot that I was, to truft myfelf to thee, though guarded by the ftrongeft appearances of innocence and diftrefs! The injured and the helplefs can find no protection in thy government, though thou boafteft thyfelf the delegate of Alla, and the friend of the oppreſſed; and I, truſting to thy ſpecious virtues, am fallen a ſacrifice to thy deceitful heart. Since Alla is the guardian of ſuch hypocriſy, I now diſclaim his authority as much upon principle as heretofore I have braved his vengeance, that I might live free from his laws.'

'Hold, O wretched inſtrument of ſin,' ſaid Miſnar; 'and ere thou quitteſt that mortal ſeat of wickedneſs, hear Him juſtified whom thou denieſt, and underſtand how thine own arts were diſcovered to me. That four ruffians ſhould quit their prey at the ſight of one man, did firſt ſtagger my credulity, and I expected at leaſt to find them return, and revenge my interpoſition; but when no one appeared to interrupt my ſecurity, I then began moſt to fear, and liſten to thy tale, as one who expected to be enſnared by the wiles of thy hypocriſy. Thy tale, though artful, did happily contradict itſelf. Thy diſhevelled garments were diſpoſed in ſuch an artful manner, as to excite deſire rather than ſhame; they were alſo dry and clean, and contradicted your words, when you pretended you had ſwam acroſs the canal. This ſtrengthened my doubts, which you at length confirmed, by calling me, at the latter part of your hiſtory, *ſultan*. Then fled my doubt, and certainty ſucceeded: I feared to follow, and yet reſolved to revenge; and Alla, in mercy, gave ſucceſs to my arm'—— Here Miſnar broke off; for her iniquitous ſpirit was fled from the body of Ulin, and the ſultan left her mangled and deformed corpſe a prey to the beaſts of the foreſt.

He travelled for ſeveral days backward, hoping to find the former companions of his miſery; and at laſt came to the place which he had left, but could find no ſigns of them: wherefore, concluding that their enchantment was broken by the death of Ulin, the ſultan returned towards Delly, ſubſiſting on the leaves which the derviſe had given him, and on the fruits of the earth; and in twelve days time arrived

at

at a small town in his own dominions. Here he lodged at a poor cottage, and where he found an old woman and her son, and enquired whether she could procure him any horses or mules to carry him the next morning to Delly.

'Alas,' answered the old woman, 'we have no cattle with us; the army has stripped us of all.'—'What,' answered Misnar, 'has the rebel army been foraging so near Delly?'

'Alack,' said the old woman, 'I think all armies are rebels, for my part. Indeed, the soldiers told us that they were the sultan's army, and that they were sent to guard us from the rebels; but in the mean time they took our cattle and provision, and paid us nothing for them; and still, every time they came, they called themselves our guardians and friends. If this is all the friendship great men can shew us, we poor people should be best pleased to live as far from them as we can.'

Misnar, although he smiled at the poor woman's manner of delivery, was yet affected at the substance of her speech; and lifting up his eyes and hands secretly to Heaven, as she went out for sticks to kindle a fire to dress his provisions, he said—

'O just and merciful Alla, and thou, faithful prophet of the Highest, I call you both to witness, with how much reluctance I have began this war, and how greatly mine heart is inclined to promote the peace of my subjects; not out of personal fear, as ye, O powers above, can bear me witness! but out of that love and affection which I owe to my people, who, as my children, depend upon me for the blessings they enjoy. O Alla, preserve me from the avarice of ambition! that while the rich and the proud advise me to delight in blood, I may remember the severities which the poor must suffer; and that I may rather rejoice to relieve one oppressed slave, than to enrich ten thousand flattering emirs of my court!'

As soon as the old woman was entered again into her house, the disguised sultan advised her and her neighbours to join in a petition, and present it to the sultan in his divan. 'A petition!' answered the old woman, 'for what?'—'To relieve your distresses,' said Misnar.

'Alas, who is to relieve our distresses but Alla?' said the woman.'—'Your sultan, the servant of Alla, will relieve them,' replied Misnar.

'What!' answered the old woman, 'can he restore to these arms my dutiful first-born, who has been so long the joy of my aged heart, but was lately torn from me, to fill up the armies of the sultan? Can he call back the brave men he has caused to be destroyed, and give life and spirits, and joy again, to the widows and orphans of India? If he can, O let him hasten to relieve the afflicted hearts of his subjects, and become as a god upon earth!

The sultan Misnar was astonished at the words and the gestures of the poor old woman, and deeply stricken by her sensible observations; for he perceived she spoke as she felt, and was animated by the tender subject.

'How seldom,' said he to himself, 'do the rich feel the distresses of the poor! and in the midst of conquest and acclamation, who regardeth the tears and afflictions of those who have lost their private friends in the public service!'

The Sultan Misnar rested that night in the cottage of the old woman, and the next morning he arose and was conducted by her younger son to a town half a day's journey farther. Here he equipped himself with mules, and in one day more reached the city of Delly.

The sultan entered a caravansera, where he found several merchants; he asked them how they dared venture to trade when the armies of the rebels were spread over the face of India.

'As to that,' answered the first merchant, ' we
have

have lived here some time, in expectation that one party or the other would prevail. It little matters to us which, provided trade was encouraged. As to the sultan's party, there was not, till within these few days, any hope of their success. The young man himself was retired from his throne, being fearful of encountering his enemies, and the Captains of the army had destroyed the prime Vizir Horam.'—' And what,' interrupted Misnar, ' is the cause of this change in favour of the sultan?'—' Ten days since,' answered the merchant,' contrary to every one's belief, as we all thought him dead, the Vizir Horam appeared at the head of the army, and assured the officers that his Lord Misnar was living, and had destroyed the Enchantress Ulin, who espoused the cause of his brother Ahubal; that, in consequence of Ulin's death, Ahubal was fled, and his army dispersed, and he expected his royal master would shortly appear among them.' The sultan Misnar was rejoiced at this news, and without delay hastened to the palace of his vizir.

The slaves of Horam seeing the disguised sultan, asked him his business. ' I come,' replied Misnar, ' to communicate to thy lord tidings of our sultan.' At these words, the slaves of Horam conducted Misnar to their master's presence; and Horam no sooner saw his master in the disguise with which he furnished him, than he fell at the sultan's feet, and congratulated him on his safe return.

' My faithful Horam,' said Misnar, ' arise. The day is not yet so far spent, but that my court may be assembled. Give orders, O Horam, that the army be drawn up, and let thy slaves proceed to the palace, and bring the imperial robes: my people require my presence, and Misnar yearns to see the supporters of his throne.'

Horam arose, and the sultan embracing him, said—
' O Heaven, I am desirous of hearing the particulars

of thy fate, but public advantage must not yield to private friendship.'

The faithful Horam then hastened to call together the princes and the vizirs of the court of Delly, and gave orders that the army should be drawn up in the royal square before the divan. The sultan Misnar being arrayed in his imperial robes, delayed not to shew himself to his people; and no sooner did he appear, than his subjects cried out, 'Long live the sultan of our hearts, who alone was able to conquer the powers of enchantment!' The sultan was overjoyed to find his people received him with gladness, and commanded money to be thrown among the populace, and double subsistence to be issued out to his army. The vizirs and officers of justice being assembled in the divan, waited the arrival of their sultan; and Misnar having ascended his throne, commanded Horam to deliver to him a faithful account of his enemies. Horam the vizir then arose from his seat, and assured his sultan that the rebel army was dispersed, and that Ahuhal was fled with a few friends to the shores of the Indian ocean.

The sultan, on this report, commanded his army to be stationed at just intervals, about a day's journey around the city of Delly, and their numbers to be reduced, and that peace should be proclaimed the next day in the city. No sooner were the vizirs dismissed from the divan, than Misnar retiring into his palace, sent for his faithful Vizir Horam, and desired him to give him a true relation of what had happened to him since his departure from the army.

'Royal Sir,' answered Horam, 'you were no soon departed, than I began to inspect the order and the discipline of your troops; to look into the method of providing for the army, and to appoint proper officers, who should take care that the soldiers had sufficient and wholesome provisions; that their tents were good, that the situations of the different battalions

battalions were in healthy places, near springs and rivers, but on dry soils, and as far as possible removed from swampy fens, or the stagnated air of the forests.

'During this time, little occurred of which I could inform my lord, as I meant not to trouble you with my own concerns, lest it should seem that I was proud of the trifling dispositions which I had made in favour of the army.

'The rebels in the mean time were quiet, and their distance only prevented me from destroying them; but on a sudden a messenger arrived, with tidings that all the southern provinces had revolted; that the enchantress Ulin was with them, and conducted their forces; that Ahubal was declared Sultan of India by her, and that she was determined to support his cause. Upon this, I took such precautions as doubtless my sultan must have read in the tablets; but my precautions seemed vain; for the next night we were on a sudden terrified with a second alarm, that the rebels were within half a day's march of our camp, which I thought, considering their former distance, must be the effect of enthantment.

'This threw our officers into the greatest consternation, who collected themselves in a body, came rushing toward the royal tent, and demanded a sight of the sultan, and declared their resolution of revolting to the enemy, unless you headed the troops.

'I was writing dispatches in the royal tent, when I heard their tumult, and my heart fled as they approached; but as they stopped for some time to fix upon one for their speaker, I had just time to slip on a slave's habit, and cut my way through the back side of the tent. I ran as swift as my feet could carry me out of the encampment; and being stopped by several centinels, I told them I was dispatched by the vizir, and shewed them mine own signet.

'But

'But I was no sooner clear of the army, than I repented my folly.'—" What have I done?" said I to myself, "I have deserted my post, and ruined the interest of my lord; better had I died at the head of my sultan's troops, or fell a sacrifice to their rage, than thus ingloriously to perish obscurely! Besides, I have been terrified without just cause; the rebel army may not be so near; I ought to have staid in the tent, and endeavoured to have pacified the officers of the army."

'And now I was in doubt whether to return, or, as I had penetrated thus far, whether it would not be most prudent to take a near survey of the rebel army. I resolved upon the last, and cautiously travelled toward the place where the spies said they were encamped.

'I arrived at the spot described, but saw neither centinels nor encampment. Amazed at this, I proceeded onward during that and the next day, but no army was to be seen, or any thing indicating their approach.

'This made me curse my folly and my credulity. "Alas, Horam," said I to myself, "how little worthy wert thou of the confidence of thy lord! and yet better is this mistake than the certainty of the rebels approach, which could not have been effected without the power of enchantment."—' Ere it was too late, I resolved to return, hoping that I should pacify the troops, by assuring them that I had in person been a witness to the untruth of the last alarm.

'But, alas! when I essayed to return, I found my feet fixed to the ground; and in a moment the earth trembled, and Ulin the enchantress arose on the back of an enormous toad.'

"Wise and sagacious vizir," said she, in an insulting tone, "I admire your prudence and discretion! and although Mahomet and his faithful crew of Genii will not permit us to overpower you, or your prudent master, unless through your own in-

advertency

advertency you fall into our snares, yet there is little to be feared from their interposition, while you become such easy dupes to our artifices. The army which I lead against thy wretched sultan is not less than forty days' march from hence, and is embarrassed by the mountains and the forests, and yet the credulous vizir fled from his charge at the most improbable alarm, and fled into the arms of one who well knows how to reward his prudence and address. Become, therefore, O silly vizir, like the reptile that bears me, and I shall in a moment transport thee into the forest of Tarapajan, where several of thy wise brethren are gone before thee."

'As she spake thus, the enchantress breathed on me with her pestiferous breath; and I fell to the ground, and crawled like a toad before her.

' Ulin then waved her wand, and sleep overpowered me: and, when I awoke, I found myself between the merchant of Delly, and the Princess of Cassimir; who, like me, had felt the vengeance of Ulin the enchantress. It was some consolation to us that our speech was not taken from us, but that we were able to communicate to each other our misfortunes.

' Mahoud first enquired of me the adventures of my life, and I had just finished them the day before my dear transformed lord appeared among us. While Mahoud related his history, your voice, O sultan, struck my ears, and I feared to ask whether my lord was in equal affliction with his slave.'

' Did you not then,' said Misnar, ' hear the adventures of Hemjunah, the princess of Cassimir?'—' I did not, my sultan,' answered Horam; ' Hemjunah was about to relate her adventures when you appeared; and after Shemshelnar, the dervise, had released you, she desired to reserve them till such time as we should meet hereafter in our natural shapes.

' Two days after you left us with Shemshelnar, who endeavoured to comfort our afflictions, on a sudden we perceived a vivid flash of lightning, which was succeeded by a violent clap of thunder; and while we were looking at each other, the wood instantly vanished, and I found myself in my palace at Delly. What became of Mahoud or the Princess of Cassimir, I know not; but I was sensible that my prince had conquered the enchantress, who had laid such hateful chains upon us.

I hastened to the divan of vizirs and emirs, who were astonished at my presence. They were met in order to appoint a sultan, having just heard from the army, that both their sultan and his vizir were fled from the encampments. A friend of Ahubal's had proposed that prince to succeed my royal master, and orders were given to proclaim him when I arrived in the divan.

'Being acquainted with the resolutions of the vizirs and emirs, I proclaimed aloud that my royal master, Misnar, was alive, and that he had destroyed the enchantress Ulin, who espoused the cause of Ahubal. At this declaration, the vizirs and emirs prostrated themselves, and gave thanks to Alla, and the trumpets and the cornets went through the streets of Delly, and proclaimed my arrival, and the victory of Misnar, their sultan, over the enchantress Ulin.

'I dispatched orders before the divan broke up to the army, with advice of your success, and commanded a part to march for the city of Delly, leaving only a sufficient number of troops to observe the motions of the enemy, if they should again unite; for I knew that Ulin's destruction would cause a dissipation of their army. Having settled the affairs of my master, to complete my joy, tidings were brought me of his approach, and Horam is again blessed with the sight of his sultan.'

The vizir Horam having finished his relation, bowed himself before the sultan, and said—'Shall thy slave give orders that an ambassador be sent to the sultan of Cassimir, to enquire after the fate of the Princess Hemjunah?'—'Horam,' answered the sultan,

'while

'while war stalks thus boldly through our dominions, it were vain to assume a state that we may in a moment be bereaved of. No, Horam, let us wait for more prosperous hours.'

Early in the morning several messengers arrived with the news of the death of Ulin, and the revolt of ten provinces from Ahubal; and soon after the provinces sent deputies to excuse their rebellion, and to beseech the sultan to pardon their offences. Misnar yielded to their prayers, but ordered some of the most faithful of his troops to march into their borders, and to encamp among them.

The sultan then redressed the grievances which his soldiers had committed, as far as he was able, and, by a just and equal law, obliged every division to furnish such a number of troops; for although no clouds were then seen to interrupt his reign, yet Misnar was assured that he should shortly be called upon to exercise his prudence, through the wiles of his enemies the enchanters. Nor were his fears unjust; Ahubal, though deserted by the provinces, was yet espoused by the Magician Happuck, who hearing of the defeat of his sister Ulin, was resolved to revenge the cause of that detested race.

It was not long before the sultan heard the Magician Happuck was encouraging the provinces who had followed Ulin, again to revolt from their sultan; but the fear of Misnar's troops overawed them, and whatever might be their real inclinations, yet they were obliged to refuse the offers and the intreaties of Happuck.

The sultan, to secure their obedience the more effectually, increased the number of his forces in the provinces, and preserved the chain of communication from them, quite through his extensive dominions.

The magician finding the sultan's forces so well disposed, and that no encouragement could prevail on the southern provinces to revolt, abandoned his design of succeeding by the force of arms, and flew to the weapons of craft and dissimulation. Though Happuck had now been employed near a year in raising commotions among the subjects of India, two provinces only owned the government of Ahubal, the rest continued firm in their loyalty to the sultan Misnar.

These provinces had raised a light army of about forty thousand men, who by forced marches harrassed the neighbouring provinces around them. Of these, three thousand horsemen parted suddenly from the rest, and by following unfrequented tracks over the mountains, and through the forests, arrived at length within two days' march of Delly. Here pitching their tents, they sent several of their chief officers to Delly, to assure the sultan that they were greatly afflicted at their crimes, and were desirous of laying down their rebellious arms at his feet.

Horam the vizir received these supplicants; and representing their contrition to the sultan, he commanded them to join the main army; at the same time sending dispatches to his general to dismount them from their horses, and to encamp them in such a situation, that they might not be able either to escape, or to annoy his army, if they should be disposed to revolt again.

The magician Happuck, who was among the officers that appeared at Delly, and who had contrived the revolt in order to get into the presence of the sultan, was greatly chagrined to find that the vizir Horam received him, and that he was not to be admitted into Misnar's presence. But, concealing his disappointment, he with the rest joined the three thousand horsemen, and marched to the grand army of Misnar.

Once a year the whole army is reviewed by the sultan in person; and it happened that the disguised magician, and his troops of horsemen arrived at the army three days before this general review.

The magician was rejoiced at this fortunate event.
' Ibrac,'

'Ibrac,' said he to the officer who commanded his troop, 'fortune has now given me an opportunity of revenging the death of my sister Ulin; this disguise of an officer is not sufficient; I will descend to the meanest rank, where I shall be less suspected; and as the sultan Misnar passes between the ranks where I am situated, I will draw my bow, and pierce him to the heart: having done this, I shall render myself invisible; and do you, in the general consternation, proclaim Ahubal the sultan of India.'

'Most powerful magician,' answered Ibrac, 'what need is there of this deceit? Since you are able to render yourself invisible, why cannot you enter the sultan's palace unseen, and stab him to the heart?'

'Faithful Ibrac,' answered the magician, 'you know not the powers which support this boy-like urchin. The Genius Bahourdi, at whose name our race trembles, is his guardian, and prevents my approach; and it is written in the volumes of fate, that no enchantment shall prevail against Misnar, unless he first allow our crafty race to deceive him. Otherwise, Ibrac, dost thou suppose, that so many of my brethren, before whom the mountains tremble, and the ocean boils, should need to league against a boy? No, Ibrac, Misnar were beneath our vengeance, or our art, did not Mahomet espouse him, and his mean vassals, the good Genii of mankind! The conquest of this boy, while thus supported, would add strength to our cause, and convince the powers of Heaven that the children of earth belong to us, and not to them.' Ibrac then furnished the magician with the cloathing of one of the common soldiers, and he was mustered with the rest of the troops.

Early in the morning in which Misnar was to review his troops, the sultan arose, and bid his slaves, who waited in the pavilion, to call his vizir Horam to him.

'Horam,' said the sultan, 'I suspect the crafty magician Happuck, he is doubtless here disguised in our camp,

camp, and if I expose myself to day, it may be in his power to set the crown of India on my brother's head.

'Let my sultan, then,' said Horam, 'proclaim a reward to him who discovers the magician, even to the holding of the second place in your empire.'

'That contrivance would have little effect,' said the sultan; 'Happuck would elude our search, and, transforming himself into some reptile, escape our vengeance, and then meditate some new device to deceive us. No, Horam,' continued Misnar, 'if he be really with us, it were folly to let him escape.'

'But how will my lord discover him amidst three hundred thousand troops?' answered the vizir; 'there is no officer in your army knows the fiftieth part of your soldiers, and where recruits are daily added to the army, to search for a particular person without giving the alarm so that Happuck might escape, would be impossible.'—'In how many ranks,' said the sultan, 'is the army to be disposed?'

'The plain,' answered the vizir, 'on which they are to be reviewed will contain three thousand in a row.' 'Bring me then two hundred of the most expert archers in my army,' said the sultan, 'and take them from those troops who are the farthest from the deserters who lately joined the army.'

The vizir did as the sultan commanded, and brought the archers before the royal pavilion.

"Go, now, Horam,' said the sultan, 'and order all the troops to be drawn out on the plain.'—'They are almost assembled,' said Horam, 'already.'

'Then,' replied the sultan, 'take these archers, and place one at each extremity of the ranks, an archer on the right of each rank; but before you station them thus, give them the following orders; be ready with your bows drawn, and your arrows fixed to the bow-string; and whenever the word of command is given for all the army to fall prostrate, let your arrows fly at the man who is last to obey the word of command.'

The troops being all drawn forth in their ranks, and the archers disposed according to the sultan's orders, the sultan Misnar came forth, attended by his eunuchs, vizirs, emirs, and guards. The loud clarions sounded, the lively notes of the trumpets were heard, and the brazen cymbals shook the trembling air.

The magician, who was impatient to perpetrate the malicious purposes of his heart, was elated at the warlike sound; and he beheld the sultan's retinue at a distance, with such joy as the eagle views the flocks of sheep on the plains of Homah.

The sultan being arrived at the front of his army, which he knew was composed of his most faithful troops, commanded silence throughout the plain.

'My brave soldiers,' said he, 'although no care nor resolution has been wanting on your parts, to extirpate the rebellion of my provinces, yet to Alla only, and to Mahomet his prophet, belong the glory and the honour of your arms; wherefore let immediate orders be issued forth among my troops, that all do together fall prostrate on the ground before the All-seeing Alla, the Governor of the world, and the Disposer of kingdoms and of crowns.

As this order went forth through the ranks, the soldiers at once fell prostrate before Alla, all but the magician Happuck, who was surprised and astonished at the order, and irresolute what to do. But little time was given him to think; for no sooner were his fellow-soldiers fallen prostrate on each side of him, than the arrows of the archers pierced his heart. The magician finding himself overpowered, and that the messengers of death had seized him, raised his voice aloud, and with what little strength was left, cursed both Alla and his prophet; but the stream of life flowed swiftly from him, and his curses grew fainter and fainter, till they were lost in death.

Those who were acquainted with the designs of Happuck, perceiving that the magician was dead, and their plot discovered, began to fly: and first, Ibrac essayed to head his discarded troops; but they not being used to march on foot, soon fell into confusion, and the forces of the sultan surrounding them, they were instantly destroyed.

The sultan Misnar saw by the confusion of his army in the centre that the discovery was made, and sent Horam, with some chosen troops, to inquire into the cause of their disorder. The vizir was no sooner arrived, than he perceived several soldiers bringing along the body of the magician Happuck, which appeared undisguised after death. 'Bid the two archers,' said the vizir, 'who destroyed the monster, come forward.'

When the archers were come forward, Horam applauded their skill and their obedience, and advised them to take the body between them, and carry it before the sultan. The archers obeyed; and the ranks before opening at they passed, they soon arrived at the feet of Misnar.

The sultan, seeing his enemy thus destroyed, ordered the two archers ten purses, containing each one hundred pieces of gold, and to every other archer one purse containing one hundred pieces of gold. To him who brought the head of Ibrac also, he gave five purses of like value; and then again issued out his command, that the whole army should fall prostrate, and adore the mercy of Alla, who had so soon delivered into their hands the chief of their enemies.

In the mean time, two only of the troops of Ibrac and Happuck escaped; and, returning to Ahubal, acquainted him with their defeat. Ahubal fled at the news, and hid himself in the mountains, for he feared lest his soldiers should betray him, and deliver him up to his brother.

But Ol'omand, the enchanter, who first counselled the sultan of India to secure his throne, by spilling the innocent blood of his brother, now resolved to revenge the common cause; he therefore directed the steps of Ahubal to a cave in the mountains, where, fatigued with flight,

flight, and fearful of pursuit, the royal rebel arrived in the heat of the day. The cave was, for the most part, surrounded by steep mountains, and a great distance from any track or path, and was situated at the entrance of a long valley, which led among the mountains.

Ahubal having slept and refreshed himself in the cave, pursued his journey through the valley, till he found his path stopped by inaccessible rocks, on the top of which he perceived a magnificent castle, whose walls reflected the rays of the sun like burnished gold.

The brother of Misnar fixed his eye for some time on that part of the castle which was shaded by the rest, for the front was too dazzling to behold; and in a few moments he perceived a small wicket open, and a dwarf come forth. Ahubal soon lost sight of the dwarf behind the rocks; but he resolved to wait there to see whether he could find any passage into the valley.

The dwarf, after being hid for some time, appeared again about the middle of the rocks, and by his course seemed to descend in a spiral path around the mountain. When the dwarf had reached the bottom, he advanced to Ahubal, and, presenting him with a clue, he told him, that if he threw it before him, and followed it, the clue would unravel itself, and discover to him the path which led up the rocks to the castle of Ollomand his master.

Ahubal having heard from Ulin and Happuck, that Ollomand was his friend, took the clue out of the hand of the dwarf, and threw it before him. As the clue rolled onward, and touched the rocks, Ahubal discovered a regular ascent, which, winding round, brought him by degrees to the castle on the summit of the mountain.

The enchanter Ollomand received Ahubal at the entrance of the castle, which was guarded by four dragons, and led him through a large court into a spacious hall, the walls of which were lined with human bones that had been whitened in the sun.

'Favourite of the race of the powerful,' said Ollomand, 'see here the bones of those who have lifted up their arms against thee, and I will add to their number till this castle be filled.' 'Alas,' answered Ahubal, 'Ulin is no more, and the vultures are preying on the vitals of Happuck! Ten provinces have deserted my cause, and the coffers of my army are exhausted!'

'Happuck,' answered Ollomand, 'despised the assistance of riches, and trusted to deceit, and therefore failed. The provinces dared not revolt while the armies of Misnar over-awed them; but I will replenish thy coffers, and Ollomand will tempt the leaders of the sultan's troops to join the cause of Ahubal. In this castle are riches and arms sufficient to equip all the inhabitants of Asia, and, when these are exhausted, we will apply to Pharesanen, Hypacusan, and all the chieftains of our race: and fear not, Ahubal, for by my art I read that Misnar the sultan shall fly before the face of his enemies'

Ahubal was encouraged by the words of Ollomand, and the enchanter having opened his design to the prince, invited him to behold the riches of his castle. Passing through the hall of bones, they descended into a square court, much more spacious than the former, in the middle of which appeared a deep and dark pit. This court contained four hundred gates of massy brass, and each gate was supported by nine enormous hinges of the same metal.

As Ollomand the enchanter entered this court, with the prince Ahubal in his hand, he lifted up his voice, which echoed like thunder amidst the lofty turrets of the castle, and commanded his slaves to expose to the sight of Ahubal the treasures of their master. The prince Ahubal, who had seen no creature but the dwarf and the enchanter in the castle, wondered from whence the slaves should come; but his wonder shortly was turned

into

into fear, when he beheld a gigantic black, with a club of ebony, forty feet in length, rife out of the pit, which was in the centre of the court. But if one was fo terrifying, his horrors were beyond meafure increafed, when he perceived a long fucceffion of the fame gigantic monfters, following one another out of the pit, and advancing to the four hundred brazen gates, till every gate had a flave ftanding before it.

When Ollomand faw his flaves were all prepared before the gates, he bid them ftrike with their clubs of ebony againft them. The black flaves, in obedience to the enchanter's orders, lifted up their ponderous clubs of ebony, and ftruck againft the four hundred gates, which jarred fo much with the blows of the flaves that Ahubal was forced to ftop his ears, and was ready to fink into the earth with aftonifhment and dread.

As foon as the black flaves of Ollomand had ftruck the four hundred gates of brafs, the gates began to move, and the harfh creek and breaking of the hinges fent forth a noife which alone had chilled the hearts of all the armies of Mifnar, could they have heard them. This difmal and difcordant jar continued till the gates were forced open by the hideous flaves. But the prince Ahubal was fo ftunned and ftupified with the piercing found, that he dared not look up, till Ollomand the enchanter, fhaking him by the fhoulders, bid him feaft his eyes with the riches of his friend.

Ahubal then lifting up his head, looked around the court, and faw the four hundred gates were opened. In thofe of the right were millions of wedges of gold and filver, piled beneath craggy arches of huge unchizzled ftone. Oppofite to thefe, he beheld an hundred vaulted roofs, under which were facks and bags of the gold and filver coin of many nations.

Before him, another hundred gates expofed to his view the arms and warlike accoutrements of ten thoufand nations, and all the inftruments of death which the inventive malice of man had ever difcovered. Firft a rude heap of ponderous ftones and the fragments of rocks,

rocks. Next sticks, staffs, and knotty clubs. Next to these, spears, darts, lances, and javelins, armed with brass or iron, or their points hardened by fire, and innumerable bows with quivers and arrows. After these, instruments of dubious use, originally designed for the assistance of men, but perverted, through cruelty and malice, to the service of slaughter and death; such as knives, bodkins, axes, hammers. On these were heaped arms, deliberately fashioned for the offence of mankind; swords, daggers, poniards, stilettos, hangers, scymetars, rapiers. In the fourth part of the court, which was behind Ahubal, were stored the more refined and destructive instruments of European war, the grenadoes, the firelock, the pistol, the musquet, the blunderbuss, the culverin, the petard, the cannon, the howitzer, the bomb, the mortar, and their accursed food, bags of powder, balls of lead, and iron shells and carcases.

Ahubal, who understood but little of these instruments, was amazed at their construction, and asked for what purposes those ghastly monsters of art were formed.

'These,' said Ollomand, ' are the arms of Europe, a part of the earth filled with industrious robbers, whose minds are hourly on the stretch to invent new plagues to torment each other. Of these mortals many are settled on the sea-coasts of our southern provinces, whom I shall persuade, through the instigations of that god which they worship, to join the forces of Ahubal.'

' Hast thou, then, mighty enchanter,' answered the prince Ahubal, ' the gods of Europe in thy power?' ' The Europeans,' said Ollomand, ' acknowledge but one God whom they pretend doth inhabit the heavens, but whom we find buried in the entrails of the earth: gold, O prince, is their god, for whose sake they will undertake the most daring enterprises, and forsake the best of friends. To these shalt thou send presents and future promises of wealth, and by their machinations,

fear

fear not but Mifnar, fhall yield to thy fuperior addrefs.

'What need of the arms, or the perfons, of Europeans,' anfwered the prince Ahubal, 'while my friend has an army of fuch gigantic flaves, ten of whom are more than fufficient to deftroy the puny armies of my brother, the fultan?'

'Alas!' faid Ollomand, 'the flaves of enchantment cannot fight againft the fons of the faithful. Though we deny Mahomet, and will not adore him, yet we cannot controul a power that muft over-rule us. Were the world at our difpofal, the mean worfhippers of Alla fhould tremble at their fate. But alas! the curb of Mahomet galls our tongues, the flefh of our lips is filled with rawnefs and foam, and our evil race muft tremble, though it cannot relent. But thefe are troublefome thoughts, and the provinces require our prefence; as Mifnar's troops are in poffeffion of the country, we will tranfport ourfelves to Orixa in the difguife of merchants, and there endeavour to forward the deftruction of Mifnar, the tame fultan of the eaft.'

As Ollomand fpake thefe words, he ftamped with his feet, and a chariot, drawn by four dragons, arofe from the pit in the centre of the court, which Ahubal and the enchanter afcended, and were conveyed in a dark cloud to the woods behind the city of Orixa.

When Ollomand's chariot alighted on the ground, he touched the dragons with his wand, and they became four camels laden with merchandize, and the chariot was converted into an elephant. Ahubal became like a merchant, and the enchanter appeared as a black flave. They entered the town in the evening, and the next morning expofed their goods in the market-place. The bales of Ahubal, the fham-merchant, being opened, were found to contain chiefly materials for cloathing the officers of the army. The troops of Mifnar hearing this, were his chief cuftomers; and as Ahubal fold his wares very cheap, he foon got acquainted with all the officers at Orixa.

In all his converfations with them, the enchanter
had

had directed Ahubal to lament the small salaries which the army were allowed; this was a subject all agreed in, and soon led to more lucrative offers, if they would embrace the cause of Ahubal. The officers, who were for the most part soldiers for the sake of pay and plunder, rather than duty and honour, soon came into the sham merchant's proposal, and in ten days Ahubal found himself in a condition to recover the province of Orixa.

The young prince, fired with his success, was about to discover himself, but the enchanter checked his ardour, and besought him to consider how many more provinces must be gained, before he could make head against his brother. The advice of Ollomand prevailed with the prince, and they sent some of those officers who were strongest in their interest, into the different provinces of the south, to corrupt the minds of the commanders.

As there was no want of money and bribery, so an easier conquest was made over the loyalty of the troops than could have been made over their prowess by swords. In a few moons all the southern provinces were ripe for a revolt, and the troops who were sent to over-awe them were most desirous of opening the campaign against their sultan. Two hundred French engineers were also invited, by large rewards, to join the armies of Ahubal, and the troops were supplied by the vigilance of the enchanter Ollomand.

On a fixed day, all the armies of the provinces were in motion, and all unfurled the standard of Ahubal; the provinces were invited to rebel, and thousands were daily added to the troops of the prince. Tidings of these alterations were sent to Delly, by the few friends of the sultan which remained in those parts; and Horam the vizir laid before his master the dreadful news of a general revolt, both of his troops and provinces in the south.

'The enemies of Misnar,' said the sultan as the vizir Horam had ended his report, 'are many, and one

one only is his friend!' Horam bowed low at his master's words. 'Faithful Horam,' said the sultan, 'I honour and esteem thee; but think not I prefer my vizir to my God; no, Horam, Alla alone is the friend of Misnar; a friend more mighty than the armies of Ahubal, or the sorceries of the enchanters.' Misnar then assembled his troops; and, putting himself at their head, he marched by easy marches toward the southern frontiers of his dominions.

The armies of Ahubal continued to increase, and Cambaya acknowledged him for its sultan. In a short time he arrived with his forces at Narvar, and encamped within seven leagues of the army of Misnar the sultan.

Ollomand the enchanter, notwithstanding Ahubal had thrown off the disguise of a merchant, still attended him as a black slave, being always about his person, till the freedom which the prince allowed him, was resented by the officers of his army. This the enchanter perceived, and therefore he desired Ahubal would grant him five thousand of his troops, and the European engineers, that he might advance before the main army, and signalize himself by a blow which he meditated to give the enemy.

The counsel of Ollomand was never opposed by Ahubal; the prince commanded the troops to attend Ollomand, and be subject unto him. The enchanter then marched with his selected troops into a thick wood, which the army of Misnar must pass, ere they could oppose their enemies; and in this wood the engines of European war were placed, to command every avenue that had been hewn out by the troops of the sultan.

Ollomand marching by night surprised all the advanced guards of the sultan, and possessed himself of the wood, where he placed the European engineers, before the sun could penetrate through the branches of the forest of Narvar. This enterprise had ruined all the hopes of the sultan, who proposed to march his

army

army through the next day, if the Europeans had continued faithful to Ahubal and his party; but one, favoured by the darkness of the night, escaped, and betrayed the whole design to the sultan.

Misnar was no sooner apprised of the enchanter's contrivance, than he ordered certain of his troops to climb over the mountains to the right of the wood, and, if possible, to gain the opposite side, and there in several parts to set the wood on fire. This was so successfully executed by the soldiers, that as soon as Ollomand was possessed of the wood, he perceived it was on fire, and had made a separation between him and the army of Ahubal.

In this distress the enchanter resolved to dispose of his troops and engineers in the most advantageous manner, proposing in his mind to secure his own retreat by the power of enchantment. But while the subtle enchanter was directing his engineers in the rear to bring up the fell engines of war, one of the cannon which was left in the wood (the flames having obliged those who belonged to it to retreat) being made hot by the raging fires in the wood, discharged its contents, and the ball striking the enchanter, carried with it the head of Ollomand toward the camp of the sultan. This put the troops in the wood in the utmost confusion, and many fled to the sultan's camp, declaring the loss of their leader, and the rest resolved rather to submit, than perish by the sword or by fire.

The flames of the wood which arose between the armies of Misnar and Ahubal, soon disturbed the peace of the rebel prince. At first, indeed, he hoped Ollomand had inclosed his brother's troops, and was consuming them by his fires. But no dispatch from his friend, filled Abudah with just fears, which were greatly increased, as in a few days the fire decreasing, and having opened a passage through the wood, he was informed by his spies, that the armies of Misnar were approaching.

The prince Ahubal having lost his friend, the enchanter,

chanter, was fearful of the event, and wifhed to fly; but his generals being rebels, and fearing their fate if they fhould be taken, refolved to conquer or die, and Ahubal was conftrained againft his will to put his army in a ftate of defence. The fultan fuppofing his brother's army would be difheartened at the lofs of the enchanter, was ftudious of giving them battle before they had recovered their confternation; and therefore led on his troops with great impetuofity toward the front of the rebel army, while the Vizir Horam, covered by the main body of Mifnar's army, endeavoured to gain the right flank of the enemy.

And now the adverfe elephants made the fandy plains fhake as they advanced, and from the turrets on their backs ten thoufand hoftile arrows were difcharged; the loud hollow cymbals founded the alarm, and the air groaned with the weight of the winged weapons. The troops of the fultan advanced with confidence, and the rebellious fupporters of Ahubal rufhed forward with refolute defpair. Innumerable fcymitars blazed fearfully over the heads of the warlike. The feet of the elephants were ftained with death, and the blood of the flain was as the rivers of Arvar. But the troops of Mifnar were flufhed with hope, and fear and difmay were in the paths of Ahubal. The prince himfelf, in confufion, founded the retreat, and the backs of his troops were already expofed to the darts of the fultan, when the fwarthy Enchanter Tafnar appeared in the air, feated on a rapacious vulture.

'Bafe cowards,' faid he, as he hovered aloft in the air, 'turn, and fear not while Tafnar is your friend. The troops of the fultan are exhaufted and fatigued, and you are flying from thofe who were deftined for your prey. Are then the riches of Delly to be fo eafily refigned, and your tedious marches over the defarts to be foiled by a moment's fear! Even now is India offered as the reward of your toils, and you prefer fhame and ignominy to glory and honour.'

The troops of Ahubal hearing thefe words, and being encouraged by a sight so wonderful, for a time stood still, unknowing what to do; till Tasnar alighting on the ground, and seizing a javelin, bid the brave support and defend the avenger of their wrongs. The sultan's army finding their enemies retreat, had followed them in a tumultuous manner, and were therefore less able to resist the Enchanter Tasnar and those who supported him. And they had experienced the truth of the enchanter's assertion, had not the Vizir Horam, perceiving their resistance, hastened with a few chosen troops to the rescue of his friends.

The battle, though not so general as before, was yet much fiercer, and Tasnar and Horam met face to face. The vizir aimed in vain his scymitar at the head of the enchanter, and Tasnar found a superior arm withheld him when he attempted to demolish the faithful vizir. But this prevented not the general slaughter that ensued, till night, which recruits the wasted strength of man, divided the armies of Misnar and Ahubal.

After the retreat of the two contending armies, the Vizir Horam attended the sultan in the royal pavilion, and informed him of the descent of the Enchanter Tasnar, and his prowess in the field.

'Alas!' answered Misnar, 'it is in vain, O Horam, that the sword is uplifted against the power of enchantment, so long as these magicians are prepared against our attacks; we must surprize them or we cannot prevail. Tasnar is joined to my faithless brother Ahubal; there is in my camp doubtless some trusty slave, who, under the appearance of betraying my cause, may penetrate into the camp of Ahubal, and destroy this enchanter while he sleeps in security; and Horam my vizir must find that slave ere the sun beholds the blood of Asia, which defiles the plains of my kingdom.'

Horam bowed, and went out of the presence of the sultan in great distress of heart. 'Where,' said he to himself, 'can the mighty find a trusty friend! or what slave

slave will be faithful to his master that has robbed him of his liberty! Better had I perished by the hand of Tasnar, than be betrayed through the wickedness of my servants!'

The vizir, doubtful where to apply, or whom to trust, returned to his tent, where he found an old female slave, who waited to deliver a message from his seraglio, which was kept in a tent adjoining to his own. Horam, not regarding her presence, threw himself on his sopha, and bemoaned his fate, in being commanded to find a trusty slave. The female slave, who saw her master's tears, threw herself at his feet, and called Alla to witness that she had always served him faithfully, and was ready to sacrifice her life for his pleasure.

Horam was rather more distressed than alleviated by her protestations. 'What art thou,' said he to her sternly, 'a poor decrepit woman! and canst thou go forth and combat the enchantments of Tasnar, the enemy of thy master's peace!'—'The locust and the worm,' said the female slave, 'are the instruments of Alla's vengeance on the mighty ones of the earth, and Mahomet can make even my weakness subservient to the cause of my lord.'

'And how wilt thou prevail against Ahubal the prince, and Tasnar the magician?' said Horam, careless of what he spoke. 'I will go,' answered the female slave, 'into the camp of Ahubal, and I will engage to poison my master, the vizir, and Misnar, the lord of our lives, as I stand before them to minister unto them the pleasing draught. And while Tasnar is intent in hearing my proposals, the steel of death shall suddenly search out the vile enchanter's heart.'

'But, knowest thou not,' said Horam, 'that death will be the consequence of this rash deed?'—'My lord,' answered the slave, 'I was, when young, bred up in the caves of Denraddin, and was taught by a sage to know what should happen to me in future times; and the sage read in the stars of heaven, that by my means should the sultan of India be delivered from the enemy that oppressed him.'

The vizir was rejoiced at the assurances of his female slave, and bid her prepare herself to appear before the sultan. The slave putting on her veil, followed the Vizir Horam, and was introduced to the tent of Misnar. 'What,' said the sultan, as he saw his vizir enter with the female slave, 'what new kind of warrior has Horam brought me?'

'Light of mine eyes!' answered the vizir, 'behold a woman who is desirous of executing thy commands. This slave assures me, that the sages of the caves of Denraddin have read in the stars of heaven, that by her means the sultan of India should be delivered from the enemy that oppressed him.'—'Then,' said the sultan, 'let her go; and may the prophet of the faithful guide her footsteps in safety and security! I am assured that Horam would not consent to an enterprize that was foolish and weak, and to his direction I leave the fate of this trusty female.'

The slave then fell prostrate, and besought the sultan to give her some of his writings and mandates, that she might pretend she had stolen them from his tent, with a design to carry and lay them at the feet of Tasnar and Ahubal. The sultan approved of her scheme, and ordered several mandates to be written and signed relative to the motions of his army the next day, which were quite contrary to the real disposition he intended to give out.

The female slave being furnished with these, and being conducted by the vizir to the out-skirts of the sultan's army, walked forward till she was challenged by the centinels of Ahubal, who seized upon and carried her to their commander.

The commander, fearful of deceit, at first satisfied himself that she was really a female slave, and then asked her what brought her alone out of the camp of the sultan.'—'Bring me,' said she, 'before your prince, for I have things to deliver up to him that will be

of

of service to his army.' The commander then sent her with the guard to the pavilion of Ahubal, where that prince and the Enchanter Tasnar were consulting in private together.

As soon as the female slave had gained admittance, she fell prostrate at the feet of Ahubal, which Tasnar observing, commanded the guards to seize her. 'Let us see,' said the enchanter, 'what service this slave can do us, before she is trusted so near our persons.'

The female slave being secured by the guards, was doubtful how to behave. 'I like not that confusion,' said the enchanter; 'have you, base slave, aught to reveal to us? or are you sent as a spy, to betray the councils of the brave?'—'I have,' said the female slave, somewhat recovered from her surprize, 'papers and mandates of great consequence, which I have stolen from the tent of the sultan, and I bring them to the Prince Ahubal, the lord of all the hearts of the Indian empire.'

The slave then produced her mandates, and the guards laid them at the feet of Ahubal. The Prince Ahubal having read the papers, gave them to Tasnar, saying—'These are indeed valuable acquisitions, and the female slave that brought them is worthy of high honour and reward.'

The slave hearing this encomium, bowed down her head, for the guards who held her prevented her falling prostrate. 'Mighty son of Dabulcombar,' said the enchanter, 'let the guards carry her forth, till we consult what reward she shall receive.'

As soon as the female slave was carried out—'My prince,' said Tasnar, 'it is indeed politic to confer rewards on those who serve us, and therefore it is sometimes necessary to do it, that the silly birds may be the better entangled in the snares of state; but when we can better serve our ends by their destruction than by their safety, it is but just that we should do it. This slave has already risqued her life for our service, and therefore

therefore she will doubtless be ready to lay it down if we require it.'

As the enchanter said this, he called one of the guards, and commanded him to bring in the female slave and the bow string. The female slave approached, being still held by the guards. 'Kind slave,' said the enchanter, 'you have already served us much; there is one thing more that we require: let the slaves fit the bow-string to thy neck, and let thy last breath be sent forth in praise of thy lord Ahubal.'

The slaves of Ahubal then put upon the wretched female the deadly bow-string, and strangled her instantly. After which they retired, leaving the dead body of the female slave on the floor of the tent.

'What hast thou done, O Tasnar!' said Ahubal, astonished at the deed. 'I suspect,' said the enchanter, 'that this female was sent on a vile errand; and see here,' continued he, searching her garments, 'is the weapon of death!' So saying, he drew a dagger from her bosom, which she had concealed with a design of stabbing the enchanter.'

'Prudent Tasnar,' said the prince, 'I admire thy foresight, but of what use is this murdered slave now to us?'

'The disguise of this slave,' answered the enchanter, 'will introduce me into the camp of the sultan, and I hope will give me an opportunity of reaching his heart, with that steel which he designed for mine. But no time must be lost; the morning will, ere long, disclose its grey light in the east.'

The enchanter then put on the garments of the murdered female slave, and stroking his face, it became as her's, so that Ahubal could scarce believe but the slave was revived. He cut off also the head of the female slave, and anointing it with a white ointment it became like his own. Thus equipped, the commander of the advanced guard conducted him to the foremost centinels of the rebel army. The disguised enchanter soon reached the camp of the sultan, and the centinels

imagining

imagining it was the same female slave whom Horam had led through their ranks in the former part of the night, suffered him to pass unexamined.

In a short time he reached the royal pavilion, and demanded admittance. The Vizir Horam, who was there in waiting, heard, as he supposed, the voice of his female slave, and went out to bring her before the sultan.

'My slave,' said Horam, as he saw the disguised enchanter, 'hast thou succeeded, and is Tasnar the foe of the faithful dead?'—'Bring me before the sultan,' said the pretended slave, 'that my lord may first behold the head of his foe.'

The vizir then led the disguised enchanter into the pavilion, where the Sultan Misnar being warned of her approach was seated on his throne. As the enchanter approached, he held a dagger in one hand, which was covered by a long sleeve, and in the other he bore the fictitious head. And now the fictitious female was about to ascend the steps of the throne, when the vizir commanded her first to fall prostrate before the sultan.

The sham female slave did as she was ordered, and the vizir seeing her prostrate, fell upon her, and slew her with his sabre. 'What hast thou done, wretched vizir!' said the sultan; 'has envy thus rashly stirred thee up against my faithful slave, that—'

The sultan had probably continued his invective against his vizir much longer, had he not beheld the corse of the dead enchanter change its appearance, and found that Horam, by the sudden destruction of Tasnar had but just preserved his own life.

At sight of this transformation, Misnar descended from his throne, and closely embraced his Vizir Horam. 'O Horam, forgive my impetuous temper,' said the sultan; 'how have I blamed my friend for doing that which alone could have saved my life! But by what means did my faithful vizir become acquainted with the disguise of this wicked enchanter, or how did he discover himself to thy watchful eye.'

'Lord of my heart,' answered Horam, 'when I carried my poor female slave through the camp, whose fate may be learned by this ghastly head before us; I bid her, when she returned and saw me, first repeat these words in my ear—" Alla is lord of heaven, Mahomet is his prophet, and Misnar is the vicegerent upon earth."—' And this precaution I took, fearful lest Tasnar, discovering our design, should invent this method of revenge. Wherefore, when the pretended slave was brought before me, and she repeated not the words that I had taught her, I was assured that it was the enchanter in disguise, and waited, till by prostrating himself before my lord, he gave me an opportunity of destroying the life of the chief of thine enemies.'

The Sultan of India again embraced his faithful vizir; and as soon as the eye of morn was opened in the east, the armies of Ahubal beheld the enchanter Tasnar's head affixed on a pole, in the front of the sultan's army.

The prince Ahubal rising with the earliest dawn of the morning, went forward to the front of his troops, and there, at a small distance, he saw the hideous features of the Enchanter Tasnar already blackening in the sun. Fear immediately took possession of the soul of Ahubal; and he ran with tears in his eyes, and hid himself, till the sun went down, in his pavilion.

The Vizir Horam, perceiving the approach of heaven's everlasting lamp, would have led on the sultan's troops to a second attack; but Misnar commanded him to forbear, that his army might rest one day after their fatigues. The great distress of the enchanters, and their unexpected deaths, alarmed the rest of that wicked race; and Ahaback and Desra seeing that no one enchanter had succeeded against the sultan, resolved to join their forces, and while one led a powerful army to Ahubal's assistance from the east, the other raised the

storms

storms of war and rebellion on the western confines of the sultan's empire.

In the mean time the two armies of the sultan and Ahubal continued inactive, till an express arrived, that Ahaback was leading the strength of nine thousand squadrons against their sultan, and that Desra was travelling over the plains of Embracau with three thousand elephants, and an hundred thousand troops from the western provinces.

The sultan instantly resolved to attack Ahubal before these succours could arrive; but the Vizir Horam fell at his feet, and besought him not to hazard his army, but rather to recruit and strengthen it. This advice, though quite contrary to the opinion of Misnar, was yet so strongly urged by the vizir, that the sultan gave up his better judgment to the opinion of Horam. And when every one expected to be called forth to action, the vizir gave orders in the camp for recruits to be sought after, and went himself to the north of Delly, to raise a second army for his master's service. The troops of Ahubal finding themselves free from the attacks of the sultan's army, endeavoured to comfort their prince, who was grieved and dejected at the loss of his friends. And the provinces of the south, to dissipate his gloom, besought him to permit them to raise a pavilion worthy of his dignity, as heretofore he contented himself with such as his generals made use of.

The Prince Ahubal, who by nature was not formed for war or contest, but only stirred up by the enchanters to be their tool against the sultan his brother, was easily persuaded to accept of the offers of his troops, and an hundred curious artizans were set to work, to contrive and erect a sumptuous pavilion for the use of the prince. To these workmen, all the provinces who acknowledged the authority of Ahubal, sent diamonds, and jewels, and rich silks, and all the costly materials of the world, to finish the splendid pavilion which they purposed to raise for their prince.

While

While the sumptuous tent was raising, the squadrons of Ahaback drew nearer and nearer, and the elephants of Deira were within thirty days of the camp of Ahubal.

The Vizir Horam being returned with his reinforcement, waited on the sultan, and besought him to trust the management of his army to him for forty days.

'Horam,' said the sultan, 'I have such confidence in thy sense and thy loyalty, that I grant thy request.'

The vizir having obtained his end, sent a messenger to Ahubal, and desired forty days truce might exist between the armies, which the prince readily agreed to. In a few hours the truce was proclaimed in the sultan's camp; and when Misnar hoped that his vizir would have attacked the rebel army with a force more than double their number, he heard the trumpets sound a truce in the tents.

Such a behaviour, so contrary to reason, alarmed the sultan, and he sent for the Vizir Horam, and demanded his reasons for making a truce with his enemies.

'My lord,' answered Horam, 'I have heard that the southern provinces are erecting a pavilion for your rebel brother Ahubal, which in splendour and magnificence is to surpass all the glories of thy palace at Delly; and being convinced that thy subjects are led more by shew and appearance, than by duty and honour, I feared that Ahubal's glorious pavilion might draw the neighbouring cities into his encampment, and thereby strengthen his army, and weaken the resources of my prince. For this reason I besought my lord to give me the command of his army for forty days; in which space, I purpose to build thee such a pavilion, as shall far outshine in splendour every glory upon earth.'

'Horam,' answered the sultan, 'I have put all things into thine hands, but let me beseech thee to be careful of thy master.'

The Vizir Horam leaving the sultan, sent to Delly for workmen and artificers, and ordering a large spot to be inclosed, that none might behold his pavilion till it was compleated, he carried on the work with great care and assiduity. While these works of peace, rather than of war, were carrying on in the two armies of Misnar and Ahubal, the reinforcements of Ahaback and Desra arrived. And the captains in the sultan's army hearing of the great addition which was made to the rebel army, while the vizir was spending his time with his curious workmen, petitioned the sultan, that one might be put over them, who loved war, rather than the amusement of females and children.

The sultan, who thought with his captains, that Horam was rather betraying than forwarding his cause, commanded the vizir to be brought before him, and in the presence of the captains asked him why he delayed to lead his troops against the rebel army. The Vizir Horam made no answer to the sultan's question, but desired his lord to bring the captains toward the pavilion which he had erected.

As soon as the sultan appeared before the inclosure, several slaves behind were employed to remove it, so that in an instant Misnar and his captains beheld the most magnificent spectacle that art could achieve. The sight of the pavilion was highly acceptable to the army of the sultan, but the captains justly condemned a performance, which had, without cause, wasted the greatest part of the coffers of India.

The pavilion was situated at one extremity of the sultan's army, at a small distance from a rocky mountain, and surrounded by a grove of palm-trees, part of which had been cut down by the vizir's order, to admit the air and light among the rest. It was composed of crimson velvet, embroidered round with flowers and festoons of silver and gold; and in the body was worked, in golden tissue, the death of the enchanters, Ulin, Happuck, Ollomand, and Tasnar.

The

The pavilion stood upon a carpet, or cloth of gold, and within-side was supported by four massive pillars of burnished gold; the cieling of the canopy within was studded with jewels and diamonds, and under it were placed two sophas of the richest workmanship.

END OF THE FIRST VOLUME.

J. ADLARD, Printer, Duke-street.

CPSIA information can be obtained
at www.ICGtesting.com
Printed in the USA
BVHW011831250322
632472BV00011B/218

9 781247 531939